ISLAND CHILD

Island Child
my early life with
R. M. Lockley

Ann Lockley

First published in 2013

© Ann Lockley

© Gwasg Carreg Gwalch 2013

Published with the financial support
of the Welsh Books Council

ISBN: 978-1-84527-417-7

Cover design: Welsh Books Council

Published by Gwasg Carreg Gwalch,
12 Iard yr Orsaf, Llanrwst, Wales LL26 0EH
tel: 01492 642031
fax: 01492 641502
email: books@carreg-gwalch.com
website: www.carreg-gwalch.com

Contents

Introduction

Life with my father, R. M. Lockley, was never boring. For the first ten years of my life we lived half on the island of Skokholm, off Pembrokeshire, and half on the mainland. We had several homes, in fact – the farmhouse on the island, a hut at Martinshaven, a house at Dale, another called Beggars Reach ... and later Cwmgloyne and Island Farm in north Pembrokeshire. My parents were perceived by many as being unconventional people, creative, perhaps restless. I certainly learned to mix with like-minded adults at an early age. My upbringing, therefore, was also to some extent unconventional. My father wrote about me in his books – but he did have a habit of 'embroidering'! This is my version, the story of my youth with Ronald and Doris Lockley, my parents, and with Skokholm.

My father's books were mainly autobiography and natural history with an emphasis on ornithology. Some of these are still in print. He had a gift for sharing his discoveries about rabbits and birds and making them interesting to both layman and scientist. He made several attempts at writing fiction, but by the time he had made a name for himself in the former subjects, he says, 'his public did not expect anything else.' Perhaps that is why he romanticised ('just a bit', he would argue) in his autobiographies.

On Father's ninetieth birthday, when he was awarded A Medal of the British Ornithologists Union, part of the citation mentioned 'his Welsh charm, said to come and go like that of a British spring day, and a tendency to make wild statements in conversation'.

To make his stories run more smoothly and to avoid repetition he embroidered some of the events he describes in such biographies as *Dream Island Days, The Way to an Island, The Island Farmers.* Because I have the diaries he kept from 1926 until 1991, I can vouch for this. I have endeavoured to tell my story 'how it really was'.

I have the advantage that most of the characters who might sue me for libel are now dead, whereas Father came pretty close to a court case for too thinly veiling some of his acquaintances. Nevertheless, no matter what I say in the following chapters, I have the greatest admiration for the talents which my parents possessed; both incurable romantics, both artistic, one with pen, the other with paint and pencil. Neither of them could be called particularly practical – their romanticism got in the way – but they were infinitely resourceful and tough.

I have drawn heavily on Father's diaries for references to my early childhood. Later I describe my own impressions in parallel with his.

My mother did not keep a diary, but I have her paintings and sketches which speak to me eloquently. Her drawings are accurate but kept to no chronological system or order: she invariably picked up the nearest book to hand and did her drawing on the first empty page to fall open!

I have tried to make my story as accurate as my memory will allow. I mention a few of the more interesting, colourful or famous people we met, who influenced events and/or made an impression on me.

We led a hard physical life. Father's diaries dwell a lot on that aspect, though there is not a lot of introspection in them. I have quoted parts which are relevant to the story and scenes which we both witnessed. I share with Father a love of words, and we had much else in common, particularly a passion for the land and its natural history, and an enduring love for Pembrokeshire.

My particular thanks go to my husband Jack for his patience, and to Jen Llywelyn for her assistance, friendship and encouragement.

Ann Mark (nee Lockley)
New Zealand, 2013

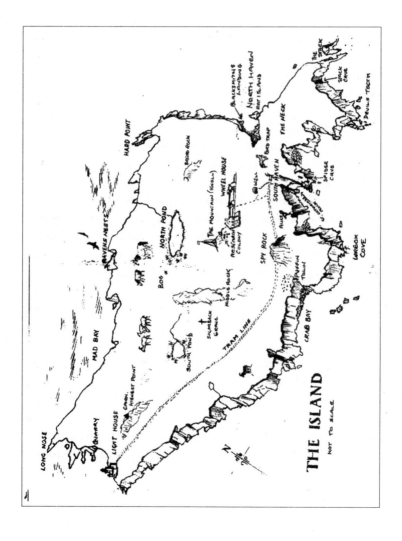

I have an early but vivid recollection of Mother and me walking up the meadow to the island house. There was no wind, I can still see our jerseys sequinned with droplets of moisture; it was so foggy that for once the gulls were silent, the only sound a bleating of sodden plimsolls on sodden ground bringing up a peaty scent from the short, matted grass. We had been ashore to get provisions, a task which involved numerous and tedious journeys from harbour to house, woe betide anyone who came up empty handed! On this occasion Mother had a large basket in one hand and mine grasped in the other. Because she was holding my hand I must have been very young. As soon as I was strong enough, my mother would have had both hands full and I would have been coerced into carrying something too. I know this memory is undeniably mine. (On checking in the diaries I have found I've sometimes been guilty of thinking oft-repeated reminiscences and family hearsay were personal memories, when in fact I would have been too young to remember or I wasn't even there ...)

1

1927 to 1928

To first set the stage: my story starts before I was born ...

White horses danced on the wave tops, bursting into sheets of spray as they broke against the red rocks of a nearby promontory. Green-backed rollers were foaming in on an expanse of honey-pale sand on the beach below the cliff top. It was Whit Sunday in the year 1927. Two men stared across the sea towards an island lying to the south, off the Pembrokeshire coast. They had arranged to visit it with a local fisherman, but he told them the sea was too rough. A day or two later conditions improved and they spent three days on this island, enchanted by all they saw ...

* * *

My father had always dreamt of living in some isolated place, preferably surrounded by water. As he wrote in one of his early books, *Dream Island*: 'To dwell alone with birds and flowers in some remote place where they were plentiful and undisturbed was an ambition early cherished ...'

He was one of the lucky ones, for he achieved his dream early in life. He found a partner, my mother, who was his equal in being incurably romantic and keen to share with him this life of comparative isolation and hardship.

Father's family were always deeply loyal to one another regardless of the circumstances. This could make life somewhat challenging for those they married, who were expected to conform and unreservedly embrace the whole clan.

My paternal grandmother hailed from Milford Haven, daughter of David Mathias, Master Mariner. He and Granny married in August 1895. They had six children: Enid, Kenneth, Kathleen, Aline, Ronald (my father) and Marjorie. Later on, the younger generation (i.e. my cousins and I) referred to these four sisters collectively as 'The Aunts'; en masse they tended to be a formidable bunch.

Father was somewhat spoiled because his mother said he had a weak chest. At eleven he was confined to bed for some weeks after being rolled on by a horse; at twelve he suffered a bad attack of appendicitis. His four sisters doted on him, and continued to do so for the rest of his life. I have no early memories of Grandpa Lockley because he was an incurable gambler and embarrassed his wife and children by borrowing money from anyone foolish enough to help pay his debts. Finally, apart from a few infrequent visits home, he was banished by the rest of the family before I was old enough to remember him. Granny L, assisted by my Aunt Enid, started a private primary school to earn enough to make ends meet.

Grandpa Lockley

Because Grandpa Lockley was an embarrassment to the family's deep sense of propriety, for many years none of them ever talked about him in front of the younger generation. The fact of his existence came out into the open one day when my Uncle Ken, with his wife Marie, had just returned from a visit to Grandpa L. Aunt Marie, unaware that the subject was taboo, was heard to say: 'Father is quite the best-looking man of the family'! There was a stunned silence from the assembled aunts, then everyone started talking at once to gloss things over. Even so, a long time was to elapse before I learned the true facts, and even longer before I was taken to see him.

My maternal grandmother, Edith Shellard, died when I was three; any knowledge I have of her is from old photographs and hearsay. I was told she was quiet, shy and reserved, a fastidious housekeeper, follower of the latest fashions and punctilious with money. If this family gossip is correct, it is hard to believe that she married such a man as my grandfather Harry Shellard. I often wonder if they were truly happy, they had so little in common. He liked living in the country, she preferred the town; he was notoriously careless with money, and loved to browse in sale rooms and bring home any antiques that took his fancy. He was very sociable and loved all kinds of sport, whisky and parties.

Grandpa Shellard had rooms in Cardiff High Street where he practised as a respected and fashionable dentist. The luxurious waiting room on the first floor, was tastefully furnished with antiques, pictures and objets d'art. It was hardly surprising that a number of the more portable pieces of value mysteriously disappeared because reception and surgeries were up on the second floor! The workshop and small lunchroom were above on the third; there I loved to watch the mechanic, a hunchback called Archie, at work amongst the paraphernalia and false teeth lying all over his bench. I found a grisly fascination in studying the highly-coloured illustrations of teeth in varying states of decay or distortion on the walls: a warning, my mother used to say, of what would happen if I did not clean mine! We always came away with a hunk of pink moulding wax wrapped in newspaper for Mother to use for polishing her flat irons.

For holidays Grandpa Shellard had obtained the use of a field near the beach at Amroth in Pembrokeshire. Here he put up a little two-roomed hut as a base for family and friends to spend seaside holidays. One room was for living and dining, the other contained two camp beds. Visitors would overflow into tents, cars or on the floor. An army bell tent, which reposed in solitary state out in the field, housed the Elsan loo. I always wondered why the loo was given so much space when guests and family had to sleep wherever they could.

We had some grand times. In those days the beach was free of the ugly groynes which are there today. We spent most of our time at the eastern end of the beach, called Black Rock. Here, at low tide there is a huge expanse of sand, with a few rocks here and there. The wash of the tide leaves each boulder surrounded by its own wave-concocted pool. These become quite warm as the tide ebbs, making a paradise of different-shaped paddling pools.

At the time when my parents met, Grandpa and Granny Shellard lived in St. Mellons, a village outside Cardiff, where they had a smallholding containing a large farmhouse, a tennis court and outbuildings. They had two daughters: my mother, always referred to as Do (pronounced as in doe – a female deer; she hated her name Doris), who ran the little farm and the garden and bred black Labrador dogs; and Do's elder sister Vi, who had already married Martin Thomas, a fellow student from Cardiff University, and lived on his farm in north Pembrokeshire. They had two children, Mary and Brian, who for many years were my only first cousins. Both Vi and Do were completely undomesticated: my mother used to say it was because their mother did not allow them to practise household skills. Granny S. had no patience with novices in her domain! Consequently married life was a bit of a shock to both sisters, and neither of them had a liking for, or became efficient at, housekeeping. Vi was ever the academic. Do was artistic and hankered after a more bohemian life: after school she had been sent to study art at a polytechnic in London. She hated it. Too many disciplines were put on her work, and she begged to come home.

Grandpa S. was a keen amateur artist. He had made a name for himself in Cardiff with his oil paintings. He befriended Edgar Thomas, a flamboyant character and well-known figure in the streets of Cardiff, with his mane of white hair and his habit of wearing a long flowing cape; a gifted painter, now considered to be a leading Welsh artist of his time. Grandpa S. engaged him as my mother's private tutor when she insisted on leaving the polytechnic; she became Edgar Thomas's complete disciple, admiring his eccentricity as well as his talent.

About 1922 Granny Lockley helped finance my father into starting a small poultry farm near St Mellons. His sister Enid joined him to do the housekeeping, and the other sisters were frequent visitors too. Inevitably the Lockleys and the Shellards, as near neighbours, came to know each other.

Grandpa S. held big tennis parties, organised walks, cycling trips and picnics in the nearby Black Mountains. On one famous picnic he was reputed to have run three miles across country to the nearest village to buy mustard when he discovered he had none in his ham sandwich. He was immensely popular with all the young, who always referred to him as 'Pop Shellard'. Reminiscences of their escapades were told ad infinitum by the grown ups, reducing them to paroxysms of helpless laughter. This oft-repeated scene brought on many a snigger from the younger generation. The Lockley girls were very athletic and played lacrosse to international level; they taught my mother to play so that she could join them and play in village matches. Father played hockey for Monmouth and Ken played football. A mutual love of literature and nature brought my parents together. They were both keen amateur naturalists.

Grandpa Shellard always liked to have the latest and most powerful car. He and Father often went on explorative jaunts, sleeping rough and observing nature. Although they had been on jaunts to Pembrokeshire before, and had visited the islands of Ramsey and Skomer, they had never been to Skokholm island, a little further south. At Whitsun 1927 they determined to visit Skokholm – they were the two men who had stared at the island across the sea. Both Grandpa S. and my father fell in love with everything they saw there. From that moment on my father could not get this island out of his mind. He decided he must buy it, but the asking price was too much. Then they discovered it was up for rent. When he told my mother about his discovery she was wildly excited and expressed a longing to be taken to see this island and its wonders.

12 July 1927. Father writes:

Today Do and I discovered our love for each other ... we spent the day together on the Brecon Beacons ... August 5th ... Great happenings during the last month, Do and I being more or less engaged, have been very happy together, we propose to go and live on Skokholm Island, negotiations have reached an advanced stage ...

They fixed their wedding day for 12 July the following year.

In late September, after ticklish negotiations, the owner, Colonel Lloyd Phillips of Dale Castle, agreed to lease the island to my father for twenty-one years at £25 per annum, providing Father compensated the present tenant and took immediate possession.

Most of the family were up in arms about Father's leasing the island: the isolation, giving up the poultry farm: the forthcoming marriage ... how would they earn a living ... their age difference was too great (he was twenty-four and she was nearly thirty-four) ... the house on the island was a ruin ... neither of them had any savings ... and so it went on. Both mothers were against the union.

Father promised he could make the old farmhouse habitable by making money from breeding chinchilla rabbits, fishing, sheep farming, trapping wild rabbits and selling them for meat and fur. They both said they could live off the land. Mother said she would elope in order to take part in rebuilding the island house and get away from her parents, who were bickering because she was not going to be home much longer to look after the farm.

My father always said the only reason my mother promised to marry him was so that she could share his life on this island – he even referred to this in his books, but my mother would have none of this, and there is no mention of it in his diaries.

2

Island Life Begins

As soon as he had successfully negotiated the lease for Skokholm, Father quickly disposed of the poultry farm and moved to Pembrokeshire, staying on the Codd family farm near Martinshaven, where the locals kept their boats. He engaged a Marloes fisherman and boat owner, Jack Edwards, to help with the work and teach this 'greenhorn from up country' how to handle a boat, learn to read the tides, to fish, make lobster pots and cope with island life. Among my father's papers I found an undated newspaper cutting which tells us much about this remarkable man:

DEATH OF JACK EDWARDS AN APPRECIATION by R. M. Lockley ... he loved the sea and was fearless, a mariner born, a complete master of small boats and well versed in the lore of local tides and winds ... Jack Edwards was to teach me all I knew about the sea ... thanks to his physical efforts Skokholm House was rebuilt ... he entered into the spirit of adventure and retained his love of Pembrokeshire Islands to the last ... he had a quiet strength, self effacing modesty and shining honesty ... sad to think his health in later years was such that he was forbidden to do anything strenuous, but he could be seen in summer out fishing ... doctors orders gone to the four winds of the west ... For me Jack Sound is forever associated with this great soul Jack Edwards ...

Jack owned a double-ended ex ship's lifeboat, the *Foxtrot*. Having no engine, she was totally dependent on sail or oars. One of the first things my father purchased was a boat both light enough for hauling and with an outboard motor. He bought a sturdy little 16-foot clinker-built craft with a 3 h.p. engine for £50, which he christened *Storm Petrel*. On 20 October he and Jack loaded the *Foxtrot* and the new boat with furniture, winch rope, rabbit traps, oil stove, fuel and stores; they took the *Foxtrot* in tow behind the *Storm Petrel* and made Skokholm within an hour. Island life was about to begin in earnest! They made many more journeys with such loads. A local man called Dicky Edwards was engaged as full-time trapper. He lived with us, and often on his own on the island when he was trapping. (Dicky was illiterate, hence the comment below.)

October to November are notorious for gales. Many were the frustrations of being marooned onshore or offshore by bad weather or engine trouble. So often they had to row or put up sail because the little engine had let them down or needed new parts. Throughout all these enforced interruptions, and in spite of his frustration, hardly a day passed when Father failed to record what was going on in the natural world around him. He generally recorded his daily activities pretty fully, invariably interspersed with observations on nature.

November 8th. I am 24 today and I am realising my greatest ambition, which is to live happily forever on a bird-island, lonely, set in the sea, with the dearest girl in the world wishing and longing and going to be with me soon. How little I could have dared hope for a few months ago, and how often I have dreamed of this! ... loaded the Foxtrot with windows, door, paint, boxes, bags ... half a ton of cement and a bag of lime, with some difficulty launched the loaded boat, and presently ... sailed fast for Skokholm, arriving in 53 minutes ... a grand morning's work ... An hour was spent hauling

Jack's 23 foot boat, probably the longest boat ever to be hauled up the Skokholm winchway ... many birds I saw today ... How glad I am to be on Skokholm again. Brought Dicky a letter, which I read to him.

In his diaries Father often quoted how fast they went in the boat with the help of one tide stream or another. In his book *Letters from Skokholm* there is a good explanation, with little diagrams. Theoretically, local fishermen said, you should launch your boat at slack water so you have plenty of time to start with the first of the tide's current moving in the direction you want to go, but it was not always as simple as that, especially if the wind was going against the current.

Father hated gin-trapping the wild rabbits on the island, because it was not an efficient method of reducing their numbers and quite a lot of birds got caught in the traps. The vagaries of the weather made it very difficult to get rabbits ashore fresh and in good order. So often they were thrown over the cliff as too stale, or rejected by the agent on the mainland for the same reason.

In January Father and Jack finished patching up the roof of the island barn with the original tiles quarried on the island, then grouting with cement. They decided to make this building weatherproof first because it needed the least attention and would then be a dry place for sleeping and eating. It soon became imperative that Father had a hut at Martinshaven, where he could stay near the boat and keep stores when he was ashore. He procured some land adjacent to the harbour for one shilling a year rent.

'The hut' today is barely recognizable. Now a shop and information centre for the islands and the Pembrokeshire Coast National Park, it is called 'Lockley Lodge'. In fact, my father sometimes referred to it as a lodge, whereas to my mother and me it was always 'the hut'.

An incredible stroke of luck came Father's way on 25 February: a small schooner was wrecked on Skokholm, to which Father got salvage rights. She was laden with 100 tons of coal and enough timber and various fitments, which would help towards rebuilding the island house. That day was an exciting and memorable one for my father and his assistant and mentor, the faithful Jack. They had been ashore to get a load of timber and corrugated iron. On their return as they approached South Haven there the schooner was, with all sails set, fast on the rocks in a creek facing south-east below Spy Rock. She was the *Alice Williams*, 1854, of Falmouth.

Father, Jack and Dicky spent all the next day wrecking, which gave Father a few qualms as to the legality of it. The following day he was able to assuage his conscience and make things legal when he went ashore and telephoned the Lloyds agent, who advised to 'salve all they could and make a deal later!' Eventually he offered £5 for the wreck, which was accepted.

Father, with help from Captain Beer (who was called Captain Crystal in Father's books), Jack's uncle, Dicky and Charles (a schoolboy who had previously written asking if he could stay on Skokholm) toiled for eight days, using two winches to haul gear and several tons of coal safely above reach of high water. This episode is described in several of my father's books.

By 14 March the wreck had broken up and a south-easterly gale continued. Father and Jack spent much time saving useful timber and spars blown back into 'Wreck Cove' (from now on this little cove would be so named).

My father worked extremely hard to get the house habitable. Stores and building materials had to be loaded from Martinshaven beach, unloaded in South Haven and carried to the house. Sand to make concrete was humped by the sackful up a steep and stony path cut in the cliff at North Haven, the only sandy beach on the island. In a letter to my mother, Father describes feeling ill after carrying sand all day.

My mother sent a regular supply of cakes and vegetables down to Martinshaven. The letters my parents wrote to each other during the year of their engagement are recorded in a book called *Dear Islandman*, published so late in my father's life that I edited it for him; the letters were a revelation to me, so full of hopes and fears and romance, before either Ronald or Doris had been touched by fame or disillusionment. They compared themselves with Oisin and Niamh from the Irish legend *Oisin i dTir na nOg*. Many years later I saw a performance of this legend by The National Folk Theatre in Tralee, and discovered my parents had used a good deal of licence in comparing it with their romance!

It is one of the best known and best loved tales of the Fenian cycle. Oisin, poet and warrior of Fianna meets beautiful maiden Niamh Chinn Oir from Tir na nOg, she asks him to come with her to her land of everlasting youth. After a while he wishes to return to Ireland. Niamh lets him go, but warns him not to touch the ground there or he will become old and die. Of course, he finds the Fianna all dead; on seeing two men building a wall he reaches down to help them pick up a stone, falls from his horse and is transformed from youth to withered old man. It is a sad tale, but a memorable performance and an extra pleasure for me.

My mother had been carefully nurturing a number of chinchilla rabbits (not to be confused with the South American rodent of that name), which she and Father hoped might make them a fortune in fur. A large 'rabbitry' was built for them, but even before this was completed, the ones already sent to the island did not thrive, and their winter pelts were never luxurious enough; certainly Father did not have time to look after them.

By the end of March the barn roof was watertight, the walls whitewashed, chimney sealed and red stone hearth, open grate and hobs constructed. Eventually *Alice Williams'* wheel was placed in the breast above the fire. From then on this building became known as 'the Wheelhouse'.

In the first week of April my mother and Grandpa Shellard arrived for a week. They brought over plants, seeds and more chinchilla rabbits. The first 'instate' meal was eaten in the Wheelhouse. After admiring the improvements, much time was spent planting up the garden and enlarging the kitchen in the cottage.

On 12 May work started in earnest on the house. Reluctantly Father ordered grey asbestos tiles, because slates would involve too much heavy hauling. Father writes:

> one need not be too particular as to horizontals and perpendiculars … owing to the lean of the walls, which are quite haphazard … doing the kitchen floor with cement from North Haven sand coloured with Venetian red powder over a rough base of cinders and contents of the midden … shells, limpets, bones, crockery, nails, broken traps and stones etc … May 19th… boated tiles across and hauled up to the house with great labour … May 20th: did not get up until 10 a.m. having rather overdone it yesterday … lazed in the sun, dreaming dreams on a bed of campion and watching hundreds of puffins flying about the harbour ... the mason, had gone off on another job … I am really glad as I want to build my own home myself … as well as possible … with the material at hand.

It is interesting to read what Father says about the floor of the old house: 'carrying on with patching up the old living room floor, as I do not intend to put this in afresh. It is largely made up of wreck and flotsam timber and I am patching it with the same'. This was in 1928. On a visit to Skokholm in 2001, the warden told me that they were going to have to renew the floor of the sitting room, adding in a horrified tone: 'You know, the floorboards were just laid on the bare earth!'

On 6 July 1928 they took delivery of a load of my mother's furniture, a flock of chickens and twelve chinchilla rabbits.

3

1928–1930

For a brief time in May my parents thought about getting married on Skokholm, but they found the island belonged to no parish, not even one on the mainland. So they decided on St Brides, a little church on the coast just north of Martinshaven. Father declared, 'I am now adopting St Brides as Skokholm's Official Church.'

My parents' wedding duly took place on 12 July 1928. It was a small and simple affair attended by just a few of the family, including both sets of parents. The church ceremony was followed by a picnic reception in St Brides Haven. The Storm Petrel awaited them on the shore below the church, and from there they sailed away for their honeymoon, first to Skokholm, then a glorious sail up the Cleddau. The weather was good and the winds fair; in the ensuing days they visited Ramsey, the Bishop Rocks and Grassholm. I am moved to quote the diary here:

a dozen seals basked in the sun at low water on the rocks and sang mournful shanties as the sea rose and washed them gradually from their resting place. After a bathe we slept in the long soft grass on the quiet eastern slopes of Grassholm and heard no petrels or shearwaters to disturb our fitful sleep ... August. These days are marvellously tranquil and happy in weather and heart, working on the house with my wife; putting the fire grate in the living room, rebuilding the roof of the porchway ... getting the house ready for visitors, Do distempering the walls of the sitting room, I putting a stove in the kitchen ...

With friends and relations to stay, a cricket match was organised, Skokholm versus the mainlanders from Marloes village. They were enchanted days for the newlyweds, ferrying friends and relations to and fro, making improvements, painting the loft, framing the sitting room fireplace with part of Alice William's taffrail. Corrugated iron was put on one of the outhouse roofs to make it into a dormitory for the boys. The Wheelhouse shanty from the wreck, which was an odd bull-nosed shed shaped like the bonnet of a car, was rolled into the shelter of the old haggard to house the chickens in one end and a bucket loo in the other. They made expeditions with visitors to other islands and played 'glass bowls' in the evenings: this was a unique form of 'hand croquet' invented on Skokholm, played with glass lobster pot floats and wire hoops, the bowling surface slightly uneven but manicured like a bowling green by the rabbits! Smashing one of the floats caused instant disqualification!

There was great excitement in September over a gramophone, a wedding present from Granny S. The precious cargo was conveyed from the hut to the boat on the bicycle! They returned to the island in pouring rain, carrying provisions, gramophone, records and bags of lime. That gramophone was still with us in 1946. It was contained in a large wooden cabinet with doors which opened in front.

With winter coming, serious rabbit-trapping began, also accounting for many birds: 'Among recent dinners we have dined off water rail caught in the traps – quite delicious even to bird lovers.' Getting rabbits to the mainland in good condition caused desperate journeys when the weather really was, as Jack always phrased it: 'in no shape for going'. One bad experience Father describes very graphically in his diary with rough sketches of the *Storm Petrel* mounting gargantuan waves, he described it as 'an experience that one likes to have had, but can never wish to have'.

If a gale came up unexpectedly in the night and the boat was on her mooring they had to wait until the tide was full before they could reach her berth at the winchway. Once or twice they very nearly lost the *Storm Petrel*. I remember watching this procedure on many later occasions. First we had to pull the boat near enough to the landing stage for someone to jump in, pull her out again away from the rocks, then bail out enough water for her to be sculled to her berth.

A large rock, strategically placed by nature and shaped rather like a lopsided A-frame, shelters the bottom of the winchway, leaving a passage with just enough room between it and the cliffside for a small boat to slip through at high tide into a small area of slightly more protected water, thus easing the sometimes tricky manoeuvre of disembarking and attaching a wire rope to start winching the boat up her rocky berth. Years later, with my cousin Brian, this was one of our favourite places to play, waiting for the tide to ebb so that we could wade across and climb to the peak of this rock, which, for some forgotten reason, we christened 'St Catherine's Island'.

In November the biggest storm my father had ever seen began to blow in earnest from the south-west. They threw ropes over the cottage roof and tied it down with stones, but tiles flew off the porch Father had just completed. A gap of 12 feet was blown in the yard wall, almost carrying away a corner of the Wheelhouse. November and December were busy months catching, killing and carting wild rabbits, carpentering, and tending to the chinchilla rabbits. A chore for the men was to bring a sack of coal from Wreck Cove each day.

Father had taken to getting up before dawn to write, a habit which he continued throughout his life. He had, much to his satisfaction, already had a few articles accepted concerning his observations on nature and life on

Brian and me playing with our toy boats on St Catherine's Island

Skokholm, and he had started to draft out a novel called the *The Island Dwellers*.

Jack and Dicky were sent home for Christmas and my parents were alone on Skokholm for the first happy time: 'Christmas Day 1928. A bit blowy and wet, spent mostly indoors except a visit to the lighthouse where Do presented a sponge cake to the men'.

At the end of January 1929, after much soul-searching, my parents decided they would have to dismiss Jack and Dicky because they could not afford to pay them. The chinchilla rabbit enterprise looked very shaky; not least because of a shortage of fodder and above average attrition, for various reasons. The season's catch of 1008 wild rabbits fetched £132, not including a bad debt. Father wrote to the Royal Society for the Protection of Birds to ask for help to run the island as a bird sanctuary.

Mid February was very cold with frosts and a huge snowstorm. The diary makes dismal reading: birds dying of cold and starvation, the more predatory ones feasting on the weaker. Mortality among birds and young chinchilla rabbits continued. Gradually the weather improved, and many members of the family came to stay, including Uncle Ken, an astute businessman, who had long ago predicted that his brother's chinchilla scheme was not going to pay. By April signs of spring appeared, with primroses, celandines and scurvy grass, and the arrival of puffins, chiffchaff and grey wagtail. The goats had kidded and the hens were laying. The RSPB sent a cheque for £25 in consideration of my parents' desire to abolish traps. They invited Father to become an honorary watcher for this district, which he accepted. Even so trapping went on for some while.

Uncle Martin bought nine lambs and nine ewes for Father, who was looking forward to being a shepherd! These were unloaded at Martinshaven, then for the boat journey each one was tied by one hind foot securely lashed between two forefeet. Jack happened to be on the beach, and he offered to come over with my parents and stay for a few days so that he could teach them to make lobster pots with the withies they had bought. On 19 May, in glorious weather, Grandpa Shellard stayed for a few days, and he painted two pictures: one of South Haven and one from North Haven. We have both these pictures still, a constant reminder of how lovely the island can look in May.

About this time, Father was ringing shearwaters to find out their incubation period, which is as yet unknown. He said: 'Some of the results of daily scrutinising are remarkable, inasmuch as some pairs neglect the egg for days at a stretch, and are remarkably casual'. These observations were the beginning of his original research on Manx shearwaters, a turning point in his career. On 12 July, my parents' first wedding anniversary, he wrote: 'we have spent a year of marvellous happiness, and the future seems full of quiet enjoyment and lovely peacefulness of tranquil shepherd's life'.

Shepherding on Skokholm was never easy, with predatory gulls and ravens attacking afterbirths and the eyes of cast sheep. The number of dead birds scattered around attracted the greenbottle fly, which increased the numbers of infected sheep, who then tended to skulk among the rocks where they couldn't be found.

Sixty-six tons of building materials were landed at South Haven to re-stucco the lighthouse. Father thought Edward the donkey was not up to hauling such heavy loads, so he made an offer to buy a pony to do the job and hire him out for 7/- a ton. With Uncle Martin's help a pony was purchased for £7.10s, a thirteen-hand chestnut stallion, broken to saddle and harness. Martin lent a saddle and started Father off at 5 p.m. on the journey from Mynachlog-ddu, in the centre of inland Pembrokeshire, to Haverfordwest. The following excerpt says much for the stamina of both pony and rider!

> I turned off the main road and trotted, walked and galloped through the lanes and villages to Haverfordwest. It was my first saddle journey, and sore I was when I got in at 9 p.m. After digging out the stableman to give my pony food and water, I went to bed at the Castle Hotel … I was in the saddle again by 8.40 … trotting along the level, walking down hill and galloping up hill. I arrived at Marloes at 12 noon, just as the good folk were leaving chapel. I walked pony sedately past the people in their Sunday best …

By this time in the narrative I felt sorry for the pony, rather than Father. He knew little about horses, never learned to 'rise' to the trot, or that generally one should not gallop a tired pony uphill.

Thirteen more ewes plus pony were taken over next day in Jack's boat, they rowed all the way with Mother steering. They landed the sheep but had to wait for the tide to come in before landing the pony, who apparently stepped out quietly and walked up to the winch without any fuss, an amazing achievement, when his feet had been tied together for so long and the winchway being so steep and rocky. They named him Punch.

Father was elated in October when Jack agreed to come and work for them permanently, summer and winter. Either my father had decided he was too inexperienced at fishing, or my mother discovered she was one month pregnant; for whatever reason, it was a timely and advantageous move, with so much work to be done: mending walls and fences, catching rabbits, tending the sheep, preparing lobster pots and going back and forth with rabbits in winter weather. Added to this, during the coming months they hauled all the building materials up the track for the lighthouse repair using Punch, sometimes assisted by Edward, the lighthouse keepers' donkey.

For a time both Jack and Dicky slept in the house until we had put a roof on one of the outbuildings to make a men's dormitory.

Later that month Marloes village was agog with news of a wreck on Midland Island in Jack Sound. Half the village were watching from the Deer Park. First thing the next morning Father and six fishermen went out to investigate, but to their chagrin the Angle lifeboat arrived just as they got there. The following morning Jack and Father rowed out to the wreck. They were very surprised to find a Maltese fireman who had somehow missed being rescued! Before taking the fireman ashore they 'souvenired' some monogrammed crockery and a pile of dreadful gramophone records. (I remember both these items!) The Britain

Steamship Co. sent Father a letter of thanks and a cheque for 29 guineas for the rescue.

By 10 December a great gale had blown up. The Molesey became washed off the rocks and the body of an Arab seaman was washed ashore near Renny Slip. I was quite surprised at Father's very nonchalant description of helping to drag his remains up the cliff ...

January 1930 began with many gales. My parents and Jack spent the winter on the island, battling the weather, doing the chores and making pots. In April they sold the first catch of the season in Milford: nineteen lobsters and 1 cwt. crabs, which fetched 1s 4d per lb., bringing in £3.

Father's diary has Monday May 12th underlined. My mother had spent the previous week ashore at the hut with Vi and Enid. Father had come over from Skokholm twice to make enquiries, the second time he was informed that 'he was father of a girl, both well'. They named me Ann.

On 1 June my parents were quite overcome by the reception that the lighthouse keepers put on for my arrival. There were code flags strung across the harbour spelling 'welcome', more flags on the flagstaff behind the house, and some on the front door. I slept soundly throughout the whole proceeding.

Being the first grandchild on my father's side, and with all those doting aunts, it was inevitable that I came in for a great deal of attention. There are copious numbers of early photographs of me in every state of dress or undress, posing inside lobster pots, tweaking the whiskers of enormous crayfish and sitting in the arms of every member of the family. These photographs are great testimony, supporting the diaries' evidence, and provide useful information on how things looked while I was too young to remember.

Enid left, having been incomparably useful in every way.

Jack had to see to his uncle's hay, and Father had been assisting them to get the job over more quickly, so that he could, he wrote: 'return to Queen Doris and Princess Ann, both well'. My mother was quite unfazed by staying on the island on her own with a very young child, although the light-keepers were not so far away, and could be relied on to signal for help with the lamp, even though it was a rather uncertain way of sending messages in the days before radio telephone.

On July 13th Father wrote in philosophical mood:

Yesterday was the 2nd anniversary of our wedding, and we have had 2 years of happiness, and are still content and eager for island life, especially since Ann is with us. We dream one day of living alone without a man, as shepherds, and hope that we may earn something to help with pen and brush. My book with Do's drawings [*Dream Island*] is nearly ready for printing …

Four days later, he wrote:

Take note Ronald Mathias Lockley, that fishing does not repay you the cost of the labour, materials and expenses of your engine … meanwhile we aim at a flock of 100 to 150 ewes, which will probably pay better than any general farm, since we need employ no men except in the rabbit season ... and if you can possibly afford not to fish next year, then your time will be more profitably occupied in farm work and doing all those works which shall add to the comfort, convenience and safety of your home and future life, and thus give your mind that certain amount of leisure by which it shall not feel starved, but shall have opportunity to philosophise and train itself, loving always a plain way of living and thinking.

I often wonder if Father took note of that little address to himself in later years. 'Plain living', as he saw it then, was to change quite considerably before long! Their desperate financial situation was somewhat eased when Trinity House called for two labourers for the next three months to plaster and paint the lighthouse, at 1/3d an hour. Father volunteered Jack and himself. October brought a red-letter day: the book *Dream Island* came out, 'and has good reviews, and Do has press notices of some oil paintings she exhibited in Cardiff. Jack began reading the book by the fire the same evening, from his frequent grins it was clear that he liked reading about himself and the history he was part of'.

In spite of Father's optimism about sheep farming, the lambing during March 1931 was pretty disastrous, with bad weather, lambs born dead, ewes with some kind of septicaemia, ravens, crows and gulls pecking at cast sheep, and lack of fences. A little dog was added to the menagerie, a terrier cross called Biddy, apparently as a companion for me. I think now that a good sheepdog would have been a much more practical solution to some of their problems.

A load of lime was delivered in April and stored temporarily in the storeroom of the hut, then transported to Skokholm, a huge job which made them 'very sore from shouldering lime all day'. In spite of sore backs, next day they set off for Milford to purchase tar and rope at the chandlers, while my mother waited in the boat and warmed my bottle in the outflow from the iceworks!

When I read about my babyhood it sounds as if my nine lives were spent before I could walk, not least in the many adventures while trying to get the boat ashore in rough weather. While I was in my wicker cradle it was always placed amidships beneath a thwart to hold it steady, but many times it would be awash from spray, or when a wave came over the stern at launching time. I certainly grew up with a healthy respect for the sea; later on I hated it enough to become extremely nervous every time my parents proposed going out when the weather was rough. They seemed to think they were invincible; the Marloes fishermen thought they were foolhardy!

One such adventure happened in May. In pushing out against a stiff northerly breeze at Martinshaven we were nearly swamped by the incoming breakers. Father had waded out up to his shoulders to get the boat into deep water, but was pushed back by the waves. After that failed attempt the boat was awash, so they rowed up to a fisherman's buoy for Mother to hold on while Father bailed. By that time my bed was almost afloat. The buoy started to drag and the boat began drifting towards the beach again. They rowed to another one, which dragged too but gave them enough time to finish bailing and start the engine. On arrival in South Haven, Father unloaded the engine, stepped ashore, lost his footing on the weedy steps and fell into the sea up to his neck! Fortunately he threw the engine onto the shore as he fell.

On my first birthday, 12 May 1930, we had a celebration ashore where the Thomas family greeted us with birthday cake with one candle, which was apparently sampled by me and my dog Biddy. We returned to Skokholm with a cot for me.

On 16 July 1931 My parents took delivery of a little green Morris Minor 8 h.p. van on an instalment system, paying £30 down. We had this van for a long time and it served us well. It had a hard life, carrying anything from building supplies, sheep, fish, bait or uncomfortably seated passengers. My memories of it were far from favourable. It had two doors at the back, each with a little oval window, but only two seats. Most often I had to sit on the passenger's knee. I dare say when it was new it did not make a grating noise when put under any strain, but by the time I was old enough to remember it well, such was the racket when going uphill that I became quite anxious and earnestly leaned forward, convinced this would help us to the top! My greatest pleasure was in starting the van, when Father used my dangling foot to press the starter button, handily situated on the engine housing; this became such a habit that woe betide him if he forgot!

Prices for wool and for fish were very low. One day my parents were so disgusted with what they were offered for their fish they took them down to Cardiff, but fared no better there. The following week the propeller flew off the outboard motor. New parts took eight days to arrive, and in the meantime they had to use the oars to go back and forth and see to the pots. Hard work,with help only from an inexperienced Barnardo boy called Ivor, who had replaced Jack.

In August Colonel Morrey Salmon and his wife came to stay. Morrey was a keen ornithologist, and a pioneer bird photographer, well-known in Cardiff for his natural history observations. He had visited most of the Pembrokeshire islands years before we ever came on the scene. Father used to send his articles in rough handwritten drafts to Morrey, who would painstakingly type them out for publication. I have some of the originals, and can imagine that Morrey would have been heartily relieved when Father saved enough money to buy a typewriter of his own. Nevertheless this was the beginning of a lifelong friendship.

In September Punch was castrated. He had become very wild, chasing the sheep and goats. He even reached over the fence one day and picked me up. Apart from a few bruises, I was none the worse for being hoisted up by the seat of my pants. Having the van gave my parents so much freedom to move around and my father's diary is full of visits to relations and friends. So much for the lonely island life which Father fondly refers to so often in his books.

My parents more or less decided to spend the winter ashore at the hut and to finish off its conversion into two rooms. This was overdue because originally Father had used sawdust as insulation between its plywood lining and corrugated iron exterior – how the mice loved it! Dick planned to stay on Skokholm to trap rabbits, which Father and a man called Folland ferried across whenever weather permitted the trip. This day Folland refused to go … but my parents' needs must:

wind west south west and seems to be moderating slowly, at 1.30 pm. Do and I pushed off in a vain attempt to reach the island. Ann was under cover in the boat and safe from the spray that shrouded us during most of the stormy passage, when we got down to Jack Sound we encountered a very heavy sea … it was breaking enough to fill the boat- we reluctantly turned back again … Nov. 11th: Still a gale veering moderately, rather forlornly we again set out at 3pm. But encountered such a heavy breaking sea below Jack Sound that common sense forced us to return to Martinshaven. Had a letter from Putnam's publishers, asking whether I could write a book on island life for them. Was feeling pretty bucked for the rest of the day! … 12th … wind N.W. by W. pretty fresh, but we again set out in some big seas, the engine stopped near the Stack … but the north stream prevented us from drifting too quickly. We found the gale of Tuesday had carried off the mooring ropes … while Do held the boat afloat I went up and fetched 94 of the freshest rabbits, leaving provisions for Dick … Cleaned the plug and carburettor … a very wet return passage in clouds of spray ... blowing hard, the engine stopped off Jack Sound, we nearly drifted onto the Benches before I started the engine in time ... engine stopped again but we were now safe and rowed before the wind into Martinshaven, after a voyage which was a triumph but a hazard. We were all wet through.

My mother never had any qualms about going to sea in any weather; in fact she was one of those people who seemed not to know the meaning of fear. Slim and barely 5 foot tall, she was an excellent boatwoman, and could manage the heavy oars or the winch whenever occasion demanded. Many a time she held the boat steady off the shore with the oars because it was too rough to moor, while Father leapt ashore to deal with the rabbit catch.

My parents were away from Pembrokeshire over Christmas until 11 January 1932. Having seen all their relations in Cardiff and in London, they visited publishers, and Woburn Park and Whipsnade zoo in the snow. In between, Father was finishing off *The Island Dwellers*. Because my parents had been ashore so much that winter the gossips spread the rumour that my mother was pregnant, much to her consternation. Eventually she had to explain that it was not a rumour, the new arrival was expected in June, but this was not the reason they had spent time ashore.

Bad weather prevented them from crossing to Skokholm until 20 January. Eventually the rough weather abated and both parents were delighted to be back on the island. They found the sheep were well, but the house was overrun with mice, and rabbits in the garden. Father's positive thoughts of the previous November were reversed. He felt sure he would never face another winter on Skokholm:

Perhaps an absorbing interest in the land by farming, ploughing, I might wish to stay. My interests seem to be literary and at present I have a strong desire for the companionship of trees instead of desolate rocks. How it is to be achieved I know not ... I think of a cottage somewhere on the Cleddau ... in more expansive surroundings with trees and books, long walks both river and estuarine ... I may be able to work with new zeal and enthusiasm with this wayward mind and pen.

How fickle are my Father's whims and thoughts ... this last has a prophetic ring. However, on 14 February he wrote:

calm anticyclonic conditions ... today warm and windless almost, a very great joy to be on the island with such weather and spring in front. Righted the boat after tarring and puttying. [She was as leaky as ever after the winter's neglect.] How many moods I have. Today, very much in love with an island life ...

Edward the donkey died; I do not remember him, of course, but the poor beast suffered from bad feet because, unaccountably, Trinity House (the lighthouse authority) stipulated that 'he be shod once a year'. The Marloes blacksmith always chose to come to do it in late spring when the gulls' eggs were right for gathering! He did a good sideline making 'donkey foot door knockers' from the old shoes still nailed to the twelve-month growth of poor Edward's hooves. While our ponies were on Skokholm they were never shod, but we had to trim their hooves regularly because they grew at a prodigious rate with no hard ground to wear them away.

Lots of different birds were caught in the gin traps. Apparently we once dined on two blackbirds, a woodcock, a lark and an oystercatcher, 'all excellently cooked by Doris'. Mother became adept at turning out good dishes with strange ingredients. I don't remember turning up my nose at any of the more exotic things she concocted, but I was a bit faddy about the more mundane.

In late February my parents looked at a modern cottage shortly to be vacant, near the Cleddau river, the rent £20 per annum.

By early March preparations for the summer on Skokholm were in full swing. The last of the coal was brought up from Wreck Cove. The last of the trapped wild rabbits were sent away and the traps pulled up. Father was resigned to making more pots, fishing and keeping sheep, since he and Mother were certain to be on the island most of the summer. He wrote:

The thought of having a home amid trees in sheltered ways of the Cleddau makes island life more lovely than ever. No longer do I feel the invisible chains imprisoning me to the barren rocks. I shall have a refuge in the woodlands to fly to: though I may never use it, the knowledge is very delicious … All the goats have kidded … we have kept three … We had Jonathon II [the cockerel] for dinner, his usefulness is over, being related to all our hens … he was remarkably tender … hung for a week, steamed and roasted.

4

A Transitory Life

On 31 March 1932 we took possession of the house on the Cleddau, inspired by the splendid view down river, my parents named it 'Beggars Reach'. A few days later they took a couple of mattresses over there, in order to camp in the house when necessary. Shepherding went on with mixed success and the ever unpopular fishing: But there was still discontent:

> When will I learn wisdom, never to waste time fishing; so far I have not covered expenses of the gear and labour – about £10 at least, never again ... when I told the agent today that I would not be fishing while I was house moving etc. he raked out all the old charges he could find for bait, even one from last year ... this is how the fisherman gets treated by the middleman ...

The weather did not improve this dire state of affairs. In May a howling sou-easter battered the store box in South Haven, and all but one crab escaped. On the 12th I had my second birthday. My mother made a birthday cake with two candles: chocolate sponge decorated with chocolate and cherries. One or two loads of furniture had already been taken straight up river via the haven to save cartage by road.

My father's diary said that 29 May was a sad day, for I was sent off with Aunt Kathleen in her car to stay with Granny Lockley until the birth of the baby. The following passage is very poignant:

> Do and I drowned our sorrows in a tour through Jefferston, Penally, thence to the Bishop's Palace at

Lamphey, where we stole in without troubling to ring the bell and climbed about the old ruins, possessed by wagtails, spotted flycatchers, toadflax and wall flowers … After lunch towards St Govan's Head where we made our pilgrimage, the 73 steps down the ravine to the tiny chapel of St Govan, where Do laid flowers on his humble stone altar while I explored the foreshore beyond this charmingly placed hermitage …

I wonder if my mother prayed then for the child in her womb. Knowing her, I very much doubt it, and if she did, her prayers were in vain. On 10 June, after a difficult breech birth, a beautiful eight and a half pound boy was born. The baby seemed perfect in every way, but only lived for a few minutes. It must have been devastating for both my parents. Father blamed himself for not cosseting his wife more, but he would have found that difficult: she hated anyone to fuss, and she was remarkably fit. I am sure in this day and age she would have been advised to have an earlier birth or a Caesarean.

They never gave me any inkling of this unfortunate and unhappy event. Maybe it was too painful. I was more surprised than sad when her friend Joyce told me when I was about seventeen. I never spoke of it to my mother. She had enough misfortune in her life at that stage. Now much, much later, I feel a very deep sense of loss, and reading about it in the diary makes me unutterably sad. How different life would have been had my brother lived. What a pleasure it would have been to have a brother near to my age, a companion, confidant, a shoulder to cry on, someone to share the responsibilities inevitably thrown on an only child.

I did not return home until early July, in Uncle Ken's new £265 Morris Oxford car. Father wrote, 'I think she recognised us, but was shy at first'.

The next months Ivor (the Barnado boy) and Father spent commuting from Beggars Reach to Skokholm to tend the sheep, usually leaving my mother and me behind. She was working hard to create a garden there, hoping one day to soften the raw look of the modern stuccoed house with trees and shrubs. Father had at last purchased a typewriter of his own, but despaired of making enough money to keep them in their present lifestyle. He was earning a little writing articles for *The Countryman*, but not much income from the sheep. He hated bargaining with the dealers, not to mention the added costs of transporting them from the island. The *Storm Petrel* was almost past repair. She was tied across the middle from gunwale to gunwale because she was starting to open up. Another boat needed to be purchased very soon, but they could not afford it.

Even though my parents had these worries, family and friends came to visit and frequent sightseeing tours were made around the county. At one time they were dining off venison from the Lawrenny estate – traditionally donated by Mrs. Lort-Phillips for the 'poor of the district', much to my parents' gratification and amusement. It was delivered to their door by her man. Later on we must have gone up in her estimation because we were often invited to the Castle for afternoon tea.

Father persuaded the Royal Society for Protection of Birds to pay the rent for Skokholm, and a notice painted by my mother was erected in South Haven:

DREAM ISLAND SANCTUARY
RESERVED
FOR BIRDS AND FLOWERS
LANDING WITHOUT PERMISSION
STRICTLY FORBIDDEN.
R.M. Lockley

When the official agreement was received the rent was raised to £26 in consideration of the landlord waiving the shooting and sporting rights, and in return for us keeping the island as a sanctuary as heretofore.

Now that I was growing up a little bit and my mother was free to come and go, Ivor went to work at Coedcandlas, the farm next door to Beggars Reach. In September the three of us called on *The Countryman* office in the Cotswolds. On this their first visit, both sides seem to have been mutually impressed. Father described it thus:

> after discussing my articles Robertson Scott took us round his fine Cotswold manor house ... Mrs. Scott showed Do her domestic arrangements which chiefly give evidence of spending unlimited money. So, having exhibited us as curios, "reared on a strictly lobster diet", we departed!

While waiting in the office there, my mother saw the receptionist/secretary scratching her eye through the frame of her large horn-rimmed spectacles! Her explanation was that 'it makes me look more like a secretary!' She introduced herself as Joyce Westrup. Subsequently she became one of my mother's best friends. She was eccentric, stimulating company and an accomplished cook. My first memory of Joyce was going to her cottage for a meal after another meeting with Robertson Scott, and turning up my nose at the deep purple colour of some mushroom soup. Knowing Joyce, I daresay it had been made with Shaggy Ink Caps!

Father's first attempt at a novel, *The Island Dwellers*, arrived in the post. The reviews ranged from good to poor. I even found an old cutting from the *Egyptian Gazette*: 'What Mr. Lockley lacks in construction of this novel he makes up for in his undoubted power of description ... for those who know this rugged corner of Wales, this book will be in no way disappointing.'

Now that Ivor had gone, my mother had to help with the sheep and fetching rabbits from the island. The light-keepers asked to do the trapping on a half-share basis if Father would ferry what they caught to the mainland. A flag was to be raised when they have caught a minimum of thirty. So back my parents went to live in the hut at Martinshaven to be near the boat. In October's notoriously stormy weather, many times the keepers threw the rabbits into the boat because it was too rough to approach the landing stage too closely:

October 8th: Nasty groundsea in South Haven … too rough to land Ann, so Do stayed in the boat with her and held onto the mooring ropes. Almost as soon as I had jumped ashore and gone up to the house, Do lost both the oars when a huge swell shook the boat and carried them out of the rowlocks. What a predicament she was in: Ann very troubled and ready to cry sitting in the stern, Do holding on, not daring to let go, having no oars to manoeuvre the boat to face the breakers head on … what a life we lead, perils too near to be comfortable, yet starry sky the still sea and warm sun on other days make the hazards worth while. The wash from the rocks brought the oars within reach, and she was retrieving them when I returned with the rabbits.

On 7 January 1932 Father 'Arranged to take Reuben Codd's rabbits from Skomer'. Too frequently the engine went wrong and spare parts took time to be delivered, but the rabbits couldn't wait, so they had to take to the oars and the sail. To avoid the breakers in Jack Sound they rowed to Little Sound, then put up sail. Halfway across a squall hit them and stripped the sail right off the yard below the rope. Poor old sail, it had done wonders since it had been sewn for them by Jack five years before. Now and again a foray was made to Beggars Reach to enjoy a very welcome hot bath after a wet crossing to get rabbits. The price for rabbits improved by the end of the month, making their adventures more worthwhile.

On 3 March, my mother's birthday, the family gave her a primus oven for 72/-. It was a boon, because hitherto she only had the use of a couple of primuses and the old coal stove, which was very slow. The primus stove lasted until we left Skokholm in 1940. It was basically a tin box with shelves and a hole in the side to insert the primus.

Rabbit catching was over by mid March as the price suddenly fell. In April they gradually started to move all the furniture out of Beggars Reach, some to the island and the rest stored temporarily at Coedcandlas. My parents had decided they could not afford the high rent, and anyway they needed to be on hand for lambing on Skokholm. In moving one lot of furniture and personal gear, the van door 'came slyly open', were Father's words! The van and the high wind had made so much noise that they did not notice that all their possessions were strewn for miles. They arrived in Haverfordwest before they realised what had happened. On turning back, they found that an AA man had followed picking up various items and stowing them on his carrier; he reported a traffic jam where a basket of stuff had fallen in the middle of the road. The loss of one of Father's almost new brown shoes was the most lamented. This problem with the van doors had happened before on two earlier occasions while Father took sheep to the mart, which entailed a long chase over adjacent fields to retrieve those which had escaped!

May 12th was my birthday. I was three. In the evening we took a trip over to Skokholm taking a load of stores and coal, the *Alice Williams* supply having finally come to an end. All this preparation was in honour of a visit from Julian Huxley (Sir Julian Sorell Huxley, evolutionary biologist (1887–1975), brother of Aldous and Andrew), who asked to come in order to do a paper on puffins. Julian was enchanted with the island. When taken to Grassholm he was even more enthusiastic, and suggested they make a film on gannets in the coming year.

August: the island was now an official bird observatory (the first in Britain), and the rent was being paid by the RSPB. A bird-ringing trap had been constructed at the end of the garden where there are mallow, blackcurrant and elder bushes as extra cover. Col Morrey Salmon and his family came again, and Morrey and Father did a photo-census of the gannets. on Grassholm. When they had finished, they found that the difference between their individual counts was only seventy birds, 5,045 against 4,975. How the population has grown since then! The Grassholm colony is now reported to be something near 39,000!

Great was the excitement when Father received news of his first ringing recovery: a gannet found off the French coast. A serious census of all the birds on Skokholm was undertaken. Much to Father's delight Morrey purchased a plate camera and developing equipment for him. We were inundated with enquiries from people wanting to visit the island as a result of reading Father' articles.

The moment we had completed the finishing touches to a fancy sheep dip constructed below the well, Father wrote: 'just as I decided to give up fishing now I feel I could wisely give up shepherding and devote my whole life to writing articles and books ... and observing wildlife.'

Much of September was spent ringing birds at every opportunity and building a fence right across the island to confine the sheep. This ploy involved many visits to the Wick on Skomer for fencing timber. In late October Father decided, after several unsatisfactory attempts to hire a man to trap wild rabbits, that he would tackle it himself. By early November he had pulled up the traps in disgust after an unsatisfactory catch and on numerous occasions finding rabbit paws left in the gins. We all returned to spend the winter in the hut, which was now more roomy and comfortable. Weekly visits were made to Skokholm to check on the sheep.

Now, free from the rabbit-trapping, lots of excursions were made, the most important being a meeting to discuss the impending International Ornithological Congress scheduled to visit the Pembrokeshire Islands. We went to Dinas Head to walk the cliffs and to Orielton Estate to view the wildfowl decoy and lake. That day I remember being allowed to stroke a tufted duck that the game keeper produced from a sack. On a subsequent visit I remember watching a corgi, specially trained to entice the ducks up the funnel of the decoy. Father loved both Dinas and Orielton. I wonder, when he was writing this in his dairy in 1933, what he would have thought if he could have read his destiny; both these places were to play a notable part in his future.

We went on to see Robertson Scott again (the editor of *The Countryman*), who, according to my mother, remarked on my pallor, saying that I 'was as white as a maggot'. (I was sure to have been suffering from the 'mainland' cold!) We stayed with Joyce, the editor's secretary, and went for an excursion to Wychwood Forest, near Oxford, where Father found a grey squirrel's drey in a beech tree; he climbed up and shook the naked babies out onto the ground, much to Joyce's consternation and to mine. In 1934 there was grave concern that the recently imported grey squirrel was going to spread, to the detriment of the more attractive native red one. Unfortunately, all efforts to exterminate the greys were in vain.

We made a round of the boatyards in Cardiff, looking for a replacement for the *Storm Petrel*. While making up his mind, Father walked the streets to find a cheap doll's pram for my favourite toy dog Bow-wow, finally tracking one down for 4/11 at Peacock's bazaar. A day or two later, having found no boats to his liking, Father placed an order for an 18 foot long, 6 foot beam clinker-built sailing boat with centreboard, mast, yard and sprit, to be built complete for £46.10/-, to be delivered at Milford by the end of March.

Meanwhile we were making frantic preparations to move to Skokholm for the summer. The sheep were short of feed because rabbit numbers had not been kept down by trapping.

On 29 April we took delivery of the new boat, Father called it by the same name, *Storm Petrel*. We were thrilled with the look of her, painted white with varnished seats and gunwales, the 26-foot mast looked formidable. The local fishermen said it was 'way too high'. Grandpa Shellard was determined to make the maiden voyage in her, carrying his wife's ashes, which he desired to scatter on the island. I think that this was most inappropriate, because from all accounts Granny Shellard never liked the island and generally thought it an unsuitable place for her daughter to live.

In April the old *Storm Petrel* made her last voyage to The Wick to get timber. There is an old belief in Pembrokeshire that you should not destroy your boat when she is finished with; she should be hauled out and left to rot in peace. Bearing this out, lying against the banks of the lane to Martinshaven the rotting remains of a number of old boats can be seen, their bare bones softened by nettles and cow parsley growing between the ribs. True to this tradition dear

'Old *Storm Petrel*' was hauled up the slipway to end her days at the top of the cliff where the lighthouse railway track begins.

Father was fed up with hired men and the lack of birds in this particularly cold spell. Adding to his aggravation, a woman visitor, thinking to be helpful, brought in a 'lost' lamb, which was not lost at all, just temporarily separated from its mother. Father resolved: 'not to come to the island until mid-May in any year, to sell the sheep and unwanted tools etc ... and devote the rest of my life to the production of profitable illustrated articles on country life and natural history subjects'.

Finishing touches to the Wheelhouse were completed, and it was now a fully-equipped mess room. Julian Huxley was due to arrive on a second visit. On being asked if I remembered him, I apparently replied: 'Yes, long like a caterpillar', and from then on during my childhood I referred to him as 'Mr Caterpillar'.

On 6 June I was shunted off to Rhyd-y-gath to stay with my aunt and uncle, while my parents, Julian and two cameramen arrived to make the proposed documentary, *The Private Life of the Gannet*. The Trinity House relief boat took out their supplies, which comprised eight barrels of water, a barrel of cider, tents, stores and bedding, masses of personal gear belonging to Julian, and camera gear.

The weather was mercifully fine and warm during their whole stay. They worked fairly solidly each day from 6 a.m. until 8.30 p.m., with a short break for meals and a two-hour siesta after lunch. The ten-minute film was a big success; it won an Oscar in 1938 in the category Best Short Subject (One-Reel). I still have a copy, which I enjoy both for the nostalgia and its old-fashioned style, delivered by Julian, like the old newsreels, loudly with short, staccato sentences, none of this stage whispering as in today's wildlife films!

The filming of The Private Life of the Gannet: *front: Julian Huxley, Do behind*

Towards the end of the month we were invited to stay on Caldey Island. Joyce came too. Our host was The Hon. Mrs de Reyes King and her consort, who had a holiday house there. She ran the Little Theatre in Bath and the Everyman Theatre in London and was a very dramatic figure. We were lavishly entertained and shown round. Father wrote: 'everything bright and colourful here with a well appointed table which gives us a feeling of lotus eating!'

In July we were preparing for the highlight of the year. Skokholm, Skomer and Grassholm were on the itinerary of the Eighth International Ornithological Congress. Noticeboards to indicate various routes about the island to bird colonies and nest sites were hastily erected. Near the house a board was put up with the history of the buildings, and space for all the members' signatures. The following day Father went to Pembroke Dock and met members of the congress, who were to travel to the islands on two destroyers, *HMS Windsor* and *HMS Wolfhound,* both cleverly procured by Morrey Salmon. The Congress' visit was a great honour for my parents, and put Skokholm on the map as the first Bird Observatory in Britain.

July 8th dawned calm and cloudless. Skokholm was the Congress members' first stop: My mother, Jack and I were on the landing to meet the first boat. After the first few people had landed Jack was on hand to show them a puffin sitting in its burrow in South Haven. They were then directed by the notices to various places of interest under the supervision of Morrey Salmon and Mother. Father was busy at the shearwater colony behind the house to show them how he was doing his research.

My parents felt extremely proud when the three of us were called out after lunch to hear what Father describes as a 'pretty little speech in thanks to us, made by the organiser, Mr. Stressemann', with references made to the seabird research which Father has done so far. The voyage to Skomer had to be made right round the western end, the destroyers being too large to pass through Jack Sound. Meanwhile Father was having the time of his life in a speedboat belonging to the commander of the *Windsor*, taking the most important member, ex-King Ferdinand of Bulgaria, and Stressemann for a circumnavigation of Skomer. Father referred to it as:

a pleasure much appreciated! We went slowly, examining every interesting colony, shag, cormorant, guillemot, razorbill, kittiwake, once we saw a great black-backed gull devouring a puffin ... At the Wick no words could express their admiration of the vast colonies ... bit by bit we did the coast of Skomer, I steering and driving this beautiful little boat ... Ferdinand did not land on Skomer, but subsequently the papers showed pictures of him leading a party of the Royal Ornithological Congress up the steep cliffs of 'Skomer'!

In reality the press photographs were taken on Skokholm, where King Ferdinand, much afflicted by gout, had difficulty walking even as far as the house! The story goes that he was given a stool in order to bend over enough to see into a puffin hole!

Afternoon tea was served on Skomer North Haven beach for those who had walked the island, then they steamed slowly for Grassholm. (The papers said they dashed full speed!) Here they made two circuits of the island going as near as they dared to the colony on the west side. A blast on the destroyers' whistles sent all the non-breeding birds into the air, but none of the breeding birds moved. Home via Broad Sound, where we picked up the evening 'shearwater assembly'. Father wrote:

> it was great fun to be on the bridge and giving advice as to which flock to chase, I don't think the British navy has ever chased shearwaters before! We made it to Pembroke Dock by 9pm. The *Windsor* docking without a jar, but the *Wolfhound* had to make a second attempt and even then jarred into us.

I recall parts about this big day: being amazed by the hordes of people suddenly landing in South Haven, one of whom presented me with a soft toy rabbit which she produced from a brown paper bag. I distinctly remember that after she'd handed me the rabbit, she screwed the bag up and threw it over the cliff! My second vivid memory is arriving back at the docks on one of the destroyers and hearing the above-mentioned crash and sound of splintering metal when the destroyer *Wolfhound* accidentally pranged the *Windsor*. So ended a tremendously exciting and proud occasion for my parents: 130 people signed the visitors' board, the weather stayed fine, a feather in the cap for Britain's first bird observatory.

We all went off to Rhyd-y-gath to sleep. Father wrote: 'It has been a day of days … I think everyone was pleased with the whole experience. I know Ferdinand was, he promised to send me his portrait!'.

In July we had a big day on Grassholm ringing 2,000 gannets and some kittiwakes. Jack was catching for a visitor, Mother was catching for Father, while I followed behind close on their heels, holding a rope of spare rings and trying to avoid the stabbing beaks of the larger nestlings. I loved going to Grassholm, chiefly because we never went unless it was dead calm! But I was not so keen on walking among the colony when the nestlings were mature enough to reach out and peck my legs.

In August W. S. Bristowe, the arachnologist, came to Skokholm. He had a birthday during his stay, and I remember a 'spider-birthday cake' my mother made for him. She iced the top with an orb-web decoration and in the middle sat a ball of brown wool with eight wire legs and two button eyes!

Bill Bristowe was pleased to find the rare Nelim silvatica on the roof of a small cave near South Haven, a long-legged, web-weaving spider. It makes very fine cocoons about the size of a small ping-pong ball which hang by a strong silken cord. Henceforth this cave was dubbed 'The Spider Cave'. It was a favourite of mine, because I could get in through a slit-shaped hole in the roof well above high tide mark, and be first to count the spiders or show one off to visitors. Larger folk had to wait until the tide was out and clamber in by a bigger entrance where the sea comes in.

In his Book of Islands, Bristowe talks about that visit to Skokholm. He mentions the wildlife, sheep farming, fishing and birdwatching keeping my father blissfully happy, and his wife supplementing his skills with her painting and study of wild flowers. (By then my mother had little time for her painting and father was intermittently discontented with farming and fishing ... but on those fine days in August this would not have been be apparent!) He also says that the effects of isolation on their little daughter of four was already looming in their minds and was illustrated by watching her with other children, thinking that whoever was staying at the time would have been the first children I had encountered (almost true). I had, he said, learned to play by myself, but not to share with others: clearly, island hazards were on their way! (True!)

By the fire in the Skokholm house;
fire surround made from the taffrail off the Alice Williams

When I look back I think I must have appeared somewhat precocious. Admittedly I was more comfortable with adults. I can distinctly remember showing visitors round when my parents were busy, and holding forth on 'the habits of the island birds; did they know that the shearwater deserts its babies and that it was not a puffin even though the

Latin name was *Puffinus puffinus puffinus*?' – I blush to remember that now, because so many of our guests were very well-informed. What a spoiled little 'know-it-all' I must have appeared. If other children came to stay I delighted in showing them the sights, but I always felt a sense of relief when they departed and I had the place to myself again. There were exceptions, including my cousins Mary and Brian, whom I worshipped, and anyway they were older and refused to be bossed around. We all looked forward to the arrival of the two Salmon boys, Norman and Hugh, who came with their parents Morrey and Queenie every summer until war broke out, and more than once they stood in as very capable wardens when my parents were busy elsewhere. I have many photographs of we three children; in retrospect, times like eternal summer.

We had our den behind the Wheelhouse yard. It was the remains of the galley from the *Alice Williams*. We thought it was a palace. We divided it up into rooms with partitions made of discarded sail, hung our washing from the enormous cleats which were still bolted to the sides. We even built an elaborate bathroom at the rear, complete with bath (a discarded galvanised tub) and toilet (an enormous oval-shaped iron cooking pot); none of us ever had the courage to use the latter, even though we dared one another to do so.

South Haven was the warmest place to bathe, but it was too deep for children not yet able to swim. With the Salmon boys to back me up I implored our unwilling parents to take us to North Haven's cold but sandy beach. Another of our favourite playthings was the old *Storm Petrel*, which was hauled out at the end of the slip. There we three sailed with driftwood mast and sacking sail as pirates to the South Seas, or pretended to row for our lives because the engine had broken down (in reality, something we had all experienced!). Daringly we sometimes sat on the gunwale nearest to the cliff, with a drop of 50 feet to the rocks below. No one told us it was dangerous. When we were at sea we were never allowed to do this, in case we fell overboard – this we put down to the inconsistency of grown-ups!

Sailing the seven seas in the old Storm Petrel.
Hugh Salmon, me, Norman Salmon.

It seems quite unbelievable to me to read in Father' diary for that September that my parents had decided to move back to Beggars Reach. It had obviously always been in the back of their minds as a nice place to spend the winter.

After several postponements due to inclement weather, a calm day eventually came when we could move all our sheep off the island, plus a good deal of furniture. For £12 Mr. Rouse's tug and a barge were hired for the day. The postponements involved frantic messages sent by Morse code between Skokholm light and St. Anne's, always a clumsy and prolonged procedure in those days using a

Morse lamp. Quite often it took a long time for anyone to respond. Some of the messages seem so trivial for the amount of time and trouble entailed: on 6 September, for example, Mother and I were on the island and Father ashore. He'd received a message from Spiderman: 'Bristowe wants rare harvest spider found at roots of damp vegetation, collect while you wait, crossing as soon as possible Ronald.' On another occasion I had left my mother's sandals, which I was supposed to be carrying, on the beach at Martinshaven, and a message was sent for Reuben Codd (the local coastguard, and son of the hospitable Codd family) to go down and collect them before the tide came in!

A suitable day dawned so we were up early and had all the furniture down to the landing by the time Rouse appeared at 8.30. The sheep had been locked in the yard overnight. A hard morning was spent in tying their legs. The two light-keepers, with Punch pulling the pony cart, did the work of carrying from the yard to the end of the tramway. From there the sheep had to be carried by hand down the slipway to the landing steps. The large barge took four-fifths of the sheep, the rest being in another boat, some in the *Storm Petrel* and the rest on the deck of the tug, which towed the two laden boats and the *Storm Petrel*. Father describes it as:

> a pretty cavalcade. We made Llangwm Ferry in two and a half hours and were almost as long unloading, the chief business in cutting the bonds which lashed one hind leg and two forelegs of each sheep and throwing them into the water. Mr. Merriman sent a dog and one son down to assist. One sheep was dead and several were weak after their long bondage and fast. I gutted and paunched the dead sheep at the ferry cottage.

I remember small bits of this day very clearly: being fascinated by the big wake of the tug with all the little wakes from the towed boats coming along behind, and feeling sorry for the sheep struggling to free themselves from their bonds. I have vague recollections of spending the early afternoon in the van that was used to ferry countless loads of our possessions up to the Beggars Reach. It was a tiring day for all. The sheep settled down to graze on the sweet green grass in Merriman's meadow, which they found much to their liking after the close island herbage.

At the end of September Father spent a strenuous few hours sorting the sheep for sale at Haverfordwest, along with oddments like shearing machine, wire and rabbit traps. For now, sheep farming was at an end! After the sale Father went at once to the Castle Hotel for a bath to clean off all the sheep muck, before catching a train to Scotland; he was going to help build, in partnership with W. B. Alexander (a keen ornithologist and ringing expert), a bird trap on the Isle of May. The only memory I have of 'WB' was his rotundity! He never missed a chance for a swim, even in the coldest weather. My mother told me his party trick was to take down the Trinity House lifebelt which hung near the landing stage, throw it into the water then dive through it ... a dangerous procedure in view of his figure.

Early in November Father went up to London on his own to see a preview of the gannet film at a meeting of various ornithologists. He wrote:

the film was splendid and very well received. I thought it very cruel of Huxley to allow himself all the honours on the title of the film placing me under his name: 'assisted by Ronald Lockley'. After all the whole idea was mine and he only stepped on the island, so to speak, with everything arranged for him by me ... As our agreement was a half share of everything ... There was no mention of me at all! ... It is all very hard on me that he should walk away with all the honours.

Father never forgave Julian for his omission. One can hardly blame him, because the same thing was to happen several times thereafter: his name was not in any of the publicity, film reviews, or, what most rankled, in the agreement. Father found Julian apologetic and anxious to make amends, and in future we found that he always had a good excuse for everything he did. In spite of everything, Father and Julian remained friends for the rest of their lives.

Father returned to Beggars Reach on 17 November. The following day, he went for a stroll by the river and thought nostalgically of Skokholm as being the happiest place! He started digging a pond near the house: it leaked badly!

Just before Christmas he travelled to London again to see the premiere of the gannet film. Just before the film circumstances were somewhat fraught:

> had to change into a dinner suit at Moss Brothers ... then meet Do who was looking rather unusual with a big bruise on her forehead and two black rims under her eyes, as if I had been bullying her [in fact, the result of a bad fall]. I was slightly unusual with brown shoes, as Do had failed to bring my pair of black ones with her. I had to rush and have my brown ones blackened at an hotel!

I was the cause of Mother's fall. We had been staying with Grandpa Shellard at Penarth. I had called out in the night and Mother had fallen down their steep back stairs going to the kitchen to get me a drink.

Before we returned home, I was taken to see a performance of *Peter Pan*. I was apparently amused and bored by it, but enjoyed the clapping and the crocodile – the only things I remember!

Father would be gratified to learn that today the idea of leaving roadsides to nature has been widely adopted. Such were his thoughts during our journey back to Wales:

My mind is intensely active while I am driving the van, all sorts of brilliant ideas dart through it. Today I became obsessed with the idea of starting a movement to encourage people to adopt grassy stretches of the highway as wild gardens and to get them to plant and tend informal wild flower masses; there are thousands of people ... who would do this.

5

1935

It was mid January, and the new *Storm Petrel* was still upriver. My parents wished to see how things were on Skokholm so they went over with Warren and Hugh Edwards, two Marloes fishermen, the diary says:

> we launched their boat and characteristically they had no sail or tiller, Do steered with an oar and we three males rowed. Ann sat in the stern and made topical remarks. It was calm, shags and razorbills at sea, gulls and oystercatchers in South Haven ... it was certainly nice to be at home this quiet day ... the trouble was that too much of our hearts is left behind on this island of ours.

Father received £40 from the publishers Witherby, an advance royalty for the book he was writing, *Birds of the Green Belt*, about the birds round London. Mother got £10 for her sketches in it.

In February we befriended some neighbours, two old Canadian brothers. Father wrote: 'they entertained us with their rolling stone yarns. I have invited the rollingest stone to dictate his memoirs to me.' Later on George Harris (the rollingest one!) was to spend many years with us, and Father wrote a book about him called *A Pot of Smoke*. They were not in fact Canadians, but George had once had a ranch in Alberta; now he'd returned to Pembrokeshire where he was born, to spend his semi-retirement with his brother in a cottage in nearby Lawrenny where they grew vegetables for sale.

In March Father was doing further research for *Birds of*

the Green Belt, and I was parked with Granny L. That was probably a good thing as far as I was concerned, because from then until well into April my parents spent all their time going on birding forays, sleeping on a bed of straw in the back of the van, the dust from which gave them both hay fever. Uncle Ken was on leave, and Father made shameless use of his comfortable car for short journeys. After one of their trips Mother arrived back with a big bruise on her forehead and the van had a star-like pattern of cracks on the windscreen. Apparently they had collided with a telephone pole. Father was studying the map and Mother fell asleep while she was driving! I remember the cracked windscreen was still with us well after we returned to Wales.

Before our departure an expedition was made to Woburn Park and to Whipsnade, with seven of us tightly packed in the van. I have a few sketchy recollections of seeing lots of bison, and an ostrich snatching an applecore from my mother's hand.

Father recorded on 20 April that we spent the day getting the Skokholm house in order, attending to visits from relations and guests, and making a trip to Grassholm. Additions to the family were my pet rabbit and two young ravens, which Father had taken from a nest.

Now that I was nearly five, whenever we landed at Martinshaven and it was just my parents and me, it was my job to be of assistance in winching the boat over the pebbles up or down the beach. We had about five skids. The skids were solid bits of driftwood, liberally smeared with old grease and fat. As each one appeared from under the moving boat, I had to retrieve it and stagger over the pebbles to the other end and place it in front of the keel. I hated the job and always hoped someone might be on the beach to assist. Then I would be free to fossick along the beach to see what 'treasures' I could find.

By early May we had built a new garage with a cement floor. The old one beside the Martinshaven hut had been made into a new room, which was light and attractive, though as yet unlined. Temporarily my parents had let the island to visitors, because the work of caring for paying guests was too much , so we were all living in the hut. They talked vaguely of school for me.

In June Father was offered a trip to Iceland with two ornithologists. In fact he never made it to Iceland itself, having been persuaded by the steamer's captain that the Westman Islands would offer more birds. On his return he recorded: 'Do met me with Ann and both protested against a small moustache, and voted for its disposal, as with the beard grown earlier in the spring.'

Late in September they finished clearing up everything on Skokholm for the winter, put bedding away safely from the hordes of mice who inevitably raided the house in cold weather, put the engine away in the new garage and pulled the *Storm Petrel* up tight to the winch at Martinshaven. The Skokholm Bird Observatory record book showed that 1,600-odd birds had been ringed that season.

In October my parents dropped me with Granny Lockley at Boxlane Lodge in Hertfordshire, while they went off on a bird exploration to various Scottish Isles. They returned on 3 November. I had been left behind because Granny had found a very exclusive little school for me, held in a small building in someone's back garden! I was neither impressed nor there for very long.

My parents returned in early December to try and sort out their financial woes. They were in debt by £500 without any prospects of ready money coming in at present. *Birds of the Green Belt* was finished and in the publisher's hands. Nevertheless, we enjoyed a good family Christmas spent at Boxlane Lodge and the New Year seen in with charades and champagne at the neighbours'. I have no recollection of my first party, but apparently I enjoyed it, in spite of being ill the night before. I do remember poor Aunt Aline washing my vomit-ridden bedclothes in the bath and complaining bitterly – poor Aline had obviously drawn the short straw and been assigned the job! She was the least domineering of the aunts, and therefore a favourite with my mother – who, doubtless, had been out somewhere at the time looking at birds.

In spite of my parents' parlous financial state most of January 1936 was spent attending a good many exhibitions, researching seals at the British Museum and Skokholm history in the Public Records Office. One event I was allowed to attend was an illustrated lecture by 'Grey Owl'. Father thought it:

> a pleasant talk propogandic of the Canadian Parks and the conservation of beavers and wildlife generally. He spoke well, where we were expecting from the newspaper criticism, a dry and platitudinous discourse, he left before the end of the films and saluted us in picturesque Indian fashion.

I remember this occasion so well. Grey Owl was wearing buckskins like the ones I had seen in picture books, and his wife had a real live beaver on stage. At that time Grey Owl was very much in the news. I still have his two books, published at that time, about his efforts to save the beaver from extinction. He was, in fact, Archie Belaney, born in Hastings in 1888, who had emigrated to Canada at the age of eighteen, and reinvented himself as half Native American.

On the way home we spent a few days in Penarth, where

Grandpa Shellard had been looking after my pet rabbit and our recently-acquired lurcher. I have pleasant memories of staying in Penarth on numerous occasions. My grandfather's house was right on the waterfront. On rough days it was great fun to go for walks when the sea was pounding in over the edge of the promenade and to see, from the comparative safety of the pavement, how close to the waves we could get without getting wet. I was very daring: on Skokholm this was something I could never do! The Penarth house seemed to me immutable; the grandfather clock slowly ticking in the hall, the sound of Kathleen playing her grand piano, deep carpets, deep armchairs and hundreds of pictures. After Granny S. died Grandpa's sister-in-law Gertie and her unmarried daughter Kathleen, a gifted pianist, had come to housekeep for Grandpa S.

On 12 February my parents went to the village of Dale in Pembrokeshire to look at a house on the waterfront which had attracted them both. They were charmed by its character and quaintness. It went by the rather grand name of Richmond House.

Later in the month Father wrote of sad news from the island:

> a notice from Trinity House that poor old Punch was killed during the relief on February 15th. He apparently broke his halter and backing over the cliffs, fell to his death on the rocks below. As he was desperately nervous of going near the cliffs I can only think he was mishandled … I am claiming compensation. We were very sick about the grand old boy.

We found out later that Punch had been tied up by an inexperienced keeper near the limekiln in South Haven. He should never have been tied where there was so little room between him and the cliff. Normally on lighthouse relief days he waited by the sheep yards until he was needed. He was sadly missed by everyone. In his summer coat he was quite handsome, slightly bigger than the ponies we had later. Being on his own he sought human company and often got up to mischief, as my baby bruises testified. He was extremely inquisitive, and everything had to be closely inspected. One time when a roller towel inexplicably went missing off the line, it was found round Punch's neck.

The sad loss of Punch was compensated somewhat by the news from Julian that the Duke of Bedford was going to present Father with two Soay rams and six ewes; he thought that since this breed hails from St. Kilda they should do well on Skokholm. We were delighted, but first Father had to request permission from the landlord, Col Lloyd-Phillips, who was enthusiastic about the prospect.

Towards the end of March we moved all the furniture out of Beggars Reach and stored it at the hut. It was a tight squeeze, and much of it ended up in the garage. The new room, though comfortable, was still not complete.

The very next day my mother went over to Dale to plant currant and cotoneaster bushes in the allotment-like vegetable plot, which, apart from a small back yard, was the only garden belonging to Richmond House.

At the end of March we went the rounds of the Preseli hill farms in search of ponies. I was very excited. My heart was set on a skewbald or a grey, but there were few of those to choose from. In the end we bought a bay mare and stallion. We were busy with the preparations to spend the summer on Skokholm. Three new nanny goats and a kid were purchased, as only one goat had survived the winter. From Father's diary:

May 5th: Up at 5.30 to load the ponies, the Soay sheep, the latter all individually crated as they came off the train, a load of lime, timber and insulating material. Captain Thomas of the Trinity Relief boat took it all with the utmost good humour ... although it was calm at dawn, it came on to blow half a gale from the S.E ... at Skokholm we took off the relief gear ... then the goods and the sheep using the crane. By this time the tide had ebbed ... when we tried to get the mare to step out of the tender onto the steps, she refused, we bundled her out finally, but she slipped down ... and a wave swept over her. In trying to lift her up I got a shove from her that sent me into the sea me up to my neck. I was hauled out by two seaman while the others coaxed the scared mare up the steps. We went off for the stallion, but this time we tied his legs and put him in a cargo net then bodily carried him out.

I witnessed all this drama with great excitement from the top of the landing stage. I was desperately anxious that no harm would come to the little mare – never a care for Father up to his neck in the sea! The sheep crates were lined up in a row well away from the cliffs. At the time we had a very charming guest staying, Pat Venables, who had a most unfortunate stutter. He wanted photographs of the sheep before they were released. The ram was unceremoniously dragged from his crate by the horns, which did not show him to his best advantage. Pat was so excited: 'Hold the bloody rrrr ... rrrr oh hell, the cock sheep's head up', he was heard to say. From then on the ram was known as 'the cock sheep'. Next time he was ashore, Father belatedly received a letter from the Duke of Bedford: 'On no account release the sheep immediately, as that could be fatal!' They were grazing contentedly when we looked for them next day, but they didn't allow anyone to approach closely.

When I look back on my early years, living as we did in different homes made life very interesting. We always seemed so busy, so it does not surprise me that later on I found school so boring. Father was, my spite of his faults, always stimulating company, extremely gregarious despite his assertion that he wished to live alone on an island. My mother was more reticent and content with our isolation. Her nature appealed to a certain kind of person, and they remained her staunch friends throughout her life.

I often wonder what motivates other people. I have never been one for self-analysis, so when I am asked questions such as: What traits do you think you might have inherited from your parents? Or, Was your upbringing a good preparation for your future life?, I am really stumped for answers. I know I am not a martyr to unreasonable situations, as my mother was. It is true I was exposed to, rather than shielded from, the cruelties of nature. Early on I acquired that certain callousness that is required to be a practical farmer. At the same time, I was in a position to appreciate the wealth of nature liberally provided right at my feet.

6

1936–1938

12 May 1936 was my sixth birthday. An increasing number of events recorded in Father's diaries from this time on are shared experiences that I remember well. Many years later we had family arguments about where, why and how certain events took place; to prove he was right, Father always said: 'I can prove it, I wrote it in my diary!' But those diary entries are still his own point of view and very much coloured by his aspirations, along with his naive inability to see the opposite point of view.

Father had 'a futile argument in the local press on the right of landing on Grassholm. He wrote: 'I first protested about Reuben Codd's advertisement of a monopoly of landing people there, now Sturt and Betty have weighed in with a lot of personal and malicious interpretation'. Father thought it was his right to land as fishermen had always done. He said he had saved Grassholm when it caught fire (someone had visited the island and left a cigarette end burning on that peaty soil), and made it famous so that the Codds and the Sturts stood to profit from taking more visitors there. However, I doubt if it would even occur to him to put himself in their shoes; he was 'a Johnny-come-lately', taking all the limelight without consulting them or making any kind of formal or written agreement. I daresay in this particular case any 'agreement' might have been difficult: Mr. Sturt was an irascible gentleman whom life had not treated kindly.

My Father hated a row and throughout his life went to enormous lengths to avoid one. This often got him into trouble. He always assumed that everyone was going to fall in with his plans. When I grew up I often pointed this out; a look of hurt and innocent surprise would come over his face, which I am sure was *mostly* genuine!

In spite of the way my father described our life in his early books, in practice my parents' romanticism and pretension to live the simple island life never really came off. There were too many commitments on and off shore: rabbits, fish and sheep to sell, guests, relatives and friends to contact. The more articles and books he wrote, the more correspondence arrived, and it had to be dealt with. As a result we were forever travelling one way or the other whenever the weather allowed, and too often when it didn't! I can remember nightmare crossings and idyllic ones, but I never realised until I read the diaries how nomadic we were.

My father always referred in print to 'the remote island of Skokholm': it was 'remote' in the sense that no one had lived there for a long time, but it was not 'remote' as the crow flies or when the weather was good. However, in those days of heavy open boats driven by hopelessly underpowered little outboards, having to negotiate a tide race and land stores in rough weather, it certainly seemed very remote at times.

Having so many visitors made life pretty hard for my mother, and even when she had some help, it was intermittent. Catering facilities were still primitive. She was not cut out for domesticity, nor was she particularly systematic, so she made extra work for herself. Father said she took too much trouble over these chores, and hinted that it was a privilege for guests to stay! Mother rightly maintained that if guests were paying a lot to come, they were entitled to three good meals a day. Young men were given a cheap rate if they worked for their keep, but as Mother pointed out, they were the ones who had the most prodigious appetites.

I remember being bored to tears waiting at the Co-op in Haverfordwest, where we bought all our supplies. Everything had to be taken off the shelf by the assistant, wrapped in brown paper and tied with string. I dreaded the words 'and is there anything else, Mrs Lockley?' Invariably this meant more waiting, with Mother deep in thought. The highlight of shopping days was the purchase of a batch, a flat, soft, white loaf, which we spread liberally with butter to eat on our way home. Whenever my aunt Enid came to stay, my mother would thankfully hand over the organisation and the shopping to her.

It had been more of a 'simple island life' in the 1740s, in the days when Skokholm was last profitably farmed. I know that at times my mother wistfully imagined that as the life we might have led. In the eighteenth century rabbits fetched a good price. The walls round the various fields were constantly maintained with stone and topped with furze, which restricted the rabbits to the outer areas. Cattle were 'swum' over from the sandy beach on the mainland opposite. The island's mild climate encouraged good grass and clover to grow and some cultivation was carried out. The tenant farmer seldom went over to the mainland, so work would go on without interruption. A system of beacons signalled the occupants' needs to the mainland.

In Victorian times the agricultural depression made the island unprofitable, the walls fell into disrepair, and the rabbits took over the whole island. Fishermen and rabbiters visited spasmodically, and camped in what remained of the old farmhouse.

When I was younger I never gave a thought to the unusualness of our itinerant existence between our various dwellings, or the reason for my parents' constant comings and goings. Apart from having to go to school, I never minded being uprooted from one venue to the next. Rather the opposite: I welcomed the changes. There was always something new to be investigated or rediscovered, so life was never dull. Nevertheless, some things in my early private life were constant: my two totally imaginary friends Brada and Carto, and Bow-wow: when I was about three I was given a large pyjama case in the form of a dog. I never kept my nightclothes in his zipped-up tummy, but instead he was my constant companion. I named him Bow-wow.

Me with Bow-wow.

Brada, Carto and Bow-wow shared all my earliest adventures; we went everywhere together: in the van, the boat, to bed. Of course, Bow-wow was the only one who suffered any wear and tear, and he even received regular haircuts, so he became balder and balder, and his neck longer and skinnier from being dragged about in all weathers and conditions. I daresay my parents sometimes wished that he, too, existed purely in my imagination, because I refused to go anywhere without him. My joy was complete when Father bought that 4/11d. pram for him. It was more than I'd ever had: a pram was hardly practical transport for an island. When I was a baby my mother carried me about in a rug wrapped round us both, gypsy fashion.

I have a theory now as to why I chose the names Brada and Carto. In 1933, Heinemann published a book called *Tschiffely's Ride*, by A. F. Tschiffely. He had ridden two horses called Mancha and Gato from Argentina to Washington DC. The book was a sensation and was much discussed. I was always picking up words from grown-ups' conversations, and it is more than likely that I metamorphosed Mancha and Gato into Brada and Carto, and attached them to my imaginary friends. (Another time Father taught me the word 'incomprehensible'. I had no idea of the meaning, but used it often. I apparently used to say to him, 'You are incomprehensible' – he did not know how true it was!)

When my parents went off on expeditions I was left with Granny L. at Boxlane Lodge (Hertfordshire), or at Rhyd-y-gath with Aunt Vi. I was quite happy in both households. They felt like extra homes as well as our other four abodes: the hut, Dale, Beggars Reach and Skokholm. I felt as if we lived in them all simultaneously!

I am put in mind of something Dylan Thomas wrote in his story *A Child's Christmas in Wales*, when he said: 'I can never remember whether it snowed for six days and six nights when I was twelve, or whether it snowed for twelve days and twelve nights when I was six'. I can seldom say 'when' early events took place, but I can always pinpoint 'where'. For this reason I have related my most vivid recollections quite randomly according to their venue.

About 1931 Betty Sturt had married Reuben Codd, the coastguard. I believe old Mrs. Codd was disappointed in the match. She was deeply religious and wanted Reuben to have a career in the church. She was a dear lady and always very kind to me. On visits there she would provide me with a paper bag in which to collect the dried florets off the escallonia hedge by her back door. I was fascinated by them, perhaps because we had nothing like these 'treasures' on the island. I remember the dark kitchen and coal range, on which a large black teapot always stood, the tea becoming more and more brewed as day wore on. My mother said it tasted vile, but she never liked to refuse a cup because old Mrs. Codd was so good to us.

Betty and Reuben lived in the coastguard's cottage nearby. They had three children. I played with the elder daughter, June. She and I were sometimes sent up the hill to the Deer Park with a snack for Reuben when he was on coastguard duty. I remember one very hot dry day when June and I had been arguing about who had lugged the basket the furthest. When we reached the lookout Reuben put out some water for a few sheep he grazed up there. Four of them came dashing up as soon as they heard the bucket rattle and all put their heads deep into the bucket at the same time. Now, as clearly as then, I associate that scene with the stand of an admired (by me) fruit salver we once had, consisting of four water buffalo carved in wood, their heads down and facing inwards, supporting a large brass dish.

The only flat ground near the hut was a narrow grass terrace in front, where more often than not there was a box containing some unfortunate incarcerated specimen of wildlife; something my parents wished to study or photograph, or recovering from some accident. I remember an adder which Father persuaded Mother to hold up by the tail while he took photographs; she promptly dropped it when it started to loop up close to her fingers. For a long while we had a cock chaffinch we called Spink, while he recovered from a damaged wing. I was also very taken with a parrot we looked after for a few months.

While we were in one of the cramped transition stages of altering the hut, some bird acquaintance or other came to visit. As he threaded his way through the stacks of impedimenta in the one completed room he stepped on the plaster head of one of my dolls. I had always hated this doll and had refused to have anything to do with it. Being shy I said nothing about the breakage. I can still hear the 'crunch' and his abject apologies about my 'dolly'. (I never referred to *any* doll as a dolly!) My mother insisted that I would be glad to see the back of it, but the poor chap was so contrite he sent me a bigger, better and more expensive doll a week later. I liked it no better than the old one, and I let Mother give it away.

On a number of occasions when we spent time ashore, I would return to the island feeling off-colour. I did not have a chance to build up a resistance to any of the common diseases which affect children, notably the common cold, always referred to as 'the mainland cold'.

On any prolonged visit to the mainland I had to bring along my pet rabbit. I adored her. She was grey with a snowy white shawl, front paws and blaze, her pink nose forever twitching. So I called her Bunnynose, always prefixed by me as Darling-Bunnynose. On the island she was not confined, but never strayed far from the house. On the mainland Mother was terrified that a stoat or stray dog would find her. One time when we brought her ashore she was due to have her first litter and there was nowhere safe for her to make a nest. Father was away, and I spent all day playing with June. I came home to find a grand wire netting pen erected in the field above the hut. Alone and unaided my mother had made it all herself, and just in time: the following night my Darling-Bunnynose produced a huge litter. Needless to say I was in raptures. Later her progeny were quietly allowed to escape: 'One pet rabbit is enough', I was told. Besides, she had been consorting with the wild rabbits on Skokholm. In future she had many more litters of this kind, some distinguishable by a white shawl over the shoulder; for some years, rabbits could be seen on Skokholm with the mark of Bunnynose, or so I liked to believe!

6 May 1935 was the Jubilee of King George V and Queen Mary. A celebration sports day was held in the nearest village, Marloes, with running races for everyone. I came fifth out of eight in my age group, which was remarkable considering I had not run a race before, but I liked the idea of lining up among all those other kids. I remember being given a solid push by Father and told to 'start running – a penny for the winner' (but in the end we all got pennies). Each child was given a souvenir mug with tea in it. I had never been offered tea before and I thought it was horrible. I remember Mother surreptitiously tipping it out into the hedge.

I was too young to remember the days when my parents first discovered Beggars Reach. It was a far cry from the house on Skokholm or the hut, being a modern bungalow in cream-coloured stucco. Mother revelled in the modern plumbing and a chance to create a sheltered garden. Everywhere we went she gardened; even at the hut she grew a few vegetables. The grounds round Beggars Reach were littered with tins and bottles left by previous tenants. During our second intention to stay permanently, we ordered lots of trees to plant, to try and mellow the surroundings. My job was to throw all the offending rubbish into the bottom of the holes, then hold the trees steady while my parents (or more often just my mother) filled them in.

Coedcandlas next door was in its heyday one of the finest old farmhouses in the district, well-known for a stable full of horses and gardens full of home produce. It was then owned by W. G. and Annie Thomas, who were the grandparents of the famous writer of best-selling racing thrillers, Dick Francis. Dick was born there in 1920, and spent his early years attending the local school in Lawrenny and developing his love of horses. When the Thomases died the Merriman family bought the property. I can remember only a slate-flagged kitchen, always cool and inviting, and in the back garden a most luscious raspberry patch. I remember sitting under the canes and reaching up to stuff myself with raspberries, egged on by Mr. Merriman's daughter Cleddy.

I always enjoyed visits to nearby Lawrenny Castle, where the Hon. Mrs. Lort-Phillips held sway. We would have polite afternoon tea on the terrace with cups and silver tea service just like the one Granny Lockley used. After tea I was allowed to go and look at Mrs Lort-Phillips' deer in the park, and the budgerigars in her huge aviary.

Aunt Vi and Uncle Martin's farm, Rhyd-y-gath – 'cat's ford' – was so named because the shortest way to the village of Hermon was over a little stream, said to have been the access to the farm in days gone by. There is a charming little waterfall upstream, where we used to cool off in hot weather, and now there is a little footbridge over the ford.

The farmhouse at Rhyd-y-gath was typical of the older ones in Pembrokeshire. Some of the walls were up to four feet thick. The floors of the kitchen, table room (a sort of staff dining room) and north facing dairy were all flagged with slate, some with hollows where a constant traffic of clogs had worn them away. In the dairy, also floored in slate, were slabs for salting bacon and shallow pans for setting milk for cream before the days of separators. The dairy doubled as a cool place for food storage – no one around at that time had a fridge or even electricity. A flight of stone steps outside led to the maid's room above the kitchen, probably designed so that the servant girl would not have to pass through the parlour to go to her room. Typical of many local farmhouses, the front door opened onto a tiny formal garden with a wall to keep the animals out. The kitchen door faced the same way, but was open to the yard and all its mud.

Down a path at the side of the house there was a little slate-roofed hut containing a two-holer loo set over a stream. It really was the most unhygienic arrangement because the stream ran down in front of the piggery and into a duck pond at the bottom of the yard, in which the domestic ducks swam and the cows waded and drank on their way to be milked. Zoonosis was obviously not considered any problem! I got myself shut in this loo one day. Presumably I wasn't strong enough to lift the door, which always sagged on the flagstones. I screamed and yelled and cried my eyes out, but the distance from the kitchen and the noise of the stream drowned out my howls. Finally my aunt came to the rescue with a garden fork which she pushed under the door to lift it inwards.

Traditionally, also built separately from the house was the *gegin fach* (little kitchen) which contained all the impedimenta of an outside laundry. Beside the *gegin fach* was the culm pit. Culm is a mixture of anthracite dust and clay, which was moulded into patties to heat the kitchen range. They burn slowly, almost like peat.

Apart from having to drink cows' milk (unfamiliar and strange-tasting after my usual diet of goats' milk), I loved to stay at Rhyd-y-gath, a real working farm with lots of baby animals to play with. I gave the cowshed a fairly wide berth because cows seemed such large animals and smelled so different from goats, and I hated being squirted with milk straight from the teat, which seemed to be the milkers' favourite sport if I poked my head round the door at milking time. I helped feed the calves and the Pembrokeshire corgis, which Aunt Vi bred. I bear a scar on my arm to this day from a sheepdog protecting her pup whose leg I inadvertently caught in the kennel door.

The men let me ride on the gambos, which are two-wheeled farm carts. These were made especially long and narrow for restricted Pembrokeshire gateways. There were carthorses and half-draught foals destined for the pits, and Mary had a pony.

When we spent Christmas here, after opening presents after breakfast it was traditional for the men to spend the morning shooting rabbits by ferreting. Neighbours joined them and walked over adjoining farms to look for, and shoot, pheasant and woodcock. At midday we would have an enormous hot dinner of turkey, ham and Christmas pudding. My father and I hated the latter, so we always had fruit salad made especially for us. Then it was a time for quiet naps or desultory games by the fire in the front room, where Aunt Vi had her grand piano, and for the younger ones to gloat over their presents. My cousins Brian and Mary were older than me, which meant for once I could not have my own way. They teased me mercilessly. I did not really know how to handle this situation, but it did me the world of good.

At the top of the stairs there was a little box room in which Mary and Brian kept their toys. Brian had Meccano, which I thought very sophisticated, but most of all I envied them their immense rocking horse. He was superb, dapple grey with flowing mane and tail, red leather saddle and bridle and real stirrups. He was too big to fit in the box room, so he stood, like the proud steed he was, on the landing at the top of the stairs. Brian could make him rock so violently he'd move along the floor, but when I attempted to duplicate this manoeuvre I only succeeded in tipping myself off and chipping a chunk off the top of the banisters. It was very hard trying to keep up with two cousins who were older. There were many tears of frustration.

We used to call Rhyd-y-gath 'the land of cream and honey'. We enjoyed cream and butter, honey from Uncle Martin's bees, and a surfeit of fruit and vegetables from his garden and glasshouse. A whole cartload of strawy manure was spread over the rhubarb bed at the top of the garden every autumn; both to feed it and to keep off the frost. Old pots and buckets were never thrown out, but saved to place over each rhubarb crown to force and blanch the rhubarb stalks into being delicately pink and deliciously tender.

It was the custom on most north Pembrokeshire farms for the staff to have all their meals provided, breakfast and supper included. The clackety-clack of clogs on slate flags heralded the men's arrival in the table room for meals. No one seemed to shed their dirty footwear unless they were invited into the parlour. Cawl was the staple food and general favourite: it is simply home-cured bacon and leek broth, followed very often by the same piece of bacon removed from the pot and served with potatoes.

Pig killing was a special event and full of local ritual. The victim was always a sow, fattened to bursting point after her first litter. This meant that the lean on the side bacon was almost invisible under a thick layer of fat! I was morbidly fascinated by the whole process, right from sticking to disembowelling. The only job in which I could take part was to be given a patch of skin to 'dewhisker' after it had been scalded! In some districts the small intestine is kept to make 'chitterlings'. I have never seen them made in Wales, because I can clearly recall the sight of Fly, their sheepdog trailing yards and yards of intestine behind her as she made off to the midden to bury it! The pig's tail was always cut off and given to the maid, who would tie a pink ribbon round it, then send it to someone in the post. I am sure there is some ancient custom from which this might be derived. Faggots, wonderful offal meat balls cooked in the pig's caul, were traditionally made the same day; the back steaks were another treat, always cooked and eaten while they were fresh.

One of Aunt Vi's sidelines was to sell fresh cream in little glass bottles with a cardboard insert in the neck. Much of the cream was made into butter. On churning days, as soon as the butter had 'come' and she had strained off the buttermilk and the 'washings', Aunt Vi's maid May used to let me make a little pat of my own. The butter was rich in colour and, with no electricity or refrigeration, sometimes rather strong in taste if the cream had been standing for long.

Some of the outbuildings had been replaced by more modern ones. A few of the old ones built with facings of local stone and the cavity filled with a mix of mortar and rubble still remained. In these the rodents revelled in the easy digging. When the rat population grew too large, a rat hunt was mooted. This was an exciting event not to be missed by staff and visitors alike. Ferrets were put into the largest holes and water from a hose into those at ground level. Armed with sticks and pokers we'd wait with bated breath, the corgis and the sheepdogs all alert, with noses quivering and ears pricked in anticipation; suddenly the rats started to emerge and all hell broke loose as dogs and sticks flew in all directions. Afterwards Brian and I would go round and poke the dead rats just for the fun of watching the dogs rush up and bite them all over again from top to tail, thinking they'd come to life again!

Other times I spent long periods with Granny Lockley at Boxlane Lodge. It was a convenient place to stay whenever my parents had business in London. I can still see my mother sitting at the dining room table there, doing the pen and ink illustrations for *Birds of the Green Belt* (Witherby 1936) and being told by Father 'to get on with it, for God's sake.' My mother found it very hard to work to a deadline. In those days it was a painstaking and long drawn-out process to make a 'top copy' with her black and white vignettes. The house, all on the ground floor, was long and low, with imitation lead-light windows, which I thought were entirely beautiful. There was a tennis court, big garden, paddock and an aged gardener called Cripps, who scared me to death.

Granny, being a bit of a snob, liked to associate with those of her neighbours she thought were 'correct', especially the ones who would play bridge with her. There was Mrs Green across the road who always had a large jigsaw puzzle on the go in her entrance hall, where everyone had an irresistible urge to contribute at least one piece before leaving. There was Mrs Brett, who had a large grown-up family and an enormous store of board games, and always had time to play one with me. Both these ladies spoiled me utterly, but they also made me aware that they were very conscious of their 'place'.

In January 1936 a lot of snow fell. Boxmoor Common was alive with people having fun. Mrs Brett held a tobogganing party. She produced a Swiss luge and a four-man sledge. Her tortuous drive above the common was like the Cresta Run, and many a guest landed in the hedge bordering it. Father, not to be outdone, decided to try out the luge. Taking me on his lap, he proceeded down the Common at high speed. As usual I was unsuitably dressed in woollen kilt and socks ... the snow thrown up by the open luge went up my knickers. At the bottom of the hill we ran over some brambles hidden in the snow. Tearfully I showed Father my scratched and bleeding thighs. I'd had enough of these mad grown-up antics. Once more it was my Aunt Aline who sympathised and walked me home.

Granny L. thought I might be bored while I was staying with her, so she bought me a tortoise. I loved him dearly, but he wasn't a very interesting playmate. I preferred her sheepdog Bruce, who would go completely mad and rush up the paddock and into the wood at the slightest mention of 'rabbits'. I was happy to play by myself in the garden or pester someone to read to me. With four doting aunts and their young friends popping in and out I was pretty well indulged.

I was invited to a party by a little girl from up the road. I had never been to a party for little girls, and felt quite lost among so many self-assured children my age and hardly any grownups. Afterwards I complained to Granny that my party dress 'wasn't pretty enough'. The hostess had announced just before tea: 'All you girls with pretty dresses come and get a paper napkin before you start.' I misinterpreted her words, thinking my dress did not qualify me to partake of the lurid jellies and hundreds and thousands provided.

On another occasion this same family held a huge Guy Fawkes party. I had a very bad cough, (doubtless the 'mainland cold'), so with another child in the same condition I watched proceedings from their bathroom, from where, we were assured, 'we'd get the best view of the fireworks'. I was quite relieved when it turned out to be a very short party: the box of untouched fireworks accidentally caught fire and went up in a very impressive but remarkably short conflagration!

Granny was very religious. She taught me to say my prayers, 'Gentle Jesus, meek and mild, look upon this little child, pretty mice implicitly' and 'Our Father witchart in heaven, haloed be thy name'. Just so much gibberish which I gabbled off dutifully, without understanding a word. I don't know what my mother thought when I came home, because she was an atheist. She was, however, much amused by my interpretation! I was not required to say any prayers at home.

After moving most of their chattels to Beggars Reach and getting almost settled in over a couple of winters, my parents started to look around for somewhere nearer the sea with easier access to the boat and the islands. Father was too impatient to linger over house-hunting and soon got bored. My mother and I enjoyed it. I don't think she ever really liked Beggars Reach: too far from the sea and a modern house with little character. When just the two of us went house-hunting, we played a game of 'what we'd do if we lived there, and where I could keep a pony and a rabbit and which would be my room'. Our imaginations ran riot; my mother gardened, landscaped, renovated and decorated, with no thoughts about what it would all cost or how gargantuan the task! I remember particularly a little cottage near St. Ishmael's, called Goose Green – the very name fired our imagination. It was the sort of glorious warm day when everything looked sublime. Nicely situated on the inner part of Milford Haven, the garden overgrown with docks and horseradish, the house with its crooked winding staircase and tiny bedrooms. I was reminded of the house the crooked man found when he walked a crooked mile. We thought it ached to be loved and lived in.

In March 1936 we found Richmond House, an unusual sort of place on the sea front in Dale, and took possession at the end of the month. It was tall and narrow, squeezed between the Griffin Inn one side and a grand porticoed house on the other. Our front door opened straight onto the street, the back door onto a tiny little yard with high walls and a solitary apple tree. It had four storeys, two rooms on each, with a big attic at the top. There was a good bathroom but no electricity, and the calor gas lighting we put in proved to be temperamental. The beams supporting the floors were all old ships' timbers and masts. The front windows looked over the sea wall and straight up Milford Haven. The deciding factors for taking this house were the view and the proximity to good boat moorings.

The sewage systems for most of Dale's waterfront houses left a lot to be desired: all waste went under the road in front and out onto the beach below the sea wall. We were encouraged not to pull the chain unless the tide was in!

It was not until July that my mother, and the governess hired for me at the time called Evelyn Hardy, had time to redecorate the house. Wherever we went my mother could not resist decorating at least one room with her usual trademark – this time the master bedroom – in deep cream with a bold wagon red stripe right round it at shoulder level. She and Evelyn then went mad in my little bedroom painting a seascape all over one wall.

Over the years the frequently resurfaced macadam road had built up in front of the house. Consequently we stepped *down* into the hall from the front door. The dining room was off to the right, then there was a passage to the kitchen at the rear passing a deep coal cellar. In a really good southerly storm the waves came over the sea wall, across the road and in under the front door, flooding the dining room and hall and filling the coal cellar. This happened once when Granny L. and I were alone. I will never forget the sight of the waves breaking over the wall and hitting the dining room window. It felt like being below decks! The coal cellar flood was a disaster. It took so long for the water to drain away.

I had my first experience of a proper school at Dale primary. My short attendance was by no means regular and could only have been for a few months in total. I did not learn to read, but I learned my two times table by rote. I also learned to happily mix with and enjoy the company of other children from the village. Stilts made from tins were the craze at the time; the beach was littered with them. Our favourites were golden syrup tins with lids. We'd thread a piece of string through the rim on each side, knot each end to make a loop just long enough to hold comfortably while standing up, a foot on each tin and away we went. The school was surrounded by huge blackthorns dripping with sloes; we used them as rewards for winning our stilt races at playtime.

There were two playgrounds, one for the boys and one

for the girls, separated by a high wall. Separate latrines with a common roof stood at the furthest end of the playground, each containing a spacious six-hole long-drop. We were usually turned outside at playtime. If the weather was cold, we used the loo as a warm place to sit and gossip. If someone wanted to use your seat for the purpose for which it was intended, there was plenty of room to stand behind; no one was in the least abashed. When my mother heard about it, she was horrified, not by our lack of self-consciousness, but the fact that we used the building for shelter! Corporal punishment was the norm, boys on the bum and girls on the hand. I never got the cane – I was far too shy to misbehave in class.

Dale was flat enough for me to have a bicycle, but a new one was beyond my parents' means. They were offered Brian's old one, which was in pretty poor order. Father burned some midnight hours polishing away the rust and replacing the necessary parts. My mother then painted it red and black like a postman's bike. I rather wished she'd chosen other colours because inevitably I got teased. Before long my bike showed its age, it was always breaking down, but the wheels still turned, so my friends took me in tow.

Dale beach was ideal for all kinds of activities. At low tide it had plenty of sand with rocky outcrops. No one seemed any the worse for encountering the odd bit of raw sewage floating about. There was all sorts of flotsam and jetsam as well as sea life; favourites were skates' egg sacs, which we called Neptune's purses, and razor shells sticking up like mini-cricket wickets, which we delighted in lopping off with a stick – what sacrilege! Razor clams are now considered a delicacy. We spent a lot of time at low tide pushing a shrimp net about – the shrimps were plentiful but rather small. Sometimes a group of us sat round one of the many rock pools with an old tin each, and we'd bail out all the water so as to catch the stranded shrimps.

My mother was not a strict disciplinarian, but she did have a couple of bees in her bonnet. One was supervising the cleaning of teeth (understandable, perhaps, as she was the daughter of a dentist). The other was that children should go to bed early. I always seemed to be in bed before any of my friends of the same age. Those long summer evenings seemed interminable when I felt like anything but sleep; neither was I supposed to look at a book. It was particularly difficult for me in Dale, because I could hear my friends playing outside on the sea wall. If I signalled from the window, they asked if I was ill!

We never missed Portfield Fair in Haverfordwest. There were all sorts of sights to be seen, from food stalls to the fun of the fair. I remember well the following event which Father described:

> October 5th 1936: we saw the wall of death, where a lioness, cruelly driven, sat in a sidecar and careered round the arena, snarling at the driver who kept tapping it with a whip to keep it quiet. After the performance the lioness rushed to her den with a snarl of relief on the word of command by her trainer, the animal part of this performance should have been forbidden. There was a small zoo (children 1d and adults 2d), consisting of 3 monkeys, a parrot, budgerigars, a badger and an agouti, but advertised on the outside by an African beating a drum and dressed as a South Sea Islander in a skirt of bast standing by a placard depicting a jungle scene with crouching tigers! ... and a cabaret with painted lady showing a lot of flesh.

I wanted to go on three kinds of roundabout, which left the parents exhausted – although not too exhausted to squander a lot of hard-won sixpences on the dodgems, always my father's favourite.

The island, in spite of all our moves, was where we spent the most time, and most happily. It was where my parents always wanted to be whenever they were elsewhere. I felt I was a princess there; as if the whole island and everything on it was mine. This feeling was doubtless encouraged by the fact that Father often called me 'Island Princess'. I may have been pretty unsophisticated compared to mainland children, but I had unconsciously assimilated and learned to love everything that made my parents so enjoy living there.

There was so much wildlife to investigate. Under a piece of corrugated iron at the bottom of the meadow a group of beautiful slow-worms lived, some a lovely coral colour. I loved it when visiting children thought they were snakes! If Father had left the sail lying on the slipway in South Haven overnight I could never resist lifting it to see the teeming hordes of huge sea-lice scatter. I could identify most of the birds and their nests, and even hold my own at the 'bird game', a favourite evening pastime with a crowd of bird watchers. This involved two teams sitting opposite each other, the first team would shout out the name of a bird beginning with 'A', then the other team had to think of another beginning with 'A', and so on through the alphabet until each letter was exhausted. The opposing team would count to ten, keeping the score with matches. If the opposition failed to come up with a different bird beginning with the required letter before the time limit, they lost a point. Some very unlikely birds came to light, the classic being a 'French bustard'.

I was very happy on Skokholm. I was unaware that I was living an unusual life on an island with my pets and indulgent adult company. Here my Darling-Bunnynose roamed free, and had family after family beneath the old chinchilla pens in the Wheelhouse yard. Her progeny went wild, but she never strayed far from the buildings. Strangely,

The pet ravens let me carry them about

our sheepdog did not molest her. From time to time we kept pet ravens, not because they were orphaned, but because we found them such fun to rear. They became very tame and let me carry them about. Like magpies, they were very mischievous. We fed them on rabbits, bread and milk, bacon scraps and the entrails of goats or sheep we killed. Sadly, the parent ravens hung about and called for quite a long time after the nestlings were taken. One pair (named, appropriately, Tinker and Inky) we had to take to the mainland with us because they were not fully fledged. They scattered a party of innocent tourists eating their lunch in the Deer Park by making rather aggressive advances in their attempts to share their picnic. There was a bit of a scene while Father smoothed ruffled feathers on both sides.

Skokholm in spring and early summer was at its most colourful, when the flora could rival the best alpine meadow. With their spiky leaves grazed short by rabbits, mounds of thrift surrounded the clifftops like cushions stuck with pink milliner's pins. Dark blue vernal squill and pink centaury dotted the meagre pastures; drifts of the darkest bluebells grew under each embryo bracken-patch. On the rocky outcrops of red sandstone; clumps of stonecrop and scurvy grass grew among the yellow lichen-clad boulders, more aesthetically placed there by nature than by any human rock gardener. Pennywort grew in the crevices of the ruined walls of the outhouses, their flowers like candles in round candlesticks. On the sheltered banks of South Haven's little stream there were minute wild forget-me-nots and primroses – it was always a thrill for me to find the first of these in spring. The rabbits did not permit anything edible to grow tall; the grass was cropped like a cricket pitch. The only patch of blackberries grew safely out of 'rabbit reach' inside the lime kiln, and we carefully harvested enough for one pie!

In the days before my mother finally consented to send sheets to the laundry, wash days were a prolonged chore. First the water had to be heated with a primus placed under our large square copper. We agitated the washing in a fluted galvanised tub with a copper washing dolly (a wedding present), which looked like a bell full of holes on a stick. We plunged this up and down in the tub like old African women grinding mealies. Then everything was put through a hand wringer twice, once to wring out the soap and again after rinsing. My romantic mother preferred not to hang the sheets on our clothes line: she'd rather lug our big double-handled wicker basket away behind the knoll and spread them out on the heather because 'it makes them smell nice'!

Mother was equally painstaking about the garden, but it was her greatest pleasure. My father helped her dig the potato patch and keep the garden rabbit-proof. The rabbits necessitated constant vigil; they never ceased to try to undermine the garden wall or penetrate the wire netting outrigger round the top. The soil was light and red in colour like the island's cliffs, and full of little sandstone chips, which we raked away to make a fine tilth. The following season there always seemed to be just as many pebbles to rake away again! The high banks surrounding the garden made it pleasantly sheltered from the wind. There was just a tiny lawn under the front windows of the house and a border of annuals: escholzias, nasturtiums, cornflowers and shirley poppies (the latter for me to make poppy ladies by folding the petals down).The rest of the garden was given over to vegetables and a few small fruit bushes to entice the birds. The Atlantic gales foiled our many attempts to grow trees, but for a few elders with their tops blown off. Hordes of snails lived in the crevices in the walls: you could hear them on still summer evenings as they made their forays into the lettuce bed. We gathered them by the bucketful and emptied them with fiendish joy into the sea the following morning.

Bath nights involved almost as much work as washing days. I don't think we bathed an awful lot; in summer we could have a swim or a sponge-down outside. But I well remember our long tin bath being brought inside and lined up by the sitting room fire. Boiling water would be bucketed out of the copper and cold from the rainwater tank at the corner of the house. One side of the bath would eventually get scalding hot from the fire, which kept it nice and warm for each member of the family to have a turn.

Against the end of our little porch was the ruin of a lean-to shed, thought to have been used for storing fuel and peat in past times. It was a great day when this was repaired, whitewashed and floor concreted to make a lavatory and bathroom, so we could forsake the bucket in the *Alice Williams* deck-house, which we had shared with the hens.

There was still no hot water, but cold laid on and an Elsan loo. I remember the day when a very worried-looking lady guest complained to my mother that the lavatory door was stuck. With a couple of other female guests in tow, Mother prepared to climb through the window; there was an indignant shout: 'What's going on?' Father was seated there reading the paper! Soon after that my long-time playhouse, the *Alice Williams* galley, was requisitioned as another loo, the window still discreetly screened by the old curtains hung there by me and the Salmon boys!

My little mare Judy was barely eleven hands. She was no beauty, but she had no vices. Once she was caught I could do anything with her. How I adored those ponies. Father had some chain hobbles made, so that I could catch Judy by myself; otherwise it involved every available able body to chase the ponies down to the narrowest part of the island where they couldn't get away. I named the stallion Sugarback, because, unusually for a pony, he did not like

Darling Bunnynose – and those plaits!

sugar. He would mouth it briefly, then drop the sticky, salivary mess back in your hand. He was far more handsome and friendly than Judy, and the light-keepers had no trouble getting him in on relief days to haul their trucks.

When I was six I was very envious of cousin Mary's plaits. I begged to grow my hair. Mother was very much against it, but Father finally persuaded her to let me grow it. At last I had plaits! When Father went away to Heligoland to visit a bird observatory there, my mother sneaked up behind me and snipped them off without undoing them! My hair was consequently a mess, so I gave up, sat still and snivelled while she tidied up the ends back into my usual 'basin' haircut.

Mother, being so petite, looked really smart in any kind of trousers. She despaired because nothing would persuade *me* to wear them. Fortunately for me 'the aunts' kept me well supplied with the sort of inappropriate garments I preferred.

Not infrequently, on his wanderings to more remote

Me on Judy – inappropriately dressed for riding!

parts of the island Father caught a bird, and in order to bring it home to ring, he would put the poor unfortunate in his pocket. After finding one or two dead or dying birds 'forgotten' in the spacious pockets of the corduroy suit my father habitually wore, and calling him 'a wretched man', Mother took the precaution of checking his pockets every day. I sometimes reminded him myself because I hated it if the bird was dead but still warm, and would weep over the poor little carcase.

Many of our visitors came year after year and became lifelong friends. One such was a young student, a slim, quiet, fair-haired young aristocrat called John Fursdon, who looked as if island life was the last thing he was cut out for. My mother decided he needed toughening up, and straightaway she set him to carrying water from the well. After a pretty torrid introduction to the rougher experiences he became a good friend and invaluable observer who returned regularly, eventually becoming warden of Skokholm when it reopened after the war.

By 1936, the days were well and truly gone when we could have the island to ourselves. The Sturley brothers, fishermen from Dale, had been contracted to ferry people and supplies for us in their big open ex-lifeboat. Even day visitors could land and have time for a wander round the island before the fishermen went home after spending the day tending their pots. The Sturleys were intrepid seamen, and ran the gauntlet of the tide race off St Anne's Head when many a Marloes fisherman would have said it was too rough. There were three Sturleys: Edgar the skipper who tended the big inboard engine, and hardly ever moved from his place at the tiller; John, who sat amidships; and Jim, the youngest, who did most of the work at his place in the bow. I loved Jim best because he used to wear a dried starfish stuck in his hatband. When I went ashore I liked to sit next to him and watch him delve into a seaweed-lined basket and fish out the lobsters they had caught that day. One at a time he'd tie their pincers together so that they were safe from each other and ready for market ...

The Wheelhouse, still adorned with relics off the *Alice Williams,* made a fetching mess room. The ship's bell hung outside to summon people for meals or a 'bird drive'. The fire still smoked, so it was seldom used. We hung a series of brown double-handled porridge bowls, reputed to have been made by the monks of Caldey, along the length of the black-and-white chequered transom which Father fastened up to frame the crockery shelves.

In this room my mother did all the cooking on three or four primuses and a primus stove. We had a sink, which for a long time was without a tap. Water had to be brought up from the well in four-gallon cans, until much later when a pump and a tap were installed. A long refectory table and benches took up the centre of the room. At the height of the season there could be twelve or more mouths to feed. We ate like kings: gulls' egg sponge cakes for high tea, sometimes crab and lobster purchased from the Sturleys. I was chief gulls' egg collector and cracker of claws. When we were having crab my mother collected them from the Sturleys, then dumped them on the Wheelhouse floor to keep cool until she was ready to boil them. They always crawled away to the darkest corner. It was important to remember how many we had purchased in case one went astray. When we had time to troll for them we had mackerel and pollack.

In summer, when we had a lot of visitors, our fare was more conventional than when we were alone. I remember huge pear-shaped tins of ham which lasted for several days and saved cooking. Whenever we had beef it seemed to be a big sirloin roast. I can't remember ever having mince or cheaper cuts of meat. We had goat and Soay sheep from time to time, and Mother's special rabbit pie. She thought visitors would prefer rabbit if it was disguised, because roast rabbit, which we ate at other times, looked a bit bizarre when lying stretched out on a plate – especially when the head, considered a delicacy by my mother, was left on! Her deep-dish rabbit pies were legendary and a convenient food to take on expeditions, being portable and just as good hot or cold. She soaked the rabbits overnight in vinegar and salted water, a trick she learned from old Mrs. Codd, 'because it do take the "waildness" out of them!' Next day they were boiled with herbs and onions until the flesh came away from the bones. The meat and vegetables were arranged in a pie dish with three or four eggs here and there; when cut in slices the contrast of yolk and white made Mother's pies very attractive.

Anything remotely breakable dropped on the sandstone flags of the Wheelhouse floor smashed to pieces. With all and sundry doing the washing up, we had trouble keeping a supply of water glasses. A grateful guest sent us a set of 'unbreakables'. Father could not resist testing one as soon as they arrived, in spite of Mother's pleas to wait until someone accidentally dropped one. True to its label, the glass just bounced, so it became one of Father's party tricks, which one fine day turned to disaster: too late we discovered if the glass went down base first it would break into hundreds of tiny crystals ... our set did not last for very long!

In the light evenings of high summer, after reluctantly going to bed early, and not feeling in the least tired, I sometimes lay awake listening to someone push-mowing our miniscule lawn. The sound was not unlike the rise and fall of the waves, which was nearly always present. On really calm evenings, if I listened hard I could 'hear' a crackle, which I still call 'the sound of silence'. Conversely, the noise the shearwaters made when they came in from the sea just before midnight was anything but silent. It is an extraordinary sound. The Pembrokeshire people call them 'cock-lollies', which is not unlike the noise they make if you repeatedly shout it from the back of your throat! It is their way of signalling their mate waiting for them underground. When they land at their burrows their caterwauling stops abruptly as if in 'mid-sentence'.

I never tired of watching bad weather when my feet were safely anchored to the land! In a really big storm foam blew right over the island, the spume would collect in crevices and against rocks in waist-high globs like soap suds. I loved to wade into these snow-like drifts. I could spend hours watching the waves come screaming into Mad Bay during a westerly, when mounds of white water hit the sheer cliffs, sending a shower of spray a hundred feet into the air, then dropping it back in seething, hissing flood-white waterfalls to the reef below. There, briefly, before the next wave engulfed it, the flow would back out across the rocks like a curtain of green and white lace. The stream draining the North Pond would barely reach the cliff before it was blown backwards.

The continuous noise of the wind and surf tired me out; after watching it for a while as a spectacle I felt exhausted from bracing myself against it. Even indoors there was nowhere to escape from the sound. In these conditions there was a limit to the chores one could do outside, and the birds tended to skulk away in the shelter and not show themselves.

Evelyn Hardy had arrived in June 1936. I think she must have been a friend of Joyce's, introduced to my mother because she was interested in art. After helping to decorate the Dale house, she stayed on to give me lessons. Brian, nearly four years older, happening to be between schools, came too. This arrangement does not seem to have lasted more than a couple of months. Art being Evelyn's forté, I remember doing little else! I am not sure what progress Brian made, I know I made very little. We set forth every afternoon to 'draw'. Evelyn would choose a subject, then the three of us would sit down and sketch or paint the subject from life. One of these was Brian's pet buzzard, which, whenever you approached it without caution, would turn on its back and present its talons. It had been captured in the first place because Julian Huxley had an idea to populate London with buzzards. He had asked Father to capture some to start a flock, but the buzzard was given to Brian when the scheme failed to get off the ground.

When we were on the mainland we had many expeditions to other parts of England and Wales, some impressions of which are fleeting but nevertheless very vivid. We visited Regent's Park Zoo after hours when Julian Huxley was director there.

We went inland to Llandovery to do a kite count. We stayed with an old family friend, Dorothy Davies, in the hills at Rhandirmwyn. I liked this wild mid-Wales terrain, so different from Skokholm, with woods and rivers, disused mines (we threw rocks down the shafts to see if we could hear when they hit the bottom). We visited Twm Sion Cati's cave in the woods above the Tywi River: it took us ages to locate it. I was disappointed to find it looked more like a cromlech than a cave, not a fitting hiding place for this seventeenth-century 'Rob Roy' of Wales. There was great excitement when we found one or two kites. Nowadays they are common in Wales and venturing elsewhere, including Ireland: all the hard work towards their protection and rehabilitation has been a success.

No account of island life would be complete without

mentioning our neighbouring islands, especially Grassholm. Sometimes we went in the *Storm Petrel*, sometimes with the Sturleys. On Grassholm days the forecast had to predict perfect weather: one of the criteria was 'absolutely no sign of any surf against the rocks'. (Consequently, when I was about four I told a guest 'it's ALWAYS fine there!') In the *Storm Petrel*, with a little outboard, it seemed to take forever to cover the twelve-mile distance. Time passed more quickly if the mackerel were biting or a pod of dolphins appeared. Usually we used the east landing called 'The Gut', a narrow slit with a cave at the end. By clambering over rocks and swimming the pools at low tide we could go right through and come out at the north landing. The middle of the island had the most extraordinary area of closely-packed disused puffin burrows, which were all caving in. It was impossible even to walk over them without falling in, but we never missed trying to run races over them.

All the west side is taken up with a huge gannet colony. The sight of this mass of birds is indescribable. They sound a like a machine shop going full blast, and the stench … some days we were busy ringing gannets most of the day and came away smelling highly of guano and half-digested fish. It is possible to catch an adult gannet on the nest by making them look at your pointing finger then grabbing them by the neck, or sliding a wire hook over their heads. The air was full of fluffy down off the nestlings, and I remember Mother's curly hair being full of it where she sat painting a picture of the colony. After ringing, one would hope peace was restored once we had left. Father admits: 'We rather disturbed the even tenor of the colony's life, but as an experiment I think it was justified'. I often wonder if it was: the chaos caused by catching them among this close-knit colony seemed huge for the eventual number of recoveries. Down below the colony are some low flat rocks frequented by seals basking in the sun. We could not hear their eerie moans until we clambered down to the low tide mark, away from the gannet colony. If time and tide permitted we'd go for a swim in a massive rock pool there. On many a hot day the water, unlike the surrounding sea, became quite tepid: a good place to wash off the guano.

Sometimes the *Storm Petrel*'s engine played up and we had to row or sail home. Once Edgar Sturley's boat let us down, and we rowed for hours, till a trawler came along. Edgar signalled with a sack tied to the blade of an oar, and they came alongside and gave us a tow all the way to Dale. We had a good mixed-sex crowd of visitors on board. The men just peed over the side; I am sure the women were uncomfortable. I was desperate but refused to go in public in the proffered bucket. That evening, with very bad grace, my mother wrung out my knickers behind one of the defunct fishing boats hauled up in Dale Roads, doubtless remarking that I was a 'wretched child'.

We made frequent visits to our neighbouring islands, Middleholm and Skomer, especially the Skomer Wick, famous for its bird cliffs as well as its driftwood. Occasionally we sailed to The Bishops and Stack Rocks in the middle of St Brides Bay, and further afield to Ramsey Island and the village of Solva.

7

1936–1938

At this stage there are gaps in Father's diary because my parents were hectically busy with a large number of visitors, but now and again he wrote a resumé of what had been going on: the hut not finished, the Dale house being refurbished, another of the ruined and roofless sheds at the end of the row near the Wheelhouse being repaired. The arrangement with the Sturley brothers was that they should bring out visitors and supplies, weather permitting, twice a week for £1 per journey, visitors 5/- a head. This meant Father was free to stay on Skokholm and not have to go back and forth for supplies himself.

Father spent thirteen days in the Faeroe Islands in late June 1936, taking with him two Manx shearwaters from his experimental colony behind the house. He was very keen to see how long they took to reach home. He released them south of the Faeroes. Both birds were discovered already settled back in to their burrows on 10 July, the very day Father returned to Skokholm after his trip!

Father's general observations were recorded in his book *The Way to an Island* (which was published by Dent in 1941) and more detailed research in *Shearwaters* (also published by Dent).

In August Julian and Juliette Huxley, with their two sons, Anthony and Francis, came to stay at the same time as my cousin Brian. There was one episode for which Brian, as the initiator, got the blame. Trinity House had three little flatbed railway trucks; only the front truck had a brake. Starting at the lighthouse two-thirds of the track sloped gently downhill, making it possible to 'coast' all the way until the last third, opposite Spy Rock, then the track becames steeper, a real roller coaster run! Father often took people for rides this way, but always used the truck with the brake. The three boys took one of the brakeless trucks from the lighthouse. When they reached Spy Rock they gained speed with no means of slowing down, on approaching the last corner Juliette caught sight of them and yelled 'JUMP!' It was fortunate that they obeyed, because after this bend, the railway went along the cliff edge above South Haven and the truck could, at that speed, have become derailed. However, it went on down, ploughed through a lobster box left lying on the track, then smashed to pieces against the rocky bluff at the end of the line. There was fearful reckoning, I did not witness the crash, but I observed, with the malicious satisfaction of one who was not involved, an air of circumspection among the three boys for a few days.

On 14 September Sir Charles Martin brought myxomatosis to Skokholm. He instructed Father how to place the virus medium (*Myxomatosis caniculi*) under the eyelids of some fifteen rabbits. Several times thereafter, Father looked for evidence of Myxomatosis and could find none. Eventually he discovered that as far as Skokholm was concerned the experiment was a complete failure because the vector for this disease is the rabbit flea ... and Skokholm rabbits have no fleas! See *The Private Life of the Rabbit*, published by Deutsch 1964: I personally think this is one of the best books my father wrote. It was also the inspiration for Richard Adams' bestseller *Watership Down*. When Richard was writing this book he contacted Father, and consequently they became very good friends. They went on trips together, and collaborated on a book about the Antarctic in 1982. Together they were very entertaining company. They had a lot in common, both ardent conserva-tionists and fond of literature; words were their life and their bread and butter; they both liked to lead the conversation and outdo one another in flights of fancy. Richard was the smoother character with a gift for magical storytelling. Father was best described in a eulogy at his funeral: 'He had the beguiling charm of a rascally fisherman and told fantastic tales of adventure on sea and land – most of them true – or almost.'

Late in November Father wrote in the diary: 'Do, Morrey Salmon, Ann and I were picked up in a Frenchman's dinghy at 7.15, right in front of Dale house and taken to Grassholm for a trip to look at seals.' I have absolutely no recollection of this particular voyage! I remember many other times when we were entertained by these French crabbers from Brittany. To store their crayfish each boat had a salt-water well with an open hole in the bottom. The first time I saw this I couldn't understand why their boats didn't sink! I was usually given a glass of watered-down red wine and thought it was horrible! They were confirmed poachers, always sneaking in and fishing inside the twelve-mile limit. My parents generally turned a blind eye. They were more concerned the Frenchmen did not land and molest the birds on Grassholm. Given the chance, our local fishermen used to steal or cut their pots.

Our most regular visitors are too numerous to mention, but some stick very much in my mind, notably two Oxford graduates – more probably undergraduates at that time. One was a rowing blue, Anthony Harthan. They were passionate about birds and could happily be left on Skokholm to ring birds and cater for themselves. On their first visit Joyce was with us, and she nicknamed them Hengist and Horsa (I can't find an explanation why she should have called them after two ancient Jutish warriors who captured Kent!). Another regular character was a young geologist named Stephen Marchant, who invented 'night gull catching', which involved going out at night among the thickest herring gull colony in the centre of the island, creeping up slowly, dazzling them with a torch and launching a frantic rugger tackle at the same time!

October always brings storms, and the day of the 2nd was no exception. We'd had to moor the boat in North Haven overnight because South Haven was too rough. A storm blew up and the boat broke her temporary moorings and washed onto the rocks. All hands were called to get her off. Stephen was overdue to return to the mainland and had brought his luggage down to Blacksmith's Landing. They bailed the nearly submerged boat, but owing to the swell, a very tricky embarkation was required. In the process my mother slipped and fell into the sea trying to rescue one of Stephen's suitcases. Stephen jumped in to rescue her, though Father said he thought she was in no great danger! My mother, far from being grateful for such a gallant gesture, said to me later: 'That wretched man, there was no need for both of us to get soaked.'

Everyone was relieved when the old billygoat belonging to the light-keepers had to be destroyed. He had become too aggressive and had cornered a few visitors near the edge of the cliff. How well I remember him: he had a splendid pair of curving horns but otherwise he was a scruffy individual with short legs and long shaggy coat which reeked of his urine. Fortunately one could usually smell him coming and thus avoid a meeting. I gave him a wide berth. I hated the vacant look in his goaty eyes and the toss of his head which spelled, 'I've a good mind to give you a good butt in the backside'. One day my mother met him in a gateway. When he refused to budge she rolled an old cider barrel towards him. The ruse worked: he took to it with his horns and butted it away down the meadow.

Christmas was spent at Dale. I had a Christmas tree in the attic, the large space we used mainly for storage and as a playroom for me and my friends.

On 29 January 1937 Father was in rare philosophical mood. I always find this kind of entry interesting:

The days slip by magically – and I suppose I am as happy as I shall ever be in this life – work of a creative nature that brings me in a living of from £250-350 ... writing, revenue from visitors. A wife and daughter and a home by the sea, not too cut off from the little comforts that improve our little happinesses – the post now delivered twice daily, at my request ... in fact only the uncertainty of the future eggs me out of a state of lazy contentment which the Pembrokeshire weather induces in mankind ...

In February Father wanted to capture and photograph some horseshoe bats from where they clung to the roof of the Wogan Cave, an enormous cavern beneath Pembroke Castle. He borrowed a 30-foot ladder from the curator, and climbed to the top armed with net and camera. The ladder swayed perilously while Father tried to steady himself and the net, and adjust the camera, all at the same time! It was then he discovered that he had the wrong kind of flash bulbs! He captured twenty-five of the unfortunate creatures, having decided my mother and I could hang them up in a more convenient place on the cave wall while he nipped back to get his car battery and rig up a lighting system. This was a crazy scheme; although bats are comatose during winter days, they soon wake up if they are disturbed. They had no intention of being 'hung up' in a strange place, and started to fly away. We quickly snared the eighteen remaining bats, which Father took home to photograph. He thought they would survive in a neighbour's loft, but it was too warm and they started dying, so he hastily returned the sickly few survivors back to their cave, and seemed surprised to get a very surly reception from the curator. Father said: 'It was all in the cause of research!' To this day Pembroke is my favourite castle, a fairytale place to explore.

We had been haunting the boatyards for some time. Like house-hunting I enjoyed the experience of wandering about and letting my imagination run riot in such places. My parents always dreamed of having a boat large enough to take them further afield, to Ireland, Scotland and the continent. I was encouraged to join in these dreams. Amongst other prospective boats, we looked at a 40-foot long Cornish lugger named the *Primavere*, going for £200 with dinghy and gear, a price Father considered a bargain. Much to his surprise his bank manager allowed him the necessary overdraft as soon as he had obtained the approval of an engineer and a Lloyds surveyor.

The trial run in the *Primavere* a few weeks later did not go well. Much was found to be out of order in both engines. Father was so disgusted he decided to offer £180 for the boat, and this was accepted. A few days later we went to Milford, took a picnic lunch and had a 'dry land sail' in the *Primavere* and discussed the dream ship we hope to make of her. At the same time the Dale house was in chaos having the calor gas fixed up.

Father had persuaded the Post Office to remove the Dale telephone kiosk from its present undesirable site near the Griffin Inn's urinal to the grass verge on the other side of the road. We had no telephone in the house; I cannot recall where the extension bell was installed so that we could hear it, because the kiosk was still a sprint of 50 yards away!

Father had been elected onto the Pembrokeshire Rural District Council, probably to keep him quiet, because he was always ('justifiably', he said) 'banging on' about something!

The maiden voyage of the *Primavere* was beset with various problems, but Father, with Harold, one of the Sturley sons, finally got her to our mooring in Dale. It blew hard from the south-east for the next week, so we did not have a chance to give the boat a good run. For as long as we had her the engines gave trouble now and again and never stopped smelling unpleasantly of paraffin. But we had some great voyages in her, to and from Skokholm, Grassholm and Ramsey.

Wednesday 12 May 1937 was my seventh birthday, and also the Coronation Day of George VI. The Rhyd-y-gath folk came down and had a jaunt in the *Primavere*, and Uncle Martin caught a pollack. Then Brian, Mary and I went up to the village sports to get our 'handout' of a Coronation Mug each. In the evening there were fireworks and a bonfire on the beach.

Father's diary, 25 May:

Now comes a sad tale; having been at Skokholm for the day, there was a fresh groundsea, so I decided we would have to seek shelter for the *Primavere* in Skomer North Haven, I was listening to the 9 pm. news before departing when Harold came in and said the *Primavere* was drifting ... Only minutes before we had been in South Haven ... and noticed nothing amiss ... it was one and a half hours after high water, evidently she had been chafing her loose chain on a rock ... why it should have parted then is mysterious ... we were too late – by the time we had rowed the dinghy around the harbour rock she was fast in the fangs of the Devils Teeth, lifting and crashing with the swell. The falling tide held her, but the swell prevented our getting aboard. It was now growing dark, forlornly we rowed back, told Do and the three of us scrambled over the Devils fangs ... torches in hand ... and got out to where she was lying at a steep angle on her starboard side, the rocks having pierced her in several places ... We could do nothing ...

27 May:

The poor old *Primavere* slipped off the fangs, the tops of which she had smashed, and went down with the rising tide into a deep cleft between them. As we watched at 8 am. the superstructure was swept away – the Wheelhouse and cabin top recovered by the Trinity House boat which arrived later ... so vanished our dreams of cruising this summer! ... She is luckily insured, though finding the premium high I had dropped the total from £500 to £350, a mistake in view of the casualty. The loss was a sensation in the village today.

I was in bed asleep when the *Primavere* went aground. I remember crying into my pillow when Mother came into my room early to tell me the news, then later on going down to the Devil's Teeth and hearing the water sloshing through the few remains.

Early in June my mother went down with a very bad fever and bladder infection and was in much pain. Father gave no details in his diary (he never was much good at dealing with sickness). When Vi heard she immediately advised 'that Do must come ashore and see a doctor at once'; the doctor ordered her to stay in bed at Dale with a live-in nurse to look after her.

Fortunately two spinster ladies, Misses Stark and Webb, came to the rescue. They ran a business as public typists and accountants near Reading. They had recently been to stay on Skokholm and had been an instant hit with everyone. Father hastily summoned them to assist while Mother was indisposed. They coped admirably, both on Skokholm and later at Dale. Father made shameless use of their typing and shorthand skills. I became very fond of these two ladies and nicknamed them Starkie and Spider. I was to have a great deal to do with them, because Mother went off to Rhyd-y-gath to convalesce for the rest of the month, taking with her Darling-Bunnynose because they thought (wrongly, as it turned out) that it was unsafe for her on Skokholm with myxomatosis.

While mother was away, Joyce brought her intended, David Green, to stay. He was tall, dark and distinguished-looking, and Joyce was utterly besotted with him. Also staying were geologist Stephen Marchant, and Hengist and Horsa, all three of them busy ringing 600 guillemots and razorbills. I remember being very impressed with their daredevil climbing skills among the cliffs while doing so.

Earlier in the year Father had obtained a swarm of bees. They were housed in an old butter box among the currant bushes in the garden. Later he was given another swarm, this time in an old tea chest. He thought the colony would be stronger if he amalgamated the swarms. One still evening in July he donned a makeshift veil, gloves and thigh boots, grabbed the tea chest, and dumped it squarely on top of the butter box, in which he'd previously bored a couple of holes. He got stung on the nose and backed away chased by a cloud of angry bees. The following morning a good deal of excitement could be heard in the double hive. This was hardly surprising when presumably the two queens were fighting for supremacy! The rest of us watched this exercise from inside the house with all windows firmly closed. That winter the whole lot died out.

Father's diary, 24 July:

> Great excitement, a shearwater released in Venice on 9th July was found happily sitting with its mate and (probably admiring) the chick which its mate had hatched in its absence while in the Adriatic. A wonderful homing feat, the more remarkable because it had come in on a night of brilliant moonlight.

I cannot remember a time on Skokholm when Father wasn't experimenting with this little colony of Manx shearwaters living on the knoll not more than a few yards from the house. In order to do this he had cut out a square of turf above the egg chamber at the end of each short burrow. He reinforced each square with a board and wire hook, so he could then view the sitting bird on her egg with a minimum of disturbance. I often helped him to record their ring numbers and send the birds back in by the entrance. I loved the downy chicks which looked so much like grey powder puffs – but they, like their parents, could pack a vicious peck. The adults were remarkably long-suffering. When we'd finished they would shuffle back on their tummies, pushing with their legs and settle down again. In his book *Shearwaters* Father named his 'bird heroine' Caroline. Her famous burrow is still in use.

Great was my excitement when I was allowed to stay up on a moonless night to go ringing shearwaters. Apart from having to take care to avoid their pecks they are easy to catch, because their legs, built for a life mostly at sea, are placed so far back they have to shuffle up to some elevated projection to make a 'land take-off'. As well as the excitement of staying up late for our 'shearwatering', I loved it when all around was darkness except for Skokholm's red light from the lighthouse close by. Far away I could identify the yellow ones of St. Govan's Lightship, St. Anne's, the Bishops and the Smalls lighthouses.

In August my parents took the ferry to Cork to begin an excursion to Ireland's Western Isles. They returned home on 23 August, finding everything running smoothly in Dale with Starkie and Spider, and at Skokholm with the Salmons in charge.

September proved to be idyllic in every way, with pleasant pursuits, sailing, fishing, swimming and catching birds. Father sailed to the mainland to pick up a new guest, John Buxton, whom he describes as: 'a young man of classic countenance, a wanderer over the face of the earth and presumably a writer of some kind, possibly a playwright'. On this, his first meeting; Father's thoughts were prophetic; John had travelled extensively and been on various archaeological digs. Later he became, not a playwright but a poet, author, an authority on the Elizabethan era, an Oxford Don and an extremely good naturalist. But what Father did not prophecy was that this man was to become his brother-in-law!

Not long before, my Aunt Kathleen, one of Father's sisters, had been appointed headmistress of Brighton and Hove High School for Girls. This would not be the first time, or the last, that she took my parents to task over my lack of formal and consistent education. She offered to give me a place at her school, with board and lodging in her flat. In September 1937, at the age of seven, I was taken to Brighton, in a second-hand Wolseley 10 saloon car for which Father had paid a £25 deposit the day before, using the journey to Brighton as a 'trial run'.

My parents spent the night at my aunt's flat: then, as Father wrote, 'we left after breakfast leaving Ann little perturbed at our going and very happy in Kath's hands'. This was true at the time. My aunt had catered for all my material wants: a room had been decorated and furnished especially for me. Here I stored my favourite things. During my time at her flat she was constantly carting me off to her dressmaker with material to make us both new clothes. My mother was astonished at the wardrobe I accumulated.

At seven I could barely read, my arithmetic was almost non-existent, I couldn't even tell the time! I was put into the lowest form to catch up. I was strangely nervous of both children and staff at this new school where everything was so utterly different from the one at Dale. I was so overcome I just could not bring myself to put up my hand when I wished to leave the room, with disastrous results. Altogether I had an inauspicious start to my first day; I was supposed to go over to the senior school like all the other 'day girls' to have school dinner (in retrospect I didn't miss much!), but instead, after morning school I went to my aunt's flat to have lunch. Of course, she was away in her office and her maid Margaret was out. I was hungry and miserable. I lay on the sofa in floods of tears. I was not missed until afternoon class, when my form mistress came to find me. I remember being given a slice of bread and jam by the housekeeper.

My earliest written letter from Brighton says:

DEAR MOMY,
MOGROT SES I CUD PUT SOME MONKNUS ON WIDOWSTIL AND THE BURDS WILL COM, LOFOR ANN.

(Margaret always fed the birds by putting peanuts out for them on the windowsill of her room.)

My confidence gradually grew and I made friends. Chief among them were the Ashcroft sisters, nieces of the famous actress Peggy Ashcroft. They had both inherited their aunt's talent and love of theatre. Margaret Ashcroft eventually became well known for her performances on television and in the West End. At that time they lived out in the country in a row of old coastguard cottages, which were perched on a hill near Roedean, with a splendid view out to sea. They often asked me out for weekends. They were not well off, and maybe this was what made me feel so comfortable with them. I remember roaming the fields with them, picking poppies, and going down to the beach.

At school I put up with the subjects that I disliked and enjoyed the ones I was better at. Lesson time passed reasonably quickly. Aunt Kathleen had a busy work schedule and did what she could. I don't think she realised how often I was bored. I missed my pets, my outdoor activities and the constant flow of stimulating visitors I was used to. Very often weekends and evenings dragged on interminably. Life would have been a good deal worse if it hadn't been for Margaret, my aunt's maid. She was a lady of many talents, born into service, in the course of which she had travelled to the continent as a lady's maid and a nursery maid, and there she had picked the brains of French cooks. She had taught herself watercolour painting. Nothing went to waste: out of discarded materials given her by my aunt or the staff, she sewed fancy dresses for her nieces. She was never too busy to put up with me in her kitchen or her room. She had a great sense of humour and did hilarious 'take offs' of members of staff and of some of my aunt's friends. This would produce fits of giggles from me and loud laughs from Margaret, which sometimes got her into trouble. After leaving school I kept up with her until she died, when much to my surprise I found she had left me and her nieces small bequests in her will. She must have scrimped and saved from her pension and small wage. I could have wished she had spent more on herself.

Going shopping with Margaret was quite an experience. Her regular shopkeepers knew her by name and would put things by for her. She came home with the same ingredients for half the price my aunt paid. On summer days off she liked to take a bus into the country, pick herself a bunch of wild flowers and find a place to paint. When the blackberries were ripe she insisted my aunt take us in the car to gather them for jams and desserts. Using both hands and with a basket placed firmly between her feet, Margaret picked twice as many as we did.

With her family dispersed, Granny Lockley no longer needed a big house. She rented a small bungalow in the nearby village of Ovingdean. When I had chickenpox I was sent there to recuperate. (In those days we had to stay away from school until the spots disappeared) There time dragged even more. I amused myself dressing up in Granny's clothes, scuffing her best high-heeled shoes, in which I fancied myself, and counting the cows from the farm next door as they came up the lane for milking.

One day Father came to visit. I told him I was bored. He immediately proposed a walk on the Downs and the beach, ignoring Granny's protests that I was not supposed to go out. We had a wonderful day and I suffered no ill effects.

There was, however one bonus to my incarceration: I learned to read. I had a series of books about a little girl called Milly-Molly-Mandy. My mother loathed the heroine, saying she 'was a stuffy little prig'! (She was absolutely right!) Nevertheless, because they had been read to me over and over again and they were full of simple repetitive sentences, many of which I knew by heart, with nothing better to do I suddenly found I could read all the words. I was elated and couldn't wait to return to school and show my form mistress my new accomplishment, as a result I was moved up to the next class.

I had improved, as this letter shows:

> Thankyou for the letter. I am in the first form. Hip! Hip!
> Hoorah. I have a desk all of my own, Love from,
> Ann OXOXOXO [all across the page!]

The very next letter is even better:

> did you like the presents I made, I made the little book
> my self, and the cold cream is not only for your face you
> can use it wen you have been gardening and have washed
> your hands. I went out to tea with a little girl and we
> danced to the wireless music. There are lots of flowers in
> my garden.
> Love from Ann XXXOOOO [followed by a drawing of
> daffodils and crocuses.]

The advice about the cold cream was because after I had
helped Aunt Kathleen in her garden, we would come in for
a cold drink and wash the mud off our hands and then put
on a hand cream – refinements in which my mother never
indulged!!

Aunts Enid, Aline and Marjorie all got married within the
following twelve months. I already knew their future spouses
quite well, because, of course, they were thrown head-first into
the family circle and it was assumed that they would instantly
approve of everything we did. As the only Lockley niece it was
taken for granted that I would be bridesmaid to all three.
Early in 1938 Enid married Barry O'Hara: he was very
distinguished-looking, conservative and recently widowed.
Their wedding was a very low-key affair held in Ovingdean
Parish church. Enid had met him while helping to run his
household and preparatory school in Hampshire. Barry
already had two children, Terence and Meriel, near to me in
age.

At half-term I was invited to stay with my new cousins. We got on famously from the start. I had been given a jar of sweets to take as a present. Early in the morning Meriel came to my room to play, saw the sweets and asked if she could have one. I said, 'Go ahead; they're for you anyway'. Much to my surprise she had eaten half of them by the time we were called for breakfast! After lunch we lined up with the primary schoolboys in front of the 'tuck cupboard', which was ceremoniously unlocked and we were allowed 'two sweets each'. No wonder Meriel took such joy in getting into the 'forbidden fruit' – *and* before Terence had his share! Sibling rivalry and locked tuck cupboards were quite outside my experience. I had so often been presented with sweets by our visitors; they were no novelty and I didn't have a sweet tooth. As a rule Father ended up eating them. It was not until sweets were rationed during the war that I started to miss them.

Aline was next to be married, to Alan Sheffield, a teacher from Stubbington Boys Preparatory School, where they both taught. She chose an elaborately-decorated, full-length wedding dress in blue lace, and refused to be married in her mother's parish of Ovingdean. Both these decisions were unpopular with her rather conventional mother. I shared bridesmaids' duties with Alan's two nieces. The marriage was such a happy one, they had so much in common, but fate was to deliver some cruel blows. Aline died in childbirth, but their baby boy survived, only to die from croup, aged four. Alan had every right to be bitter, but he seemed, outwardly at least, the same gentle, self-effacing man we had always known, he remained loyal to our family and his sisters-in-law made shameless use of him as an escort. I sincerely hope he enjoyed their company as much as they enjoyed his.

Aunt Marjorie happened to be staying on Skokholm at

My Aunt Aline's wedding.
L. to r. Ken, Marie, Marjorie, Father, Mother, Granny L.,
Aline, Alan, Kathleen, Barry, Enid. Me in front . . .

the time of John Buxton's second visit. There they fell in love, and were married in April 1939. That wedding I know little about: at the time I was in bed with a high temperature and tonsillitis. I was inconsolable. My bridesmaid's dress, a pink frilly affair, hung at the end of the bed to taunt me. The sight of Meriel dressed up and ready to go as the other bridesmaid brought on fresh floods of frustrated tears. My mother gallantly stayed home from the wedding to look after me and read me stories between my sobs.

I put up with school, but it became less and less attractive as time went on. I longed for the term to end, and moped about, dreaming of what I would do at home. My aunt introduced me to many classic stories I might never have read otherwise. I enjoyed her attention. I realise now that she spent as much time as she could afford in entertaining me. When the holidays came I prayed for fine weather to cross over to the island, and storms to delay my return. Sometimes I was lucky and my prayers were answered; this excuse for being late was usually greeted with disbelief by my classmates.

Travelling between Dale and Brighton for school involved a tiresome journey. Any island guests going even remotely in the right direction at approximately the beginning of term were pressed into service, either to escort or to ferry me in the direction of Brighton. Mary Priestley, a keen bird-woman was one. She drove me up to London and I stayed a few days at their house and played in their large garden with their red-headed daughter. I remember her father J. B. appeared briefly from his study for meals, but I was at the wrong age to be impressed with meeting this famous author and war correspondent. On another occasion a staff member at Christ's Hospital School gave me a lift. At the time I was unaware of the long line of distinguished alumni who owed their education to this charity school, but their uniform of yellow stockings and long blue coats created a lasting impression. I remember being quite disappointed to discover that they changed out of them for playing sport.

On 25 September Skokholm was packed up for the season and my parents set out for Scotland in their newly purchased Wolseley, then took a ferry for Orkney, Shetland, Fair Isle and the Out Skerries where: 'we had trouble getting accommodation in case we demanded a water closet!' Their time on North Ronaldshay is described in detail in Father's book *I Know an Island*. I was utterly fascinated with the photographs Father took of their sheep, and I refused to believe said sheep subsisted mainly on a diet of seaweed.

On their way home my parents stayed at Penarth. They looked at a run-down cottage on his old St Mellons estate, where Grandpa intended to build. Ever since his wife had died he had been longing to return. On a visit to the site a few months later, Grandpa told the land agent he wished the cottage had burned down so that he could claim insurance, whereupon the agent put a cigarette in the thatch and the two men departed hastily!

I returned reluctantly to school in mid-January 1938. I was taken as far as Cardiff, where my Aunt Aline and future Uncle Alan picked me up. When we stopped for a picnic there was much consternation because all their sandwiches contained a generous amount of mustard, which they both abhorred. I can remember wading through mine without a murmur. I wasn't really keen on it either, but some kind of childish bravado made me say, 'I loved it'.

Late in January there was an enormous storm which did widespread damage in Pembrokeshire. Dale Roads was littered with boats, many of them washed into the meadow behind. At Martinshaven Mr. Sturt lost both his boats, and

Rough weather in Martinshaven's heyday.
Storm Petrel II *is the white boat*

most of the others there sustained minor damage. When the wind and rain abated Father reported to me: 'At Dale today the lads were sailing in the meadow in my and other dinghies with improvised sails of sacking!'

In an answering letter I refer to this storm:

> Thank you for the letter, please can I have a bigger one next time ... the sea nearly tuches the batheing houses here. If the sea has come in has it made a swimming pool in the coal sellar. I expect cunl rind [Colonel Rhind, whose garden bordered the meadow] will be grumberling because the boats floated in his garden, I hope my byscule hasnt floated into the cole-celler.

In February 1938 George Harries (the 'Canadian' friend) was getting increasingly dissatisfied with sharing the cottage with his brother at Lawrenny, so he finally consented to come and live with us. Father had been badgering him to come ever since we lived at Beggars Reach. It is hard to describe what place he took in our household: handyman, storyteller, mechanic, friend, rough carpenter; he was all of these. He soon became part of the family and loved by all. Stooped in figure, with an old beaver hat on his bald head, he looked as old as time; he was only in his sixties when he came to us, but his life had been hard: Boer War veteran, Canadian rancher, you name it, he'd experienced it! (Or said he had!) My father christened him 'The Baron' after Baron Munchausen, the teller of tall stories! From then on few people knew his proper name (George Henry Owen Harries). He figures large in a number of Father's books. I loved him dearly and spent hours in his workshop listening to tales of his childhood. Amongst other things he made me a couple of hobby horses, which I treasured. To keep me occupied he would give me a piece of wood and a spokeshave to whittle away while I listened. Later he got himself a simple lathe driven by a foot pedal and taught me to make an endless supply of chisel handles. Unlike Father he loved to tinker with engines, so our outboards went a lot better after he came to live with us! If my mother wanted some carpentry done he obliged – albeit a bit cumbersome and rough, but no sooner was it said than it was done.

The Skokholm summer season was beginning. The Baron proved invaluable because Father was writing regular articles for *The Countryman* and composing the Skokholm Bird Observatory Report, 500 copies of which had to be distributed to members. He also wrote an article about island life for the American *Geographic Magazine* (great honour, great pay, he reported). The article included a picture of me riding Judy, and as a result I received quite a lot of fan mail from American children. I was made to reply to each one!

The Inaugural Meeting of the Pembrokeshire Bird Protection Society was held on 26 February, in the Gold Room in the Mariners' Hotel, Haverfordwest. For months Father had been working towards this day. He'd spent a lot of time driving round to different parts of the county trying to persuade interested persons to be 'Honorary Watchers' for the Society. The meeting was a tremendous success. Amongst other items they adopted the

Me with my beloved Judy

constitution, Lord Merthyr became president, and Sir Evan Jones, Sir George Bowen, Julian Huxley, Earl Cawdor and Major Gwilym Lloyd George were Vice Presidents. The society was destined to be the forerunner, after many name changes, of the present Wildlife Trust for South and West Wales.

By April my parents were finding life very hectic with so many visitors:

> We shall certainly not run an observatory on the same lines next year. It is too exhausting for Do, who is so conscientious in her cooking and housework, and too willing to shoulder all the burdens thereof, believing she is the only one to do things thoroughly, and she is right – with the present company, we must run it some other way …

Admittedly there were few people (Starkie was the exception) who could handle the primus stoves and primitive facilities as Mother did. She seldom delegated jobs, even unskilled tasks, nor would she ever insist on having some more labour-saving devices. I think, as far as Father was concerned, this was only a temporary fit of depression, because nothing changed until we left the island! He loved the company and the migrant-ringing season had been particularly fruitful; a number of 'firsts' had been recorded in the daily bird records book.

I must have acquired the art of hand-milking at a fairly early age, because I don't remember ever having to learn. For as long as I can remember we had kept goats to supply us with milk during the summer. They were 'dried off' in the autumn, looked after themselves in the winter, then kidded early in the year, and the kids would run with the nannies until we needed the milk ourselves. Depending on winter's

Milking the goats

The moveable goat shelter

Pinknose and Sunshine-Snowy

attrition, we kept a few replacement nannies. Males and surplus females would be slaughtered and put in the pot.

I adored the goats and was in charge of them whenever I was home. In 1938 we had five nannies, each one with her own character and foibles. The matriarch called Longhorns (for obvious reasons) was bossy and bad tempered, she frequently put her foot in the pail and tried to butt me when I was milking her, there were tears mixed with spilled milk on many occasions. I was highly relieved when she was sent off to Rhyd-y-gath to supply Aunt Vi with goats' milk for her corgi pups – she believed goats' milk kept the worms away. There Longhorns again ruled the roost and led the cows to and from the milking shed and ate all the best blackberries in the lane before they were ripe. Claribel was my angel, brown and white with a lot of Saanen blood; her copious amounts of milk came quickly and easily. In a diary I kept later I described her:

> Now I will start to tell you about Claribel, she is brown and white and a rather small beard, two little tasles hanging on her neck, huge great teats which hold an awful lot of creamy milk, she is a bully to the other goats except Longhorns, even her own kid, but she is a quiet stander when you are milking her.

Then came Minnie, an Anglo-Nubian; we nicknamed her Banana-skins because of her striped and floppy ears. My favourites were two white nannies not yet in milk, Pinknose and Sunshine-Snowy. 'Lighthouse Billy', mentioned before, met his demise in 1936, and Mother named his replacement Corydon. He had long legs and a woolly ginger coat. Unlike Billy he was hornless, good natured and tremendously strong. He allowed me to ride him, which I thought was a marvellous idea when I had a long walk to find the goats for evening milking. This close contact was not encouraged by Mother, because I came inside covered in hair and smelling strongly of billygoat.

Sugarback, Petronella and Judy (with me)

About this time I was horse mad. I devoured every book I could find on the subject. Even so I was not an intrepid rider. I just loved to mess about with my little mare Judy. I did not much care for the stallion, Sugarback, who frightened me somewhat, always prancing about and being very 'stallionish'! My parents had never learned much about horses, though Father could ride after a fashion. Most of what I knew I gleaned from books. Judy was over-fat and looked very much like one of the cartoonist Thelwell's ponies. A kind guest took pity on me and bought me a saddle. When it arrived I was mortified, the girths were so long – the well-meaning donor had measured Judy round her fattest part, which is *not* where girths go! Using sail needle and palm, Mother patiently took a tuck in them.

In May I went off to school: The diary says: 'Ann quite blithe and ready for school'. I am not sure if this was true. I had just experienced the most wonderful holidays and didn't want them to end. I had persuaded the guests to participate in two sessions of what I called Sports Days, sometimes in fancy dress. Father enjoyed them as much as I did. He would make up the most ridiculous competitions and obstacle courses in which everyone was very game and joined in with a will. Besides I found it very hard to leave Darling-Bunnynose and the two white kids, Sunshine-Snowy and Pinknose, who were so friendly and followed me everywhere.

Pinknose always leaned up against me when I was milking, as if she too wanted to be milked, so I pretended to milk her just for fun. If only I had realised that this stimulation was bringing her into premature lactation. If my parents had been more informed about animal health, I might have been discouraged from doing this. Thinking back about the circumstances, and in the light of my present knowledge, I am certain that she developed milk fever later on. She would have been born sometime in January, stimulated into producing milk in June, and soon after that she adopted Darby and Joan, two orphan Soay lambs we had running with the goats, and they suckled from her. She was still milking in the autumn because my father mentions it in his diary. The following January she was heavy in kid. It was then one of the lighthouse keepers found her, saying she was unable to stand. No immature animal could withstand such a huge drain on her system.

In June I was informed at school that my mare Judy had had her first foal, a chestnut filly. I couldn't wait for the summer holidays to begin, but wait I had to. When at last I came home my parents were busy organising Dale Regatta, which, they said: 'has hitherto been a rather drab and restricted affair ... it went off well, despite the croaking of evil thinkers ... and a profit of £20-00-00.'

Later the same week we got a tow to Solva to compete in

their regatta. Heavy clinker-built boats like the *Storm Petrel* always came in among the last. There was scarcely any wind, proceedings were indifferent and began two hours late, no one seemed to know where to go. My parents ran a couple of swimming races for the younger children while we waited. I was thoroughly bored by the slowness of it all and I wasn't competent enough to go in for swimming races. Things improved on an idyllic cruise home, when we caught a few harvest mackerel as we loitered in St Brides Bay. Morrey Salmon and his family had, as ever, been ably looking after Skokholm while all these festivities were on.

The 31st of August was a memorable day. We all went to Grassholm: Marjorie, my future Uncle John, me, my parents and Baron. The outboard was going badly, but a breeze was helping us along with the big sails and great mast the fishermen feared so much. Mother and Aunt Marjorie swam through the big cave from South to North Gut, but I would not be persuaded. We ringed 400-odd gannets; as usual Father justified the disruption, and described our unscheduled visit home via Ramsey Island:

This creates some disturbance at this time of the year; many of the full grown young lunge over the cliff to the sea, which they mostly reach safely. A few hit the rocks a hundred feet below, but their fall is eased by their beating wings and at best they are only winded and soon recover and swim off; those in the safer areas herd together a great deal, but they seem to sort themselves out again when we leave, which we did about 7 p.m. three hours before high water, and sailed for Ramsey ... the sun set and a half-moon lighted our path, the wind dropped ... the engine refused to go except on one cylinder. John, Marjorie and Do took turns on the oars, I steered, it was not easy to pick out the rocks at the south of Ramsey, I had to make sure of not being carried through the race of the Bitches ... for half an hour we edged in against the current, and with the aid of a torch we beached on the pebbles at midnight. The farm dogs barked and the farmer and his wife got up and gave us the keys of the owner's bungalow, a pleasant refuge with a bed apiece ... next morning found the plug lead split, and the engine would only go on one cylinder ... this was enough to run us out into the flood of high water ... I had always wanted to shoot the Bitch race, we shot it comfortably, later we made a swift delicious sailing passage to Skokholm in two and half hours ...

How well I remember that jaunt! We ran races on the old puffin burrows, ate rabbit pie and had a post-picnic nap in the deep fescue, which has grown undisturbed on Grassholm for so long it makes a perfect mattress. Then we made our slow passage through Ramsey Sound, watching the dark rocks to see if we had made any progress. At last we walked up to the bungalow in the dark and were deliciously late to bed.

The famous tide race in Ramsey Sound is now used as a recreational facility. In the days when we had to try and run against it with a little outboard or sail we had to choose the right tide to do so or we made no progress at all. On another occasion late one evening we missed that moment, so we returned to Ramsey until the tide turned. Not wanting to bother the farm tenants we cat-napped on the beach and ate gulls' eggs for an early breakfast, using pieces of slate as plates.

A few days later we picnicked on Skomer to look at the seal caves, then took Aunt Marjorie and Uncle John ashore and came back by moonlight. I was growing up. Father reported: 'We had a pleasant sail home with the tide and a light north wind; Ann taking a turn alone with the big fifteen foot long oar, and also proudly steering, keeping the boat's prow in the path of the moon, for the sun had set before we reached home, to find Baron waiting on the landing steps'.

I just loved these occasions when we returned somewhere in the boat late at night – the only times, save the odd night shearwatering, when I wasn't sent to bed early! When I was too young to take an oar or the tiller I was sometimes sent into the bow with a blanket. It was a wonderful sensation going to sleep with the gurgle of wavelets passing under the boat's forefoot close to my ear.

The newlyweds, Enid and Barry, arrived for a week. Enid was in her element but Barry seemed like a fish out of water and seldom strayed far from the house. Poor Uncle Barry, this kind of life was completely strange to him. When we sailed to Skomer for a picnic he took a short walk with us as far as the house, then went back to the boat. We explored the Skomer South Haven caves. The one with two entrances is magnificent inside, a great vault and one crack running far into a grit beach at the end. We found a young seal in its white coat – it cried real tears, and another young one was splashing in a pool hard by. Meanwhile, my father wrote, 'Barry fiddled with the engine and lost a plug overboard, but a fresh north wind blew us home in an hour!'

At aged eight I could just swim, but not with any confidence when out of my depth. The big breakthrough came at long last on a fine day at the end of the holidays. Somehow I had persuaded my parents to take me to North Haven, but the tide was full so all the sand was covered. They dived in and swam to the far end of the beach where I could see them standing chest deep on the last bit of sand. 'Come on, you can swim this far,' they called: with much trepidation I slid in and swam to them, then I had to swim back! It was a great moment. From then on my confidence grew.

I had to go back to school at the end of September (1938), and the only highlight was that I'd moved up a class, so at last I was among my own age group.

8

War Looms

From Father's diary: 'With war seeming inevitable now it is difficult to know what to do. I enquired of the RAF and RNVR if I could render any services, and in both offices was surprised to find a lack of keenness to seize men ... Busy correcting the proofs of *I Know an Island*.' (This book was published by Harrap in 1938.)

After the British Trust for Ornithology dinner in London in mid November, my parents came to Brighton to see me. The rest of the family took the opportunity to come over too, so it was a grand family get-together. I ruined it all by handing round a stinking cold to nearly everyone. However, one highlight was watching the London to Brighton 'Old Crocks Car Race' – when veteran cars travel down to Brighton to celebrate the passing of the Locomotives on the Highway Act in 1896, which raised the speed limit for cars from four miles an hour to twelve! It was a terrible day, the occupants looked thoroughly miserable, their lovely hats were sodden and blowing away, but it was a marvellous parade.

My parents dropped me back at school, and on the way home they paid their first visit to the new cottage at St Mellons, where Grandpa Shellard was happily living in the country again and creating a terraced garden. He was still in practice as a dentist, so he found commuting to his surgery rather a chore. He had a lovely new studio in which he kept, as an aid to life drawing, a human skeleton hanging from a screw in its skull. On future visits I had to sleep in this room. I told Mother I was not very keen on going to bed with a skeleton, so she put it away in a cupboard. She'd had a frightening experience with it herself in her childhood when Grandpa had hung it up with its hand curled up over a rope line. During the night some vibration caused the hand to fall down against its side, and my mother woke up to the sound of clashing bones and the sight of the skeleton dancing up and down as if it had come alive!

Father had taken up an offer by the Universities Federation for Animal Welfare to make the island rabbit population a subject to demonstrate humane rabbit control using calcium cyanide dust. In late November, with Baron's help, they carted all the necessary equipment over in the *Storm Petrel*. The procedure was to close all the holes in a specified area with turf, then the next day, via a rubber tube, pump Cyanogas into those burrows which had been re-opened by rabbits during the night. The powder on contact with air gives off hydrocyanide. It was very effective and humane. However, Father thought it was a vain experiment because innumerable rabbits live among the cliffs. It was an ambitious project, which had to be done during the winter when all the seabird burrows were empty. This meant putting up with wintry conditions while going back and forth for new supplies of gas and food for five hungry people. Once more the diaries describe some hair-raising attempts to cross in unfavourable weather. By 14 December they went back to the mainland having decided to give up until after Christmas.

I came home from school by train on 21 December, apparently 'very well, growing more, taller, thinner and disappointed there is no snow in Dale! ... good reviews of *I Know an Island*, I only hope the book runs into five or six thousand copies, as we are financially at low ebb'. We had a quiet Christmas in Dale, just me, my parents and Baron; it was reported that the grown-ups had one present each, while I had twenty! (All those doting aunts.) On the last day of the year we all returned to Skokholm with supplies, gas and extra men to resume the gassing experiment.

January 14th came with rain and a sad day: my dearest goat, Pinknose, died after Father had brought her home on the lighthouse railway. I have already described what in retrospect I presume was the cause. I was in deep tears. Everyone was sad for such a dear young, beautiful pure white pet. She had looked to be in pain, and Father had been about to shoot her to save her agonies when her eyes became glassy and rigid in death. To offset this blow, Father caught a meadow pipit ringed in 1935, and felt pleased that it had stuck to the island in winter when most of its kind vanish. This was small comfort to me. Tears come to my eyes to this day as I read these details over again. Pinknose's death was so unnecessary, but we were so ignorant.

The same day I watched an oiled guillemot washed up onto the rocks in South Haven. It was too stormy for us to get near enough to rescue it. It kept trying to save itself by coming ashore, only to be washed back as another wave came in. There were more tears, but doubtless we could not have saved a bird so badly oiled. Life on the island was a hard school.

We buried my dear goat at the far end of the home meadow and I put up a cross inscribed 'Pinknose' in poker work, which Baron helped me make.

Father's diary, 16 January: 'Still a sou-west gale … caught a redwing in the trap. Ann is due to leave for school tomorrow, but content with the idea of being late, she loves the island and is never at a loss for amusement.' At that time I was mad on copying bird photographs. I had recently 'moved house' for the winter, from a cosy nook between two rocks on the knoll to the old disused hen house. This 'house' of mine could be better described as my 'special place', where I assembled my treasures, such as empty cartridge cases, sea shells, bird skulls, and whatever else attracted me or my imagination. I had the dogs to play with. I could always persuade Father to play word games, but best of all I preferred to be out of doors playing on my own.

Father and I had started to write a book together, to be called *Early Morning Island*, the story of my island adventures, part real, part fantasy. I was all for the real, he for the fantasy. Mostly he had his way because he did most of the writing; I provided ideas, which he embellished. From this time on he decided that when referring to my parents in writing I should call them M and D. I thought this was an excellent idea.

The next day made up for the sorrows of the day before. While hunting rabbits with the dogs, I came upon my second favourite goat, Sunshine-Snowy, laired in the rocks above Little Bay. I was wildly excited because she had just produced a pure white kid. I rushed back to tell M and D. When we returned she'd had a second, a piebald affair. The cave was so muddy we brought the trio back to the milking stalls. The day after that Claribel and Longhorns kidded too, so I was in transports of delight, even though I knew I would not be allowed to keep surplus nannies or any male kids. In his diary D says: 'I always slaughter the surplus kids when Ann is in bed.' As if I didn't know, and anyway their pelts were hanging up in the workshop and we had roast kid for dinner, which I thought was pretty nice! Still a tremendous groundswell continued which made it impossible to cross to the mainland. Much to my joy I returned to school a whole week late.

D finished off the book of my island adventures during the following term. He wrote and said he had run out of inspiration and wanted two more chapters. I can remember sending him some ideas which he adapted into Chapter V, 'A Japanese Garden', and Chapter X, 'Tailpiece.' When he'd finished my book he began writing Baron's biography in the evenings. I returned to the island for my Easter holidays.

We were offered twelve canaries by the War Department of Chemical Research to acclimatise on the island. I was very surprised to find that canaries are not bound to be yellow! These were all different colours, from yellow, green and brown through to multicoloured. We built a big aviary ready for them in a corner of the yard by the Wheelhouse. After we had kept them for a while we opened the cage and gave them their freedom. In one of my diaries I described them:

> we let them out, we knew they would not go far away for they had nests and eggs and young in the aviary to look after. Very soon they nested all around the house and buildings, in walls, tins, bushes, grass, in tanks and among stones, they have never nested further than the mountain [the knoll] that I know of, I suppose it is because we feed them in the aviary ... now we have about thirty canaries all different colours, yellow, green, brown, white, black, grey, fawn and speckled, well, there is'nt a canary all black, but black markings on it. Most of the young are party coloured ... there is one speckled like a chicken, I've a good mind to call him 'chicken' ... it is a jolly good thing that canaries don't like strawberries or we would have a bad time, they like seeds, all day they balance gracefully on blades of grass on the garden wall, they are the best thrashers [threshers] in the world if they did'nt eat the seed.

Me with Judy and Petronella and Lollipop looking on

D does not record the date of Judy's second foaling, perhaps because it was to be a surprise for me. Very soon afterwards Sugarback was castrated – he had become too mischievous and my parents didn't want any more foals. I was torn between wanting more ponies and being pleased that Sugarback might be more tractable. However, they were too late – Judy had already conceived a third foal.

With a steadier income from writing and the need to provide more conveniences for paying guests, long-overdue alterations were achieved. This was the time the hand pump and the large tank were installed outside the Wheelhouse. M could turn on the tap over the sink and get cold water! The loo-cum-washroom was improved. A new room was built at the back of the Skokholm cottage in the corner formed by the porch and back bedroom walls. This involved taking down the original kitchen chimney and knocking a hole in

View from the knoll: the new room can be seen left foreground

the entrance porch. This eventually became the 'Ringing Room'.

All this renovation meant we had to pay another visit to the ship-breaking yard at Milford to purchase more furniture. This was quite a fascinating if somewhat chaotic experience. The variety of ship's chandlery was staggering. People came from all directions. Waterborne clients like us would bring their boats alongside and lower goods straight off the wharf. D used to say some made off without paying, as no one in authority could possibly keep tabs on what was going over the side.

One particular item we purchased was a marvellous ship's washstand. When closed it looked like a narrow cupboard, when opened it had mirror, shelves and racks at the top, then a porcelain washbasin shaped like a bedpan on hinges. To empty, the basin tilted inwards, emptying its contents into a fitted bucket on the lowest shelf to catch the slops.

Although he denied it, D was always the showman. He really enjoyed the life we led at this time, sharing his island with so many visitors who were interested in birds, many of them expert naturalists and invariably enchanted with the island. After breakfast and after lunch every day he assembled everyone for a 'bird drive'. This involved spreading out in a line south of the well, where we made a slow but steady advance, beating the bracken to flush any small birds towards the open side of the Heligoland trap, which is shaped like an enormous funnel. It always surprised me how few birds flew straight up and over the entrance. Once the birds were almost into the funnel we all made a lot of noise and waved our sticks to drive them in towards the narrow end where there was a catching box with a glass front, through which the birds thought they could make their escape. As soon as they were safely fluttering against the glass, we closed the door at the back of the box. Each bird was carefully extracted through the sleeve of an old jersey hanging at the side. The correct sized ring would be selected, clipped on with a pair of small pliers, ensuring that it was loose enough for comfort and tight enough not to slip over the foot. Ring number, date and species would be recorded before the poor unfortunate was released.

On 12 May 1939 I had my ninth birthday, with an iced rice cake (one of Enid's recipes) decorated with candles and a silver shoe, which Aunt Marjorie brought me from the top of her wedding cake. We had a fancy dress sports day after high tea. M and Aunt Marjorie invariably came as Hawaiian maidens bedecked in bracken skirts and nasturtium leis. D loved to dress up and play the fool. Some of the guests showed great ingenuity making spur-of-the-moment costumes; one of the best that I recall represented the Pied Piper of Hamelin, who appeared in a robe of flowing beach towels, blowing a paper trumpet and dragging a piece of string with half a dozen dead mice tied at intervals!

Our students, as befitted the young and fit, always won the obstacle races, which we held in the Wheelhouse yard. The obstacles were normally crazily conceived by D at the last minute out of bits of plank, the sawhorse, ladders or whatever was lying about (the yard was invariably littered with timber and driftwood). I remember one competition in which the participants had to finish eating a raw turnip while walking a very wobbly plank. At this time Aunt Marjorie and Uncle John had arrived to learn the ropes preparatory to taking over the wardenship while my parents went on a birding expedition to Portugal. The island flowers were spectacular that year, the thrift incredibly vivid, partly due to the reduced rabbit population. D reports:

> The days seem to pass happily outdoors and it is difficult to concentrate on all the writing that is crying out to be done, this takes up most of the morning, driving birds, helping in the house and superintending in the afternoon, as well as rambling with Ann in the evening. By the time the goats are fetched and milked, high tea about 5.30 – there is only a half hour left for the garden before it is dark. Then an hour or so before the wood fire to do the bird records and hear the news, talk and drink a cup of chocolate, before going out to ring shearwaters, petrels and gulls.

Every evening during high visitor season everyone assembled in the cottage sitting room to report what wildlife they had seen on their rambles that day.

On 20 May we left the island in the capable hands of the Buxtons. Before M and D went to Portugal we had a few days in Benton Wood. D had always loved this place, and was still keen to buy it for the Pembrokeshire Bird

Protection Society (PBPS) But of course there weren't enough funds. On this visit we had been invited to stay in the restored castle. D wrote:

22nd: went to bed to the sound of nightjars reeling … 23rd: lying in bed this morning, (in the carved bed in the top floor of the big tower), I heard tree pipit, blackbird, blackcap, green woodpecker, nuthatch … a blue tit has a nest in the tunnel in the castle wall where the bell rope passes … Ann slept soundly in a room in the smaller tower above the dungeon, unperturbed by thoughts of ghosts of bygone prisoners and other bogies which might have scared a town child.

Benton Castle was originally built in the late thirteenth century. Later it was devastated by Cromwell. Dr Ernest Pegge lived in a cottage close by. In 1932 he had, with his own hands, lovingly restored the castle's north and south towers into living quarters. He had recycled the original stone from the destruction and obtained beams from the ship-breaking yards at Milford Haven. In the towers there were three bedrooms, sitting room and hall. On the various floors the garde-robes were converted into closets, bathroom, kitchenette and cloakrooms. All the furniture, doors and latches were exquisitely carved by Dr Pegge. I was quite fascinated by the whole set-up, especially the dragons and gargoyles carved on the arms of the chairs, not to mention sleeping in a real castle!

After a day or two exploring the woods and rowing up river to Cresswell quay, D left M and me at the castle in order to take a party of RAF officers and their wives on an expedition in their twin-engine pinnace for a tour of Skokholm. While there he picked up twelve shearwaters and arranged for their release in Switzerland – a test to see, should they return, whether the Venice birds homed overland in the last experiments.

M and I had a happy few days all on our own. It wasn't often I had her to myself when she was free of all her responsibilities. She totally relaxed and played 'make-believe' with me. We found the nest of a tree creeper in the depth of the wood. Down by the river we discovered a half-made shelter made of poles. We had great fun putting the finishing touches to it and it became our 'secret place'. I was into 'secret places', but this time M could share. We walked for miles and had picnics. She never had a very good sense of direction; more than once we became temporarily lost until I persuaded her to take another path! At the end of May I returned to school.

On 30 July my parents returned from their Portugal expedition, and were met in Portsmouth by Enid and Barry, who lived nearby. I had been excitedly awaiting their return with my new cousins, Terence and Meriel. There were gifts for everyone. I received a gorgeous hand-embroidered flower-seller's dress from Madeira. I wore it a lot that summer whenever I could persuade our long-suffering guests to have 'a fancy dress sports day'. My parents were full of their adventures: in Madeira being set upon by brigands and the atrocious meals on the steamer; tough limpets on a bed of rice tasting strongly of paraffin from the engine room! All good copy for books and articles.

My parents were given a royal greeting back on Skokholm on 3 August which D described:

flag flying from the mast, guns fired ... John handed me a gigantic wooden key of office with an accolade of rope stuck with used bird-rings and skeletons ... there are many puffins still left, but what interested us was the great growth of wild clover and grass, trefoil and other components of Skokholm turf, which in other years is grazed as bare as a billiard table ... I shall have to consider the pros and cons of sheep farming again ... John and Marjorie fit and happy ... they have made a small profit of £75 over the twelve weeks.

A few days later we went for a picnic on Skomer. Father went up to the fields by the old house (which is still untenanted) so as to compare its bare rabbit-eaten sward to that on Skokholm. Again it was balmy summer holidays, lots of visitors, old hands and new. D's diary reports: 'Ann is wonderfully keen on swimming now, and is fearless about the cold water, she can swim about thirty yards breast stroke.' I still wasn't very confident about being too far away from the landing stage, however.

In the middle of the month we went to Grassholm, a trip I remember well ... but D's description is far more poetic:

we were well beyond Skokholm before the red ball of the sun lifted in the east above the hazy island of Gateholm ... soon after we got among a huge school of porpoises which accompanied us for some distance, keeping pace with the boat, diving under it, almost touching the bow ... doing a thing I have never seen before – leaping into the air within six feet of us, great blue bodied, long nosed fellows ... we had a good day ringing 600 youngsters and 40 adult gannets, then had a delicious breakfast of tea and rabbit pie at 10am on the peak of Grassholm, our feet, as Ann insisted, stuck in the puffin burrows 'so as not to show at the table' ... After a swim in the gut ... bringing home a freak nestling gannet with a twisted upper mandible, I later killed it for the table.

A few days later, 'for lunch there was gannet, cold meat and pies. Those who, like Do, Ann, and I, tasted gannet, found it tolerable – rather like trout, not much meat on it as we'd hoped – it had been skinned, not plucked, but still smelt fishy'.

On 17 August 1939 D wrote, quite lyrically:

the post brought the complete copy of that beloved work *Early Morning Island*. I am more excited about this book than any so far, I feel it has an Alice in Wonderland quality. For the rest of the week I have lived in a kind of dream, trying to realise it is published. I gaze at this book and see myself loving it and I am a little ashamed of that other self who wastes so much time delving into it, but my head is slightly turned by the same post of a letter from the wife of the editor of *The Countryman* who says 'she must write at once, having read the book immediately on receiving it: the early part occasionally gave me a feeling like tears – not for sadness – but because Ann feels so clearly and expresses what unspoilt, imaginative children always long to say, inspiration and happiness of this wind-blown, clean book ... keep the letters of praise away from the author so that she may keep on unfolding as every happy child is meant to unfold and so many do not have the opportunity of doing! Thank you very much indeed for this honest and lovely book ... The editor will read it this evening.'

She had no need to worry. I cannot remember being all that impressed. I was most amused by the above eulogy when reading Father's diaries many years later: I certainly wasn't told of it at the time. I had little opportunity to brag about the book at school, because I was shortly to leave Brighton. I think I disappointed D because I didn't share his enthusiasm. The reviews were quite complimentary; I received quite a lot of fan mail, which I must admit I enjoyed answering, illustrating my replies with pencil drawings of scenes from our island activities.

Back in May we had spent a couple of days taking photographs to illustrate the book using D's old plate camera, which took good black and white photographs, but it was far from quick-fire photography. Obviously most of the photographs had to be 'staged' to fit in with the text. In this instance the subject (me) got very tired of waiting for him to achieve exactly the shot he wanted. D would fiddle with the plates saying: 'just hold it while I take another for good measure ...' or, 'let's try from another angle ...'

I remember two particularly trying times. One was when D wanted to illustrate my joy on seeing Judy's second foal, Lollipop, for the first time. As background we chose a splendid patch of thrift on which I turned somersault after somersault in 'imitation ecstasy' among the soft flower-adorned clumps, until D was satisfied and I was giddy. The other was when D made up this story about Alice the figurehead. M and I had picked some flowers for me to show her while I embraced her hard wooden figure where it sat perched on the cliffs above South Haven. It was a very awkward position and D kept changing his mind about the best view! I was very fond of Alice, but the story D made up I thought too far-fetched, even though I never failed to visit her whenever I went that way. Her raven locks were dressed with red roses, a silver cross on a string of beads graced her ample bosom. She had a classic Roman nose which Grandpa Shellard had fashioned for her after it got broken on the day her ship went aground. Each spring M and I would repaint these features after the ravages of winter.

I still cannot decide if *Early Morning Island* was a children's book or a children's book for grown-ups! We had minor disagreements about the fake and fancy parts and a real disagreement about the title. D wanted it called *A Dish of Sprats*; I preferred his second choice, *Early Morning Island*. In the end we compromised, and it came out with both titles. The birds, the flowers and the animals are all real ... even a dead rabbit with a skewer stuck up his backside to make him sit up. I know I talked to myself, to my pets, my toys and the wild things I encountered, but D went a step further and embellished these conversations. I daresay his embellishments all stem from something I said or did when I was eight going on nine. I was quite besotted with the goats, but I can't remember actually reading real books to them, but D says I did! I am sure they would have preferred to eat the paper than listen to me.

My hobby horses, which Baron made for me, feature large in the book. It is true I did not go far without them. One was 'Highty', because she was tall, the other was her foal (in my imagination) and made from an old scythe handle; hence 'Scythey'. My fondness for them was entirely due to the fact that they fulfilled all my wildest dreams of what I'd do if I had a pair of real ponies who behaved like they did. They were easy to catch, they obeyed my commands, they had few vices, they could jump over the most amazing obstacles and I could ride everywhere at full gallop. I kept them in a magnificent stable (the remains of a chinchilla hutch) full of the best hay and oats. My real pony wasn't half as biddable; in the home meadow I could catch her, but nowhere else unless she was hobbled. She was lazy and fat, and I was not yet an intrepid rider.

D often warned me not to go near the edge of the cliffs. This was a tall order because we were surrounded by them. The goats were often hiding when I had to fetch them for milking. In late summer when their lactation decreased they no longer felt the urge to be milked, so I had to go down the cliffs to coax them home. I largely ignored his words and he knew that. So many interesting things went on down there, with crevices full of seabird nests, a seal lying asleep on the beach below, or some particularly interesting bit of flotsam washed ashore. Sometimes having got down I wondered how I was going to get back up again. I would visit Rat Island, a rocky outcrop near North Haven, or dare myself to jump up and down on an overhang in Mad Bay that looked as if it was about to fall. (When I was last on Skokholm in 2010, I saw it still hanging there!) D must have guessed, because on our rambles together, or while I was helping M in the Wheelhouse, I would let slip that I had found a nest or something interesting in an inaccessible place. I daresay I related my own adventures with the odd imaginative exaggeration, so who am I to criticise Father's author's licence?

To me at that age, the creation of *Early Morning Island* had been a long drawn-out process, so when it was published it was, I suppose, a bit of an anti-climax. For I never went through any of the anxieties authors normally feel – will it sell, will it be well-reviewed ...

9

Happy Interlude

It was late summer, 1939. I remember crowding round the radio with the grown-ups while they listened to talk of war and I watched their worried faces. For me, though, the war brought about a brief but very happy stage in my island life. The diaries do not say when my parents decided I should not go back to school. Obviously they didn't like the thought of me being so far away while there was a war on. I am quite sure Aunt Kathleen disapproved of the fact that they decided to give me lessons themselves, but none of this was ever voiced within my hearing. As it turned out, my home schooling mainly consisted of keeping a diary of some of my activities in a beautiful leather-bound book, which I've found, decades later, to be an invaluable source of information. The first entry, on 1 September 1939, says: 'Horay, I am not going back to school because of the horrible war, I am going to stay on the island with M & D and the Baron.' Needless to say I was delighted not to be going back to school. No worries of war for me – I was going to stay in my most favourite place and we were going to have a real farm with more animals.

From then on my lessons usually took up what morning I had left after doing my chores. If there was anything going on that was more urgent, or we were going to the mainland, lessons took a back seat. D comments: 'Ann learns much of her lessons from *Cassell's Book of Knowledge*, whose eight volumes I bought so laboriously by instalments out of my own pocket for the love of good books nearly twenty years ago. I little thought I was buying for posterity!'

First I would write in my dairy, usually a description of

Mother and Baron outside the Skokholm house

some happening which had impressed me. Presumably this was considered to be an English lesson, although D seldom corrected my grammar and spelling. English, History (especially Natural History) and General Knowledge far outstripped my almost nil progress in any kind of Mathematics.

The same day as the first entry in my diary, D says in his: 'the German invasion of Poland, while we were catching willow warblers, whitethroats and rock pipits'.

D had been looking at farms around Milford Haven with Baron, and when they returned to Dale in the evening they found the distribution of gas masks in progress. The Admiralty had taken over Milford Docks, where the only sign of war was the movement of warships in the haven. We had to obtain permission from the Admiral for a permit to travel to and from Skokholm. D wanted to join the navy and at the same time farm Skokholm with sheep, now that the rabbits had been reduced. On 5 September we moved to a more protected and spacious house on the waterfront in

Dale. So far we had purchased sixty-three sheep. Baron had purchased ferrets. The sheep were easily loaded in two lots off the sea wall in Dale into Edgar's boat, then covered in a trawl net to prevent them from jumping into the sea. On 18 September, having just made the new house comfortable, we were in the throes of moving over to Skokholm for the winter. The hapless canaries had almost all been annihilated by kestrels and sparrowhawks, so we rigged up a one-way grille into their aviary to save the last few. Later, in a book called *The Cinnamon Bird* (published by Staples in 1948), Father describes our canaries, their habits, matings, incest and child neglect. It is beautifully illustrated in colour by Tunnicliffe.

The Soay rams had to be shot. Baron and D skinned and dressed them. The older tougher one was given to the light-keepers! I was obviously impressed, and wrote in my new diary:

D put the two dead rams in the wheelbarrow ... it is sad to kill the rams but we do not want them to marry the tame ewes, because the cross-bread lambs would be to small to sell ... Baron hung the young ram up on my swing, Baron began skining, he started at the rump cutting away like anything through the brown coat right up to the back-bone, he did both sides then the tail, it did look funny with no wool on it, then the Baron took out the kidneys and liver, he told me he liked the smell of a wild beast better than a tame sheep. Then he chopped down the back bone ... we had Soay liver for dinner.

We scythed the front meadow for hay (which I describe as 'hayemaking'). I was terribly upset because I wasn't skilled enough to cut grass with a scythe; the blade simply ran over the top. In floods of tears I ran indoors ... M consoled me by suggesting I went off and cut bracken for bedding down the stock (which we proposed running later), and I found that the short stout Skokholm bracken had plenty of resistance to the scythe blade, which made me happy! A few days later we carried the hay and stored it in the old dairy and the men's lavatory shed. (The latter I grandly dubbed 'the Dutch Barn'!) I was determined that we were going to be 'real farmers', and I was absolutely thrilled when Baron rigged up the sides of our old pony cart with fancy bits of driftwood and made it almost like the gambo at Rhyd-y-gath.

After the winter's rabbit-gassing, we were able to cut the first hay since the days when Skokholm was farmed.

I wrote out a timetable for us all as follows:

7   get up, milk goats.
8   Breakfast and wash up.
9   in the morning everyone is to work at their own work.

12.	Dinner and wash up.
1	work out side if whether permites.
4	cup of tea.
4.30	fetch and milk the goats and separate.
7	supper round the fire.

D comments: 'to which we adhered, under protest from Do.'

M still had her old milk separator. I was longing to try out a little churn M found in the market, but when we had saved enough cream to make butter I was disappointed to learn that butter made with goats' milk is always white in colour. Later M purchased some 'butter colouring' in case the visitors thought it looked unappetising. With Soay sheep, our own eggs and chicken, rabbit and garden produce, D thought, 'we can live very cheaply just now'.

We made copious preparations for spending the winter here. So that we could keep warmer we moved what we needed for eating and cooking into the back bedroom of the house, where the original kitchen used to be. I had a small trolley in which I trundled goods back and forth all day. My diary says: 'my first load was suger, the cart was full when I got it all on, I took it over to the new kitchen and put it on the table, it did not look a lot since suger is rationed'.

D's diary says:

October 2nd: ... we went peat cutting, in the cool north-east wind we dug up two cartloads or so of the fibrous turf on the South Field rock ... Ann was very pleased with this work, though the dust filled her eyes, nose and hair. She enjoyed building castles, parapets and tripods of the turves [and here he inserted a few sketches of the turves stacked for drying] ... she worked so hard that at 4 p.m. she was violently hungry, we adjourned to tea accordingly.

The same episode in my diary (also illustrated):

> After we had done all the work in the morning, feeding animals and doing my lessons and so on, we dug peat it was fun though it all blew in your hair, in your eyes, up your nose and up your sleeves, everywhere you could think of and in your ears too. For it was so windy... D dug it and I stacked it, my eyes were full all ready and so were D's. First we stacked them like brick walls only do it with spaces, then D said they do it Differently in Scotland ... he told me they stack them up on end with the grassy bits on top ... next we went over to the bog to see what peat was there, that was better still than what we had been digging on middle rock before, only it was so wet we only bothered to make about twelve stacks, D. said it would not be ready till next year, so we stacked the peat in castles on top of rocks.

Skokholm peat is very poor quality and needs driftwood to help it along, but at least it does not spark: our salty driftwood fires were forever burning holes in the carpet.

A friend gave M a Siamese cat to look after for the duration of the war. Baron adored him and straight away christened him Dewi Chocs. D had vowed never to have a cat on the island because of the birds, but he had no need to worry about this one – he preferred to stay indoors. The invasion of mice into the house in wintertime was catastrophic, so Dewi did not have to venture outside to earn his keep. Even so we still caught mice in our six little mousetraps set over and over again until bedtime. In the morning it was my job to feed the bodies to Baron's ferrets:

> in the morning I get up and get a paper bag and count all the mice from the night before and take them to the

ferrets, I love this because of their antics. With much hissing and growling each one grabs a mouse and hides it in their sleeping compartment then comes back for another, if there are two ferrets in the same cage, the second one nips in and start to gobble up the hidden one. Sometimes they had a tug of war and the mouse falls to pieces. After eating their fill they start a rather graceful sort of dance before retiring for a nap.

For the three goats which were still milking, we built very superior winter quarters with a raised platform at the back of the workshop. There they were milked, spent each night and were given a little supplementary feed to keep them lactating. Previously they had had to fend for themselves until we arrived back to live here in the early spring. Certainly we needed the extra milk for overwintering here, and eventually to feed calves and pigs. I was all in favour of these new quarters because I did not have to crouch to do the milking or get wet when it rained. Spending the winter here meant that in January I was also going to see all the new kids as soon as they were born.

We had two men staying in a vain effort to finish off the rabbits by cyano-gassing, as we had done the previous winter. This time, instead of doing it area by area, we filled in every hole on the island beforehand, in an effort to save gas.

By mid-October we bought more sheep, making a total of ninety-four. Baron and D have fenced off the neck and made the home meadow stock-proof. Later on, to conserve grass for lambing they re- built the fence across the middle of the island. We were fortunate in having so much useful driftwood to build fences and yards. Apart from the fences round the sheep dip, all the old ones had long been dismantled.

When there was insufficient timber suitable for our needs washed up on Skokholm, we'd pay a visit to The Wick on Skomer. This is a long, narrow gut; the eastern arm sticks out into the sea and curves slightly to the west. Because of prevailing winds and tides anything that floats by gets caught by this promontory and directed into the stony beach at the end. There it becomes trapped and piles up, a real treasure trove. Not only is it a great place for beachcombing, but the ledges on the 200-foot perpendicular basalt cliff on one side form the breeding ground for thousands of seabirds.

Although The Wick is just across Broad Sound between Skomer and Skokholm, we had to choose a calm day for what we dubbed 'driftwooding', because we never returned without grossly overloading the boat, and sometimes we had a bundle of timber in tow as well. Baron was in his element and had to be dissuaded from adding 'just one more nice bit of mahogany!' M was always in search of the 'perfect' chopping board.

On one such day, I was in my element fossicking among the jetsam. I found a lavatory seat, a wine crate – oh what fun I had filling its many compartments with my 'treasures' – and a perfectly preserved wooden sword, painted silver: what stories it might tell about some shipboard theatrical production! The boat, as usual, was grossly overloaded; we had spent too long in selecting the best timber for fencing and made slow headway against the failing north stream. We had to throw the timber off in a great hurry when we reached South Haven at half-tide, so as to haul the boat up while there was still enough water to get her near to the winchway.

Life was very busy with gassing rabbits, shepherding, and replenishing supplies from the mainland. D gave a series of radio broadcasts, which he disliked doing, but the money this work brought in made it too tempting to turn down. He was also working on his book *Shearwaters,* and Baron's biography.

A number of people wrote to ask if they could join us in our 'subsistence adventure' on Skokholm, although I would never have described our life as exactly that, in spite of my mother's willingness to try. Some of these people were cranks and some well-known. D was tempted, but wisely felt 'we can take none'. The hazards of war were beginning to show. Crude oil was fouling the driftwood and killing many sea birds. On all beaches there were guillemots and razorbills dying and dead. But a pair of robins resident in South Haven cheered us up.

By early December all the holes on the island had been filled in and gassed, but alas, most nights rabbits came up from the cliffs to dig. In the long run it was a hopeless task. Soon after that we ran out of gas, so we packed up ferrets, canaries and personal gear and went off to Dale for Christmas and Rhyd-y-gath for New Year. There was a spate of bad easterly weather so we did not return until a fortnight later, minus the men, having decided we could do the gassing ourselves.

We returned to the island in mid January 1940 with a goat, Jack the sheepdog (who was always violently seasick), three ferrets, Dewi Chocs, six canaries and ourselves. The weather was calm and frosty, but a big easterly storm had done wonders for the South Haven Beach and had filled in the gaps between the boulders with pebbles.We had no meat in the larder, but had some delicious woodcock, which were abundant enough on the island for ornithologists to eat! A huge gale carried off the mast and two oars from well above the landing stage in South Haven, the waves reaching higher than D had ever seen. Baron fashioned a new mast from driftwood. Then we had snow, much to my delight; I asked

Baron to make me a toboggan, but as snow is rare and fleeting on Skokholm, it started to melt before he had time to make it. I made do with one of M's tin trays on the mountain. (Now always referred to as The Knoll.)

The rabbit-gassing continued, but holes were continually being opened, and there seemed to be no prospect of total extermination without prohibitive cost.

On 4 February, according to the diaries, I begged my parents not to go ashore, as the weather was deteriorating by the minute. I can relive every moment of it still. For some reason we had Dewi Chocs with us in a basket. The boat was launched and just afloat in the narrow passage between the cliff and St. Catherine's rock below her berth. I had been told to jump aboard first. A second later a huge wave came in, leaving M and D clinging to the gunwales, dangerously close to being crushed between boat and cliffsides as they were sucked out by the backwash. Baron, who was not going ashore, got wet up to his knees, and the cat basket, which was standing ready to be handed to me, was only inches from being swept away; the desperate yowls of Dewi Chocs were matched by my howls of protest, and pleas that we haul up the boat ready to try another day. The next wave brought the *Storm Petrel* back in, so we winched her back up the precarious berth in pouring rain and called it a day. D's description reads: 'the morning had gone, we had healthy exercise and excitement, we changed our soaking clothes and had dinner.'

On 6 February a Greek ship went aground near St. Anne's Head. She was loaded with wheat, so everyone on the south Pembrokeshire coast was out harvesting the grain for their chickens! A great deal of her flotsam came ashore in Stack Bay: ladders, tins of oil, sacks of flour, spars, long lengths of timber and hatch covers. The flour sealed itself off quite nicely. Once we had peeled off the wet outside, it proved to be better quality than we could buy at that time. Baron rigged up a block and tackle at the top of the cliff to cope with the accumulation of timber. In Crab Bay an enormous drum of turpentine floated in; a lightkeeper saw it first, and went away to get a rope. In the meantime D saw it, and filled some containers in order to make it light enough to drag up the cliff. The keeper was a bit chagrined to find that eighteen gallons had been siphoned off in his absence.

On March 12th D and Baron went ashore, leaving M and me on the island. My diary says:

M was baking bread, she went down to the well to get some water-cress for tea, when she came hurriedly up without any water-cress or anything, she was panting vigrously, she turned the bread and then told me she had seen a hoopoe when she'd gone down to south haven to retrieve a tin of mansion polish, some driftwood and a bottle washed ashore ... we rushed down there, me on the north and M on the south, 'oh' I mean the other way round, I clambered over rocks and bracken storks, being careful not to let them crack under my feet, incase they should frighten the hoopoe. I peeped my head round a tump of thrift and there was the hoopoe digging in the ground for grubs, then he saw me and flew away towards the big rock as Baron calls it, but he stopped by Alice the figure head. I investigated the holes ... they were like starlings make, only smaller of course because he has a smaller beak. M and I tried to drive him into the trap ... we got within four yards of him, he or she or whatever it was put his crest up and down moderately in time with its beak, the bird had wide shoulders, and wings the same shape as a lapwings. We drove the hoopoe down the slope, across the stream without much bother, when suddenly we were just going to rush at him, to get him right in, when he flew up and over the trap and headed for the neck … we went up to the house and took the bread out of the oven. In the evening I went into the workshop to feed the hens and I nearly cried to see poor Proudy (the cockerel) dead, but all things have got to dye. Then we had nice water cress for tea.

I wonder, as a true ornithologist's daughter, if D was proud of my detailed observations! Although they are relatively frequent visitors, the sighting of an African Hoopoe anywhere in Britain always arouses feverish excitement among ornithologists and twitchers.

On 18 March M, D and I crossed over to the mainland in a stiff south breeze. Offshore big sheets of plywood were tumbling in the waves. We only picked up two pieces and a hatch cover because after that D said he felt sick and I voted for us to stop. The sheets were enormous and as wide as the *Storm Petrel*, each time we leaned over the side to grab a sheet and lift it aboard, the suction from the wide flat surface made the boat heel over and take in water over the gunwale, nearly capsizing us at each attempt. Ashore the great hunt for plywood was on, undamaged on sandy beaches but badly cracked on rocky shores. Afterwards we watched this parade of plywood floating past from St Ann's Head with an ebb tide and westerly gale. Scarcely an able-bodied soul in the district wasn't ranging the coast after such valuable flotsam.

Dale Roads was such a safe harbour that I could go for a row there in a dinghy by myself. On Skokholm the tides were too strong and there was no sheltered water. I was always keen to row our boat whenever I was given the chance, but the *Storm Petrel*'s sweeps were so heavy I could only manage one at a time. At the end of March Baron made me a craft of my own which I could row on the North Pond. The great day of launching arrived:

my boat is a sort of punt only I row it, not punt it, it's the lovelyest one, it floats like a duck … it's the most marvellous fun … And sometimes I get recked on little lumps which are scattered about on the pond … In this wonderful boat I have moveable floor boards and a moveable seat, a fixed seat in the bow and two fixed rollocs and a sculling hole, two oars borrowed from the light-keepers, and its jolly well an unleakable boat. The first day D. smashed a bottle over her and named her DUNLIN, but her name is not painted on her bow yet or a picture of dunlin on her stern … The other day I got a sack and made a sail.

Some of the adults had to have a go, but they all, save M, got wet when they swamped it. My precious boat took up almost no draught, which meant I could use it in even the shallowest parts of the pond. It gave me hours of fun, especially in high winds. Because the boat lacked any keel, my square rigging necessitated sailing before the wind! When I could sail no further, I frantically rowed back to have another go.

D bought three geese and a gander. In order to transport them to their new home each one was tied in a sack with its head sticking out. I was so keen to free them from their confinement I started to let them go on the landing steps in South Haven; D shouted, 'tie them up at once and take them to the North Pond.' Subsequently, no matter how many times I drove them there, they preferred to foul up the front meadow.

D hired a married couple, Roly and Audrey, he as shepherd on a profit-sharing basis, she as assistant cook and general hand. This gave my parents time to go to the mainland and attend to the ever-increasing business involved in running the Pembrokeshire Bird Protection

Society, which included the Annual General Meeting in Tenby. After the business concluded bird films were shown. One reel had been shot on Skokholm while my parents were away in Portugal. There were a few domestic scenes, such as the mail boat arriving, the Soay sheep and a shot of Baron milking Claribel. I embarrassed my parents by shouting out to all and sundry: 'He's pulling her teats much too hard!'

March 30th: D was delighted – he has been able to pay off his overdraft (temporarily) on receiving £30 in royalties for his book *I Know an Island* and £150 from the hired couple, being their share buying into the sheep flock.

Lambing was in full swing, and the last goats were kidding. I was in my element with so many baby animals to assist with. As ever, surplus kids were dispatched for the table. I knew it was useless to protest, but I did because baby goats are such great playmates. I was allowed to keep one pretty nanny, a pale brown with white points. I called her 'Cloudy.' It is hardly surprising that I named some of my goats after weather conditions – the weather affected everything we did on the island!

The goats were returned to their summer shelter. In their place we installed broody hens. D taught me how to prepare nest boxes for them: first a layer of turf to provide humidity, then hay to cushion the eggs, and finally a sack curtain over the front to keep the hen quiet. We placed four goose eggs under each hen. They were too heavy for her to turn, so I marked each with an 'X' so I could do it for her. Each day I took the broodies grain and water, and turned them off the nest while I threw a damp cloth over the goose eggs to prevent the shells getting too hard and to mimic the moisture which naturally comes from sitting water fowl. I always hoped the broodies would not take too long to eat, drink, stretch and do their business and go back before the eggs chilled. They tried my patience sometimes by pecking me when I turfed them off the nest, and were not obliging, but I revelled in the responsibility.

I loved helping with the sheep too. In April docking the lambs' tails was not very successful; in hindsight a majority of the disasters were due to inexperience. Nowadays the use of rubber rings for docking and castrating lambs of all ages is efficient and quick. Humid and maggoty conditions on the island often made suitable docking days few and far between. Maggoty sheep tend to skulk behind rocks where they are hard to find. If a ewe was not alert she could lose a weakly lamb, with ravens and black-backed gulls always hovering nearby to peck at the afterbirth. Sometimes ewes who are heavy in lamb or in full wool would lie down in an awkward position, which farmers always refer to as 'cast'; two of these birds would gang up on the helpless animal, one each side, so whichever way she turned her head there was a powerful beak waiting for a feast of eye ...

April. We had a few crab pots set in South Haven. One day there was nothing in the pots, but we found a huge lump of paraffin wax washed close to the landing stage, with which we attempted to make candles. They were not a great success, being rather smoky.

Much to my sorrow the ponies were banned from the home meadow, where they had been together with some young lambs. They had killed one and broken the leg of another two. They were banned from the fenced-off areas after that, and had to graze in the bog a long way from the house, where Judy had to be hobbled if I wanted to catch her. In retrospect I can't think why she was not confined in the meadow by herself. It was the young horses who were so playful when they were together.

At the end of April we released the canaries, along with some goldfinches which D had put in the aviary to see if they would hybridise! The finches were delighted with their freedom and soared into the sky never to return, but the canaries remained close about the buildings and garden.

We always visited Skokholm Stack in April. It is one of the most colourful parts of the island, having smooth rock sides of brilliant red sandstone patched with yellow lichen. Our longest ladder would just reach across the chasm which separates island from stack. At the top there is a small area covered in scurvy grass and guano. The greater black-backed gulls had almost exclusive rights there and we all hated them. They have an evil eye and are by far the worst marauders of shearwaters, puffins and weakly sheep. Their eggs were, M said, 'inconveniently large'. We usually made two visits there, not because we wanted the eggs as much as we wished to reduce their numbers. It was quite a balancing feat to return over the ladder with a basket full of eggs.

Me with Alice Williams, the ship's figurehead

We enlarged the sheep dip and did some more docking. At the same time two Bretons were fishing about the island; we lost a lamb and wondered if they were responsible. A new garden which we had created on the bluebell slope above Alice Williams in South Haven was fenced with netting to protect it from rabbits and goats. Full of new peas, potatoes and cuttings from Dale, it was a great success, being both sheltered and fertile. We motored to Skomer where we disembarked. We saw Mr Sturt and a boatload of egg-gathering villagers safely returning to Martinshaven. It was a golden opportunity for D to have a good look round without encountering or seeking permission from Mr Sturt! We wandered round picking up gulls' eggs and looking at the Wick and the house. On leaving Skomer South Haven a Breton smack was anchored there for the night with all her pots down and the crew asleep! We left them the eggs.

We always took enough gull's eggs for our own use and some to preserve for winter. Now with a war and threatened food shortages, it became a serious business. We needed a lot more for animal feed and for sale. We gathered most of them from a huge colony of herring gulls in the centre of the island between the north and south ponds. As usual it was my job to collect the eggs. I used to take the first two in each nest, sometimes more. Naturally the gulls objected to this and dive-bombed me ceaselessly. I was never actually struck but it often felt pretty close. We made a few trips to Middleholm to get some extra, only to find that the local residents had been doing the same thing. To preserve the eggs we used a tall brass-bound barrel from the *Alice Williams*, filled with isinglass. First I had to test each one very carefully to see if it floated in a bucket of water: the slightest inclination to do this and they would be put aside for stock feed. By the middle of June we ended up with 2090 eggs in pickle, about 400 taken to Dale and several hundred used for pigs, chickens and calves.

We still visited Grassholm for the purpose of ringing gannets. At one stage the RAF wanted to carry out bombing practice there. D was furious and went straight to the authorities to plead the gannets' cause. There were lots more signs of war. Convoys plied to and fro in great numbers from Milford Haven. More seabirds were oiled. The once red and black lighthouse relief boat looked very strange with her war paint of camouflage grey, and the lighthouses had shades so that only a fraction of their former brilliance showed. The orphan Soays, Darby and Joan, had not rejoined the wild flock. Joan had taken to butting the goats in their stalls and hurting them quite badly. She was put in the pot.

On 11 May, Baron was sixty-four. Because our birthdays were so close we often shared a little celebration together. I found a description I wrote in my leather-bound book:

> The Baron is a very amusing person, he tells the funniest stories I have ever heard, he also has funny words for the real ones. Now I will discribe what he looks like, he is tall and thin, with a bald head, he has a wee bit of grey hair round his bald part, a moustache, his hair is very curly, he leans forward a bit when he is walking and working, he says he's got floating kidneys. And a stone on one kidney which one day he says he will have out, he has'nt got many teeth, six at the bottom and one on top which he calls his pipe tooth, which he says is loose. He has many bulet marks for he says he has been in the Bore War, he has one back braser always undone in case of emergency, so if one brakes he can do up the other. He always says 'hoodlums' instead of 'lots', 'like old fits' instead of 'like anything', 'head over kettle' instead of 'head over heels' and 'destinator' instead of 'detonator' ... He helps all three of us by making things for us ... he has a schoolboys appetite which makes him go to sleep after meals.'

May 12 1940: my tenth birthday. I had a friend to stay, and we had the usual fancy dress tea and sports day, during which, in attempting to show off how I rode the billy goat, I was thrown and cut my lip. The next day D records that we have '13 goslings from 17 eggs and six more eggs under hens'.

We invested in some pigs and two calves, one pure white and the other a black and white Hereford cross. We called one of them Wilhelmina after the Dutch queen, who had fled to England after the Nazis invaded The Netherlands. In no time this became 'Wil-hell', because they were a constant source of amusement with their antics as they dashed about in the home meadow. They thrived on a diet of goats' milk mixed with meal and gulls' eggs. The pigs lived in a makeshift shed by the back meadow, where they were let out to graze during the day. The ponies had never seen pigs before. They were fascinated by these strange creatures, they pranced round, snorting and farting, with their tails in the air, before coming back to have another look and repeating the performance. Not only did we have pigs, we had guinea pigs! My Darling-Bunnynose had died, and in her place D bought four guinea pigs, two for me and two for the Codd children. M christened my pair Cuthbert and Jennifer. Inevitably they did what guinea pigs do best, and in no time we had lots more.

On the day we bought the pigs D recorded:

we brought over the vicar of St Brides the Rev. Tom Griffiths, the three weaner pigs, a white calf, and a barrel of tar, a pretty load ... Next morning, Tom, anxious to celebrate this visit to the far end of his home parish, held communion in the house. He made an altar of our folding gate-legged table, there placing lighted candles, Bread and Wine, while we five adults gathered on the cleared carpet. Do and Roly departed before the bread and wine were distributed. The sunlight from the east filled the little room and for a while we forgot the striving world, while Tom, rather gorgeously arrayed in blue and white, intoned a short service.

I quote this little episode because I find it intriguing for several reasons. Despite Granny L's efforts my parents never gave me any spiritual guidance, although I now suspect that deep down D may have believed in God. M most certainly did not, hence her leaving. I am sure, had she been asked, she would have turned down the idea of the little service.

I still have that gate-legged table. I would it could talk!

Even by the month of June I was unaware that all the grown-ups were feeling very worried listening to the news each day. D wrote that he felt guilty that he was dwelling in peace and beauty on his idyllic island while Belgium capitulated. He wrote: 'Hard physical work alone brings some relief and sleep to the tormented mind'. Baron wanted to offer his services as an engineer but was scarcely fit. D's book about him, *A Pot of Smoke*, had been accepted by Harrap.

On 14 June D received a tear-stained letter from Aunt Marjorie saying her beloved John was reported missing in Norway, where he was sent as a Commando because he was fluent in that language. D replied at once. His diary records something of his words to Marjorie:

I tried to convince myself that he was a prisoner or hiding somewhere. As if in answer to my anguished mind a swallow flew into the study and alighted on the ledge against the window beside me. I put my hand out and caught and ringed it. I thought of John's last message – he had spoken of a swallow that 'had not minded the snow of Northern Norway.' I was comforted by this omen. June 19th. We received the news that John was safe and a prisoner of war, so the omen of the swallow was a good one.

June 29th: A cheeky German pilot laid mines all the way down Dale Roads in broad daylight, watched by all the locals from the sea wall! We see more and more pretty patterns of tracer bullets from the Navy practising at sea … we are expecting to be told to leave Skokholm, there may be a searchlight station here. I am full of indecision and regret, everything on the island is so lovely in June, the animals and gardens thrive …

He did not mention the pigs, who had either sunburn or maybe a rash through being given too many gulls' eggs!

In between caring for the stock on the island and putting the finishing touches to his book *Shearwaters*, D looked at farms all over Pembrokeshire. A great many were too derelict or needed too much capital. There were many consultations with brother-in-law Martin at Rhyd-y-gath and good friend and farmer Stanley James, of Philbeach in Dale. At the beginning of August, after much negotiation and many visits to it, we agreed to take a semi-derelict farm of 160 acres in north Pembrokeshire, called Cwmgloyne, for a nominal rent of £25 per annum for three years, provided we made improvements. It was overrun with rabbits and the house was a dilapidated former mansion. The menfolk all thought the land had possibilities; the womenfolk were all horrified by the house, except for M who was excited by its potential. As for me, I had eyes only for the stable, consisting of a loose box and row of stalls with loft above, from which fodder could be pushed down through holes above the hayracks. I was still horse mad. If anyone asked what I wanted for a birthday it was always horse books or tack. The stable was some comfort and consolation for me because I was bitterly disappointed to be leaving Skokholm, where I had so much input, and I was worried about what would happen to the ponies after we moved.

Evacuation of Skokholm started by degrees and reached its full momentum through August and September, finishing on 1 October, when I ran up to the lighthouse with mail while D collected items still left behind and M took cuttings from the garden.

Two of the goats were already ensconced at Martinshaven so that we had fresh milk halfway. The sheep were brought over by degrees. We had learned to do this more efficiently and drove small groups to the landing stage with the help of our sheepdog, then kept them bunched with hurdles, so they had to be carried only a few yards before being dropped into the boat and covered with a cargo net. Too often proceedings were sorely hampered by the vagaries of the outboard motor, which was forced to work overtime, then D being knocked out by a bad attack of colitis for almost three weeks, no doubt brought on by the stress of leaving his beloved island and starting a new career. M had to take one load of lambs to the market by herself because D was feeling so low. Some of the lambs were rather light and crossed with Soays, which the grader rejected, but M was so fed up she let them go cheaply.

Thirteen years' accumulation of island life was taken over in time-devouring boatloads, then dispatched by lorry northwards to Cwmgloyne. Everything that might come in useful on a farm was removed: tools, corrugated iron, fencing material, timber, all the wire netting from the traps, preserved gulls' eggs, wax, oil, ropes and our two big water tanks. I was very anxious about the latter. I see from a quote in my diary: 'with the help of the light-keepers ... we rolled the tanks down to the landing stage and into the *Storm*

Petrel, then D filled the inside of the tanks with as much as he dared, which to my mind was much too daring.'

Even the wheel from the Wheelhouse, and Alice, the figurehead, were removed. When Alice reached Martinshaven she was propped up in a barrel over the cab of the lorry, which aroused some interest en route.

We took Judy and her last foal, Arabella, over in the *Storm Petrel*, with their legs tied, cushioned on washed-ashore ships' mattresses. Judy behaved very badly and struggled all the way over until someone sat on her head. These two were sold cheaply to D's friend Jim Codd because he had been so helpful with the moving. I was sad and cross to see them go, but we kept Petronella and Lollipop, who had taken after their sire and had better conformation. I was looking forward to training them so much that the blow of parting from Judy was slightly softened. I often wonder how much stress, if any, horses feel from loneliness; now, Sugarback, left behind, had only the light-keepers for company.

After the war the little railway was dismantled and goods for the lighthouse were hauled up with a motor, so Sugarback was no longer needed. Several times he was supposed to have been taken off but the moment was always postponed. In July 1957 an article came out in *The Times* entitled 'The Life and Death of Sugarback'. Poor old chap, latterly he had become very stiff and seldom walked far from where he died near the South Pond. There the light-keepers made him a little headstone. D says the article 'came anonymously from his pen', but was inspired by a letter from Dido Berry, the cook on Skokholm, describing Sugarback's last moments.

M and D were so busy they had no time to pine for the island – besides, how many times had they almost left it in days gone by? The tedium of ferrying goods over day after day was somewhat relieved by being able to throw a line overside and troll for mackerel. It was a particularly good season, providing many easy suppers for us. I was packed off to Rhyd-y-gath for the last week of the evacuation to make more space for gear. On the afternoon D and John Fursdon came to fetch me, I was amazed to see the carrier on the car piled high with rolls of wire netting and inside it was a tea chest full of canaries! They had managed to recapture the last of the birds not eaten by sparrowhawks, and had dismantled the aviary. We rebuilt it in the corner of the courtyard in front of the Cwmgloyne house. Some of the prettiest canaries had been given away. I hated the idea of them being shut in a little cage for the rest of their lives, but they were better off than those we kept: a weasel got into the aviary one day when we were out and killed a number of them.

I had had a wonderful time being on the island and not at school. Although I wasn't shielded from the war, I was fairly oblivious to it while on Skokholm. It wasn't until we'd been on the mainland for some time, and I'd been made to go to school, that I really experienced any patriotism, because we were forever being reminded to 'dig for victory' and 'knit scarves for the troops', and so on.

10

Cwmgloyne

The moment I arrived in our new home I was off to see Petronella and Lollipop. They looked very content but refused to be caught.

It was suggested I let the guinea pigs loose; they bred more prodigiously than ever. The offspring never became tame, and most, I suspect, fell prey to stoats, which solved the overpopulation! The goats I inspected next. With all the nutritious browsing they were milking much better here. M said they will have to go as soon as we get a cow because they are far too agile, and will always be where they are not wanted: a true prediction. That same day I found a host of wonderful trees to climb, exchanging cliffs for trees. I thought I might love this place after all.

The eighteenth-century historian Richard Fenton described the house as: 'a once gentleman's residence ... a small mansion ... not yet metamorphosed into a working farm house'. From the front, it had a secret, brooding look because a number of windows, just discernable, had been walled up in the days of 'window tax'. The front gate led onto a grassed courtyard, once a lawn where, I imagined, the squires' ladies walked and entertained in former days. A simple porch formed by a huge slab of slate sheltered the front door, which led straight into a large hall, with a drawing room on the left, and on the right a passage to what we thought were a breakfast room and the butler's pantry. At the end of the passage the west wing contained a table room, a kitchen, back stairs and dormitory, granary, malthouse and loose boxes: maybe in former days their hunters were kept there – or so I liked to believe!

The previous tenant had lived in just two rooms, the hall and drawing room. They looked very gloomy because he had boarded up all the other exits to keep out the draughts. M could hardly wait to take the barricades down and let in some light. When this was achieved a wide staircase with a window on each landing was revealed; two flights down to extensive kitchens, scullery and dairies, and two flights up to the half-storey containing six bedrooms. Once upon a time there had been an east wing, long since pulled down, and the stone used to build a hayshed. The whole interior of the house was in an indescribably filthy state: paint and plaster peeling off, mildew, spiders and rats, two of the three chimneys choked with debris. There was no plumbing or electricity. Mercifully the slate roof was intact.

When we got there, a mill pond and one of the two waterwheels still remained. Large gaps showed in the walls of the kitchen garden, which was choked with weeds. The farm buildings were a mixture of good and bad. The stable, apart from the loft floor, was in good condition, the pig sties, mill barn and calf sheds were adequate, the cowshed was brand new but had no water laid on. We turned the old kitchen in the west wing into Baron's workshop because it had an entrance on the ground floor.

There used to be a lodge at the entrance gate and a grand avenue up the Gloyne valley, which is now a footpath. Nowadays the house is Grade II listed, and part of it is a holiday let.

D was enjoying the woodland birds and never failed to record them.

Sept.20th: Do and I and Baron have fallen in love with this ramshackle and derelict old farm ... we sit by a log fire downstairs, our windows a disgrace without 'blackout', but it seems none can see us while the leaves are on the rookery trees south of the house – but the leaves are fast falling.

M chose to make the old scullery her kitchen. It was rather a dismal basement-like room, but it was the only practical choice, being near a source of water. Just a few yards from the back door was a rushing stream and a 'spout'. In those days few Welsh farms were without one. It is simply a mini-waterfall made by diverting part of a stream into a piece of downpipe, so that it flows out like tea from a pot. The constant flow has a hundred uses, including filling the kettle, washing spuds, and soaking dirty pots and farm socks. We had a sink and draining board, but the spout was the nearest thing to 'water laid on'.

For the first few weeks we couldn't use the fireplace there: the chimney, serving all three storeys, was almost filled to the top with nests and dirt left there by generations of jackdaws. I took away barrow-load after barrow-load, so that M could use the grate.

D wrote: 'Sept 30th: Off to Cardigan to become acquainted with the little town where we will do our shopping ... We called at the Cardigan Grammar School where the senior master was anxious to take Ann when he discovered she was a budding author.'

How could D have bragged about me like this? As it turned out the whole thing was a disaster. There had been no time for me to be given lessons at home, and I cannot imagine how my parents thought I could cope. I had never done Algebra, Geometry, French or Latin, and Welsh was compulsory. At ten, I was the youngest in the school by two years and I had arrived well after the first term commenced. I longed for the weekends when I could come home. I was in floods of tears every dreaded Monday morning when I had to cross the fields to get a lift with 'Mr Richards, Coedfryn' who would take his daughter and me to Cardigan on his way to work. D arranged 'digs' in a terraced house near the school with Miss and Mrs Evans: 'in her aspidistra cloister we settled that Ann should bring her own food and keep herself in soap and towel and Mrs Evans should cook, for 6/- a week, very reasonable I thought.'

They were kindly-intentioned, but there was little space or privacy there. When M learned that I had to share a bed with a fellow lodger, a third former from the same school, she offered to bring another bed for me. Mrs Evans welcomed the offer. Later on, however, when we brought along a folding bed, for reasons she never divulged Mrs Evans changed her mind. I therefore remained in the smallest half of the shared bed: Chrissie James was larger than me.

Some evenings when I felt suffocated by the boring and constrained atmosphere in the tiny kitchen (the parlour – the 'aspidistra cloister' – was off limits!) I would go out to a little shed behind my digs where the local milkman kept his horse. I talked to him and fed him grass and carrots. He was my salvation in moments of dejection. Except saying that I was coping with Biology, Geography and History, my school reports were abysmal. Chrissie kindly tried to help me with my mathematical subjects, but I was very inattentive, because I was so far behind and had no natural ability in the subject. To add to my woes I was frequently absent, and swung the lead as much as I could. However, I genuinely suffered from more than my fair share of coughs and colds, a grumbling appendix (though we did not know it at the time) and a bad dose of measles that November; the day I sickened for them I nearly fainted in assembly. I wobbled back to my digs where Mrs Evans held my head while I vomited into one of her fancy wash bowls (the blue flowers printed on that bowl are permanently etched on my memory!). In the afternoon she sent her daughter out to the telephone box on the corner to ring my parents to 'come and get the poor child'.

My very first letter from Cardigan says it all:

Cardigan Oct. 8th: Dear M & D. School isn't atall nice, Latin, French and Algebra as you know I've never done or they sound funny to me, the lesson I like best is gym, it is such a nice gym to do it in, we played a short game of Net ball its lovely, I'm writing this at my lodgeings.
I miss milking the goats every morning and feeding the chickens. Christina [Chrissie] is very nice the girl who is staying here... ... ...
love from Ann o x x o

Every weekend when I came home to Cwmgloyne there were new things to admire. There was much we needed in the way of implements, stock and fodder to tide us over the winter. A lot of time was spent going to local sales; eventually they provided most of what we needed. Often a lifetime of the vendors' accumulated junk was on offer as well! Some of the latter my parents could not resist. They bought some lovely old crocks and brass-bound barrels and a lumbering old cheese press for 5/-. M placed them in our amazing underground cheese room, where they looked fitting and decorative, which pleased her aesthetic sense. They bought me horse brasses, including a priceless set still on their original leather, made for Queen Victoria's jubilee, all for a few shillings.

One of our neighbours, Mr Rowe of Cwm-eog, set himself up as D's adviser! He took Petronella away to train. I became friends with his daughter Dilys, who had a pony too. I waited impatiently for Petronella's return so we could ride together. I acquired a Welsh accent all of a sudden.

Strangely neither M or D ever developed one, even though they were immersed in it in the north of Pembrokeshire. They enjoyed meeting a number of the locals at the sales. D recorded some amusing expressions, which resulted from Welsh-speakers trying gallantly to speak English to their neighbour. Referring to some heavy rain: 'it was damping heavy'. One of the dealers was heard to remark: 'my faith was small in that man'. On giving a stranger a lift home we were told to stop by a concealed lane: 'I lives by a very sly lane'.

D had never driven tractors before. His first effort gave him a nasty scare. He had been to fetch a load of oats in the sheaf, bought as 'field mows', about five miles away. On the steep hill above Nevern village he missed a gear, and the tractor ran back, fortunately wedging the trailer into a bank. Some roadmen helped him out of his predicament. Unabashed, he carried on and fetched the last load by moonlight.

'Field mows' are little pyramid mini-stacks made from about fifty sheaves. To build them well is a skilled job which eventually I mastered well enough to pass muster. When conditions were moist the sheaves didn't dry out sufficiently to bring in and stack, and mows, if well made, can be left to dry and mature in the field in all weathers. With combine harvesters and grain dryers this craft has now become redundant.

Great was my satisfaction when Baron bought our first carthorse, Jewel, a Shire mare, for only £25 because she had thrush (a fungal or bacterial foot infection), which he was confident he could cure.

Evacuees were flooding the district: some fitted in, but others returned to the city and the bombs rather than face the loneliness of the countryside! When D and I went to fetch our allocated couple this was the case!

When I wasn't given jobs to do there was so much to explore. When it rained heavily, water poured out of the mill pond to rush over the old waterwheel, which was too jammed with stones and debris to turn. M and I dreamed of a time when we could restore it. On wet days we cleaned out more rooms and distempered walls. Petronella returned from our good neighbours, well trained but no easier to catch. I was mortified when I discovered Mr Rowe had shaved the top six inches of her tail instead of 'pulling', as I had read should be done in the best circles. Having a pony to ride again was bliss. I was now a confident but untutored rider, which made it even harder to leave each Monday morning for dreaded school.

An experienced farmhand, Dai Griffiths, a local man, was hired. His sister Ethel came to help M. Dai was said to be a conscientious objector, although we never heard anything from him on the subject. He said little, but I often wonder what he thought of our 'set-up'. Although he slept in the house he usually went out somewhere as soon as he had finished supper. Much to M's sorrow, Ethel did not stay long. She found the evenings too long with this strange company (none of whom spoke Welsh), and so unlike the atmosphere in her home kitchen round a culm fire. I daresay both she and Dai found the food different. Most of the farms hereabouts lived almost exclusively on pig meat products, particularly boiled bacon and cawl. With the war on we were only supposed to kill two pigs a year, but most people ignored this and hoped the inspector would not count the sides of bacon on the racks above the kitchen table!

M was anxious to make the kitchen garden stock-proof, but up to November little progress had been made. The wall was full of gaps and fallen stones and the land therein waist-high in weeds. One day D and Michael (a young man waiting to be called up) started to patch the walls. Dai took the plough to the garden without mowing the weeds before he began; and the resultant mess of sod and stems was almost impossible to work with, except for planting potatoes and fruit trees. M was not pleased, and nearly killed herself trying make a fine tilth to sow broad beans.

As ever, D was very hurt on 8 November, because no one had mentioned his birthday. He was thirty-seven, but no one in the house remembered it until tea time!

The next day D went off to Haverfordwest for a meeting with the Pembrokeshire War Agricultural Committee to be examined on his application for loans to carry out farm improvements. Although I was not fully aware of all the paperwork which went on at the time, D, for all his inexperience at practical farming, had done his homework, and was not afraid to ask advice from all quarters. He carefully read all the Ministry of Agriculture pamphlets, which implied that in order to get the best possible results out of the food production campaign, farmers could apply for financial help if they felt unable to carry out the fullest possible programme of arable cultivations as outlined by their District Cultivations Officer. This was called the 'Agricultural Requisites Scheme'. D did all his calculations and duly applied for £1,500, which he thought a modest sum. An appointment was made summoning him before the Pembrokeshire War Agricultural Executive Committee. They said no one had ever asked for so much. There was an argument, but neither side gave in. They told D he'd be informed in a fortnight if his application was passed. He waited impatiently for five weeks, after which he decided his application had been shelved. In sombre mood he wrote a series of articles for *Farmer & Stockbreeder*.

At the beginning of December it was whispered to Uncle Martin, who worked for the Potato Marketing Board, that D's application for funds would be turned down. Uncle

Martin replied that if this turned out to be true, it would all be written up in the farming press, at which the said official sang a different tune. D rang *Farmer & Stockbreeder* immediately and begged them to try and get his article in the next issue … the assistant editor chuckled over the story of the Ministry official and was delighted with the article's frankness. D was delighted with the £6-6s a week he was paid for the articles! He said that either by design or coincidence they accepted his application two days after the publication of the first article, with the proviso that he reduce his request for seed potatoes. Such is the power of the pen!

Farm work went on. Unlike on Skokholm, any rabbits caught by Dai in his traps or by Baron with ferrets were sent fresh on the train to a buyer in Birmingham. We started ploughing ready for potatoes. Odd jobs were done in the house. D went to Martinshaven to collect a few things we'd left in the hut. One was the barrel of gulls' eggs, which had started to smell rather high from being shaken up. They were transferred to a box of bran. I remember the isinglass stuck badly to the bran, which gave us 'branned egg'. Most of them went bad, so the pigs had a feast.

At the beginning of December the *F&S* photographer arrived. He took lots of lovely black-and-white photographs of all aspects of the farm, fields, derelict buildings, Baron with Jewel, Dai ploughing, even our neighbour Rowe when he suddenly appeared with a delicious-looking salmon hidden in a sack, poached from the Nevern river!

D had become exasperated with no news from the Ag. Committee, frustrated because I had left for school without my weekly rations or pocket money, and: 'Marjorie and Mother arrive for Christmas this evening and Do is in a hopeless muddle'.

Poor M – she'd had to set to and provide a bed for the

photographer (already made up for the arrival of our relatives). She always had high standards and would never delegate jobs; Ethel had left; the house was cold and inconvenient. Unlike Skokholm, people could turn up unexpectedly at Cwmgloyne, then D would invite them for a meal or the night. I don't think he realised how difficult this could sometimes be with food shortages, rationing and an already full house; he seldom turned anyone down.

He hired Pauline, the daughter of a birding friend of his, as a landgirl. I was delighted: Pauline was an experienced rider and brought her black mare Bess with her, although now I cannot imagine why we needed an inexperienced, rather delicate-looking, seventeen-year-old birdwatcher as a landgirl. M did not like her, and the feeling was mutual. It was patently obvious that Pauline admired D immensely; with his weakness for flattery, he relished this. Years later, in about 1993, Pauline wrote a book about her experiences as a landgirl, and sent the manuscript to D for perusal. He asked me to read it, saying: 'Read this. I think it is terrible, she is far too rude about your mother'. I found Pauline's descriptions interesting and her attitude to M entirely predictable, because as far as Pauline was concerned M presented a grim exterior.

There were rarely fewer than seven mouths to feed regularly, as well as visitors. With rationing, no conveniences and precious little help, my mother was again overworked. D had this capacity to temporarily put aside his worries, down tools and say: 'Let's go out somewhere'. Too often M said she could not spare the time, she had chores or gardening to do. When she made these excuses, D in exasperation, would ask one of the staff or guests to go with him instead.

M muddled along somehow where many would have rebelled; and rebel is what she should have done. The landgirls were not given many household chores: they just had to look after their rooms, do the washing up and bring drinking water from the well. They slunk out of these time and again because M did not reprimand them. I wish she had been less conscientious. She loved the old place passionately and dreamt of a time when she could restore some of its former glory, but she never made time to do much more than start on these romantic notions. She was happiest working in the garden, which had such possibilities; it was a credit to her even though she had so little help. That summer we had wonderful crops of vegetables. Uncle Martin had sent over the makings of an orchard, which was thriving. Most of the walls had been repaired so the garden was almost stock-proof. Gardening was not the favourite ploy of the staff any more than domestic chores. Only once did I hear M rebel, and that when the garden got ploughed, so then Saturday mornings were put aside for some staff to do a short stint there.

Baron was the exception, of course. He was too busy in the old kitchen which was his workshop, ideally situated and large enough to accommodate all our tools. He had cleaned the chimney there and had placed a big armchair close to the fireplace, where, one cold morning I caught him snoring loudly, the arm of his chair quietly smouldering. I shouted loudly in his ear that he was on fire, he woke with a start and an oft-used exclamation: 'Good 'eavenslive – must have dropped off!'.

M was dying to remove an old culm stove, which had been built in front of the inglenook in the room next to her kitchen, which we used as a dining room. When I came home one Friday evening it was all done. I could stand in the inglenook and look up the huge chimney and see the stars. Halfway up the chimney was a little bricked-up doorway with a chiselled arch. I liked to think it had been for a priest to hide during the Reformation (there is a fine priest's hole in Nevern church, a few miles away), but my romantic notions were dashed when I learned it was more likely to be the doorway of an earlier house. Also revealed in the excavation was a niche for a shrine and a large pumpkin-shaped bread oven. Later on, assisted by Baron, M tried the oven out; it took all day and a great deal of wood, mess and smoke. The results were rather disappointing.

The clearance vastly improved the look of this ancient old kitchen. It turned out to be very snug for those close to the fire, and everyone else toasted their fronts – but their backs froze. We had removed the matchwood barricade which had hidden the magnificent oak banisters and staircase; there was a lot more light, but rather too much cold air. The same could be said of the hall. However, it had great atmosphere, with walls distempered and hung with our horse brasses and numerous pictures and furnished with our two antique linen chests, settle and Turkish carpet.

D took Granny Lockley, Aunt Marjorie and M to see a famous woodturner near Boncath who drove all his machinery with an ancient waterwheel. Amongst other things he turned out the most beautiful sycamore bowls. M purchased some for our breakfast porridge. Ever the romantic, she thought it would be nice to have our own oats ground at the mill in Felindre, our nearest village, for porridge. It took long slow cooking, and was raved over by some and loathed by others. It had a slightly gritty texture and pleasing roasted flavour. Personally I preferred rolled oats from the shop!

Felindre had a few scattered cottages, a post office, small shop, blacksmith, the Salutation Inn (known as 'The Salute'), a chapel, meeting room and the mill. The large millrace was fed from the Nevern (*Nyfer*), which wends its way through the village on its way to the sea at Newport. I remember the miller in his perpetually flour-dusted clothes, and being mesmerised by the 'slosh-slosh music' of the water leaving the millrace and filling each cup to turn the big waterwheel. I never missed a chance to go to the mill when we had a load of grain due to be ground as stock feed. On the long hill back home the wily horses knew exactly where each little drainage ditch crossed the dirt road. They pulled like mad over the lump, then rested back in the shafts to settle the wheels of the gambo in the rut and have a breather.

We made our private sitting room off the hall quite snug. This was where occasionally we could place the old tin bath in front of the fire and have a wallow. In this room, beneath years of mouldy wallpaper, we found a panelled wall. The panels belonging to the other three walls had been purloined for cupboard doors and partitions in other parts of the house. Some rooms remained undecorated, chiefly the original dining room, which was full of bits of furniture in varying states of repair, things my parents could not resist buying for next to nothing at sales, thinking they could one day be 'done up'! The men's dormitory still had gaping holes on the inside walls. A huge cellar-like room next to the dairy, with an earth floor and no windows, was so dark and dusty we never found a use for it. Like the so-called priest's hole, it could have been part of a former building.

We had twelve young geese to prepare for the Christmas market. The flock was driven into the mill barn for the night to starve. Next morning everyone was roped in to get them killed and plucked in time. M and Granny L. were busy doing the drawing and dressing. We adjourned to the 'feather room' (which was originally the old butler's pantry), each with a newly-slaughtered goose. None of us was expert at plucking geese and progress was slow. When Dai came in from ploughing D asked him to 'come and show us how it should be done'. Effortlessly Dai seemed to be able to get

Cwmgloyne – the Christmas geese in the foreground

both down and feathers off in the same movement. Thanks to him we managed to get them finished, even though Michael (who was still waiting to be called up) took all day to do one! Next day they were taken to the market in Cardigan and sold for 1/10d per pound.

Christmas Eve came around. Great preparations for Christmas day! M and I were excited at the prospect of decorating the hall and D was excited because he had heard a crossbill near the house! We went to the Rhos wood and sawed off a fallen spruce, which made a magnificent Christmas tree. In the evening we sang carols next door, where the Rowes invited us for games and talk. That night M was keen to enact the old Welsh custom of the Mari Lwyd (the grey mare or grey mary). This ceremony is said to have come from pagan rites welcoming the sun after the winter solstice. In mediaeval times it became associated with wassailing, hence M's insistence that we fashion a horse's head from a piece of wood, colour it grey (*llwyd*) and fasten it to an old broom handle. The Mari Lwyd still happens in some parts of Wales; traditionally the pole (or even a horse's skull) is carried by a man draped in a white sheet at the head of a procession, and the 'horse' has a flexible lower jaw. The wassailing party would go from house to house in the district, stick the horse's head around the door and sing a few verses, then the Mari Lwyd and the party were invited inside for food and drink.

Christmas Day passed very happily. Most of the staff had gone home. We had dinner in style, by candlelight, with roaring wood fires in the hall, sitting room and the old kitchen.

At Uncle Martin's invitation New Year's Eve was spent at Rhyd-y-gath, where Baron, D and I spent the day ferreting. The rest of the staff went on with the ploughing.

Writing chores kept D indoors a certain amount of time. His regular articles in the *Farmer & Stockbreeder* and *The Countryman* were a help financially as well as an incentive. His book on shearwaters was almost complete. To make some more money D took on some contract ploughing for other farmers in the district.

We didn't have much luck with our pig-killing. Our first was rather thin. Michael and Pauline, our landgirl, were assigned the job. They were both very inexperienced, and spent a long time trying to get the hair off the carcase, even resorting to Michael's safety razor in the more tricky parts! I remember being a bit scathing about their efforts, having assisted at more than one pig-killing at Rhyd-y-gath.

It snowed heavily the day school started, and D drove me to Cardigan with my rations and the rejected folding bed. To my delight school was closed because of the snow; to my chagrin it opened the following day.

The rest of January was spent ploughing, cultivating, spreading tons of lime and dung, and on wetter days putting up potato boxes and cutting timber. Ploughing was a job D loved, with a stream of gulls, jackdaws and starlings following the newly-turned furrow in their quest for insects. The odd bird would forage too close to the turning furrow in its enthusiasm to beat its mates to some tasty morsel, and become trapped, and would have to be released from its earthbound straightjacket on the next round.

Strangely enough, D does not mention the visit of Leo Walmsley, author of a number of well-known novels. He wrote asking if he and his family could stay with us while they looked for a Pembrokeshire farm to buy. Of course, D did not refuse. They arrived from Yorkshire very late one night, Leo, his wife Gerry, and two of their four children, Henrietta and Dane. I enjoyed having Henrietta to stay, she was a lot younger than me but mad on ponies. Gerry was a great help to M, even though they were so utterly different in character. I think M found Gerry's natural ebullience a little overpowering. I do not remember much about Leo, except that he was rather taciturn, and that he and D built a new poultry house out of larch poles down on the edge of the woods. They were only with us a matter of five weeks before they found Temple Druid, about twelve miles away, a small eighteenth-century mansion designed by John Nash with farm attached. Pauline and I rode over there after they had been there a few months, and the others followed in the car. M was most impressed that they had already got hot and cold plumbing and a generator for limited electricity, but she agreed with D it was hardly a priority, as Leo had done very little on the farm. I had eyes only for their spacious stabling and their three ponies lately brought down from Yorkshire. We had rides on all of them. Henrietta showed us the lake and elaborate adventure playground created by Leo at the bottom of their front meadow. I overheard my parents saying it must have taken days to construct!

As when we were on Skokholm, D's articles constantly brought offers of help 'to pioneer'. Many were totally unsuitable. However, in March we took on another competent landgirl called Eirwen; she was local, very good with the cows, and Michael fell for her!

In April the Admiralty asked D to do a survey of all the possible landing places the enemy might make on rock and beach from Tenby around the coast to Bardsey Island. For this work he would get £10 a week, travelling expenses and a farm bailiff. The Admiralty work proved to be a pleasure for D. In the process he discovered what he later dubbed 'The Red Wilderness' – a wild, lonely and little-known beach where hundreds of seals haul out.

In answer to D's advertisement for a working foreman and wife-housekeeper, Bert and Daphne Quick arrived. True to his name this big, strong gingery-haired man was found to be a trifle impatient and rough and shook up all the staff. As a result Michael became a troublesome, brooding clock-watcher. D dismissed him, but he apologised and begged D not to tell his parents, who were coming for a holiday shortly. The real truth was that his love affair with Eirwen was not running smoothly!

M was getting the help she deserved: Daphne Quick was very efficient in the house, and stirred the girls up as well.

I left Cardigan School at the end of the Easter term with a large and grateful sigh of relief. I was learning very little there, but no reasons for my leaving are given in D's diary. Perhaps Aunt Kathleen had made discreet inquiries as to my progress, and the reputation of the school. I had only been there six months and according to my school reports I had been absent for eighty days during that time! A tall blond girl called Pamela Smith arrived to be my part-time governess. I was delighted with the idea. She had written to D as an admirer of his books and asked if she could come and work for us. She was not a trained teacher, but she seems to have been hired on the understanding that she would spend the mornings teaching me, then help with light chores in the house and garden in the afternoons. D suggested that under Pamela's tuition I should continue with the leather-bound diary I had had on Skokholm. Obviously we did not act on his suggestion, as the following passage shows:

> Meanwhile I had left the County school and Pamela Smith came to teach me. But being friends with Pauline she joined the Land Army and trained at Cwmgloyn. Pamela taught me for about a month … I never went to school for some time.

Pamela thought the work the land girls were doing outside looked more exciting, so she asked if she could join them. She proved to be a strong, hard worker, and of course D gave his consent, although we really did not need another landgirl: they were no help to M.

Looking back it seems to me we had a huge labour force for a comparatively small farm: the land girls, Pauline and Pamela (dubbed 'The Pamelines' by Baron), Eirwen, Michael and Dai, not to mention D and Baron. However, we were doing contracting for other farms, and D was made Flax Officer for north Pembrokeshire; when that got under way we became very busy.

So once again I was free of school. It was an idyllic time for me. There were so many chores I enjoyed doing, but even the unpleasant jobs I was assigned were infinitely better than school.

I had to clean the ferrets' cages because Baron was so

slack about doing it regularly. Basically ferrets have clean habits. Like wild mustalids they always defecate well away from their lairs. Therefore the poor caged ferrets were obliged to use the furthest corner from their sleeping box, which was the wire netting door, which always looked disgusting. The hutches were lined up like apartments outside the workshop. The ferrets had bred prodigiously. D complained they were eating into the profit we made sending rabbits to market. Rather reluctantly, Baron sold a few and was duly gratified by the keen demand for them. It was just as well the population was reduced, because they had been suffering from some kind of contagious snuffle. M was aghast when she discovered that when Baron thought any of them looked poorly he dosed them with turpentine!

Besides farm chores I delighted in the surroundings at Cwmgloyne. In spring, beneath the rookery behind the house, a sea of snowdrops grew, followed by sheets of wild garlic. Along the lane I picked bunches of big fat cowslips and oxlips. There too grew orchids, hazel catkins and drifts of primroses, and here and there a patch of 'Pembrokeshire primroses', which come in shades of pink through to purple and lilac. Our footpath up the Gloyne valley was, alas, no longer a woodland one: we'd sold the timber during the winter. A gang of charcoal burners used the lighter wood at their camp at the bottom of the valley. However, the rookery trees remained intact, though D had threatened the rooks with death on several occasions, because they ate prodigious amounts of our newly-planted grain.

I spent as much time as I was allowed with the ponies. Pauline taught me more about the finer points of riding. Now Lollipop was three years old Pauline offered to help me train her. Slowly and carefully we went through each procedure, first using long reins and lunging, then the same with a saddle on, but on no account was I to ride her until all the preliminaries were gone through. I was getting impatient doing this day after day. When Pauline went home for her day off I decided I could wait no longer. I tested my weight on Lollipop's back, she stood still, so I got on very gingerly and rode round a small yard behind the stable. On Pauline's return, she looked very displeased and implied that the damage was done so she might as well have a go. I was mortified when Lollipop promptly bucked her off! When we took Lollipop out with Petronella she quickly became more tractable. I was so lucky neither pony had any vices. I don't remember ever being bitten or kicked, even when we took outrageous liberties with them. We often fell off trying to do circus tricks. It was entirely my fault that the ponies' only disadvantage was that they were hard to catch. I was far too impatient and never learned the trick of keeping them apart, or taking them a tit-bit and cuddle when I had no intention of catching them.

My diary was non-existent and D's extremely sketchy at this time. He recorded:

> We have all been twice to Skokholm … once with the object of taking photographs for the book *Shearwaters* … The second to take over a Soay ram, again presented to us by the Duke of Bedford … for making up the Skokholm flock … We have bought another cow and five calves.

Aunt Enid, recently widowed, brought Terence and Meriel down for the August holidays. For the next six years they spent this holiday with us. We have never forgotten the good times we had.

My cousins were breaking their necks to learn to ride. I felt the same about teaching them. No doubt I was rather too smug about it all, but I did work hard and walked miles

Teaching Terence and Meriel to ride at Cwmgloyne

while they rode. I well remember when Terence thought he was competent enough to ride at a canter. I suggested he tried it in the more confined space of the haggard. Everything went well for a few minutes before Petronella shied at her reflection in a pool of leachate from the silage stack ... Terence went one way and pony the other! At least Terence had a soft landing! Needless to say Meriel and I were convulsed with laughter, while Terence stalked off in high dudgeon to change his stinking clothes!

D allocated chores for us to do each day before we were free. Quite the most unpopular job we were given was to clean and refurbish the calf shed. Before Leo and D built a new one, this had been temporary quarters for the hens. The floor was knee-deep in years' worth of filthy straw, which we stacked on the midden. Prior to giving the walls a coat of whitewash we had to sweep away a thick accumulation of debris and dust off rafters, partitions and crevice-ridden stone walls. In doing so we disturbed a writhing mass of red mites left by generations of starlings, sparrows and hens. How we itched. But we had to finish the job before dashing down to the swimming dam. We had cause to be grateful to Michael's parents who, on a visit a few weeks previously and to keep themselves amused, had dammed up the stream below the house to make a pool. We used it a lot that hot summer. It was lovely and clear until someone dived and disturbed the mud from the bottom. The 'spout' at the kitchen door provided clean showers.

Our memories are fine and sunny like Grassholm days. I don't remember much rain, although D's diaries recorded plenty at the wrong time for harvesting. I clearly remember one exceptionally windy day when Meriel and I swore we had become airborne, in spite of aerodynamically-minded Terence's caustic remarks. We had tied some old curtains to our arms and legs, climbed to the top of the haggard wall, and, with arms outstretched and curtains billowing, we jumped!

Aunt Aline and Uncle Alan came to stay in the course of a camping holiday. They pitched their tent on the front lawn. Someone left the gate open, a big sow wandered in, investigated their tent, ate their toothpaste, dirtied their bedding and punctured Alines's lilo ... which caused much secret hilarity on our part.

D's diary for 14 August records a memorable picnic. Some rode the ponies, Aline and Alan bikes, and the rest of the family travelled by car to a rendezvous on the top of Carn Ingli, our local craggy peak above Newport. There we had tea, picked whinberries, saw Grassholm and Ramsey on the skyline, heard the air-raid warning and the all clear from Fishguard, before returning home. We had many such picnics; sometimes to Poppit Sands, our nearest beach. If the car was full, we rode the ponies, bikes or, as the last resort, the carthorses!

The abundant sycamores around the farm made fantastic climbing; like mountaineers who tick off their conquered peaks, we ticked off our trees. Some were too sheer in the trunk for us to make a start, but sometimes we could gain access via another tree with branches lower down. One such challenge was a huge sycamore which Terence and I had studied carefully before we made our attempt. On gaining the top we congratulated ourselves and admired the view. Suddenly I felt faint and experienced a devastating pain in my lower tummy and an urgent need for the loo; I voiced my predicament. Appropriately Terence announced: 'Shit, I'm off' and was halfway down before I'd got my trousers off. Needless to say I had subsequently to make a very careful descent. Terence had made a monumental leap into the limbs of the neighbouring tree in his haste to disappear, but he was a true friend and never divulged to the adults what had happened, or I would never have never lived it down!

In spite of D's reluctance to keep cats, we would have been overrun with rats without any. We still had the useless Dewi Chocs, who seldom ventured further than a chair in the inglenook. M procured two more, which she was assured were excellent ratters. Her favourite was a big black and white neutered male she called Cinders. One day D came into the kitchen with a dead rat held by the tail, and seeing Dewi Chocs asleep by the fire he couldn't resist throwing the rat at him. With his blue eyes as round as saucers and hair on end, Dewi fled upstairs as fast as his little chocolate legs would carry him. At the same moment Cinders sprang from nowhere and made off with the rat, hissing as he went. Dewi really was a wimp! Over lunch one day there was a discussion on the swimming ability of various animals. I decided to put our curiosity to the test. Cinders wisely evaded capture, but we took M's other cat, Torty, and Dewi down to the swimming dam and threw them in. Torty swam out immediately, shook herself and made for home. Dewi started yowling the minute he surfaced and didn't stop until he was back in the kitchen, where he finally shook himself dry, thus eliciting M's sympathy.

When one of the carthorses was in season, D ordered the stallion to come to Cwmgloyne. Both the stallion and his attendant made a grand spectacle in the days when they 'walked' through the county, the stallion a picture of rippling, prancing muscle, his feathering washed and combed, mane plaited and adorned with bunting and cockades, the attendant in waistcoat, matching cap, corduroy breeches and highly polished leather gaiters. The day they arrived D told us to make ourselves scarce; a patent invitation to disobey. Being told we were not to watch was purely because D would have been embarrassed! He never knew that we sneaked back and hid in the cowshed, where we watched the whole fascinating performance through the window. Far more dramatic than watching the bull!

Temporarily to help with the contracting another local boy was hired, we called him Dai bach (little David) to distinguish him from our Dai Griffiths. M put up a bed for him in the dormitory. We apple-pied his bed three times. On each occasion we asked if he'd slept well: 'Oh yes, very well, thank you'. It was obvious he never found anything amiss. On our final attempt we put thistles and holly in his bed. On sheet-changing day M found a lot of squashed greenery in his bed, and the sheets too clean to have been slept in. She made enquiries; with no hesitation he replied, 'Them cotton sheets is too cold. I sleeps between the blankets'. He never felt a thing! We reckoned he must have slept with his boots on!

We'd had a wonderful summer holiday in spite of my tendency to be bossy. I got my just desserts one day.

Probably I was put out because Terence and Meriel did not fall in with some 'plan' I'd made. (I was forever making plans and then being disappointed because they did not eventuate!) They must have become exasperated, and upended me into a huge two-handled fish creel full of goose down which had been put aside to make pillows. They left me there to extricate myself, by which time I was crying with frustration, properly 'tarred' with tears and feathers. I went to wash in the spout, where M was peeling potatoes. She laughed at the state I was in and I daresay made her usual judgement: 'Wretched child!'.

My cousins went home. Over the holidays in discussion with them it had become obvious how much schooling I had missed. With many a sigh of resignation, I was booked for Carmarthen High School. D said I would get more individual attention there, but I would have to be a full boarder – more sighs from me. Uncle Martin was justifiably scathing and advised against this school. He said the standard was low with too much emphasis on the Anglican church. How right he was on both counts! Mary and Brian went to the grammar school, but they had never missed any early education. If I had joined them it would have been a repeat of my disastrous two terms at Cardigan.

Miss Rees, a masseuse from Carmarthen, came to give me remedial treatment for what my parents thought was a slight spine curvature. D writes: 'Ann looks in abounding health but we are giving her this treatment as a precaution, at 10/6 a week'. I was given massage and various exercises, one of which was to hang by my arms from a bar twice each day for as long as I could bear, which caused me much embarrassment. Admittedly I was inclined to slouch: all through my school days I was given a 'C' or worse for posture. As for the curvature, I have been fortunate enough to be free of back problems. I think my parents suffered from 'only child syndrome'. When I was six M was convinced there was something wrong with my feet, because my little toe curled under slightly. She sought advice and was told to use sticking plaster to prop up the offending toe and to be sure I never wore anything but open sandals. It was a great waste of sticking plaster. Fortunately neither obsession lasted long!

September 24th was a black day for me: 'Ann started at Carmarthen High School'. No other comment from my parents, they were too busy finishing the harvest and threshing.

Most time-consuming of all was the gathering of the first flax crop. There was a big demand for this strong fibre to make canvas, aeroplane fabric, ropes, hose pipes and so on. Local farmers were fairly sceptical about working with a crop they had never even seen, let alone grown. D agreed to grow 15 acres. The root is used as well as the stem and the seed, so it has to be harvested by 'pulling' rather than 'cutting'. In spite of the late sowing and the exceptionally dry weather, our crop turned out reasonably well and proved the most profitable one on the farm. The Quicks left, much to the landgirls' joy, and M's sorrow. D said he could not put up with staff complaints any longer.

My parents still found time to attend a few clearing sales. Often any miscellaneous items were left until last. If something did not get a bid it would be lumped in with the next item. I remember M coming home with a nice kitchen chair and some moth-eaten stag horns – she was made to take the latter because she wanted the chair!

D wrote a hilarious account of one sale:

a cheap sale, I got some bargains among the £60 of stuff, including a steer and heifer, 12 big ewes, and various machinery and furniture ... Do and Joyce arrived in the car to pick us up in time to buy two huge old coloured bottles for 6d. It was getting late when some items were sold by candlelight in the old kitchen; a picturesque scene: the auctioneer standing on a table ... the heavy jowled owner standing behind him with one hand thrust forward holding a candle at a dangerous angle so that buyers could better see the wares held up by an assistant. I must not go to any more sales, having come to the limit of my account overdrawn in the bank.

11

Carmarthen

Boarders at Carmarthen High School were required to write home every week. Fortunately the staff did not read our letters, but we had to provide proof that we had written. D kept a number of my letters written from school (strangely none after September 1945). He stuck them in a book which I still have. They give me some amusing insights into school life, some remembered well, others forgotten, some confusing because I neglected to date them. A majority of the early ones ask after my pets, the latest happenings on the farm, a request for some item, then a plea to come home for the weekend. An early letter, undated, probably in October 1941:

I got your letter this morning, I wish I could come home this weekend, its going to be so dull on Sunday. We went to harvest festival yesterday, it was dull.

Will you send me my blue County School jersey to go with my kilt. I think I am getting on alright with my school lessons. I have a friend who is keen on horses and riding and climbing trees and all the things I like doing. Sorry this is bad writing and paper, but I am in a great hurry, I could not post a letter earlier because we are not aloud to post letters in the week, but I managed to post one with a day girl … How is the farm going. How are the new piglets, I hope they are strong. How are Petti and Lolli, they ought to be having a lazy time, unless you have brought the trap home, which I hope he has.' [M and Joyce had seen a little pony trap for sale, but it was a long time before someone had time to go and fetch it.] Miss

Reese [the masseuse] took me out for tea and gave me six biscuits and a packet of dates they were lovely.
Love from Ann. XOXO P.S. I am sending you a bill for my uniform'

It wasn't homesickness, more a dislike of school, boredom and lack of stimulation in the subjects I hated. My cousins Mary and Brian had digs quite near. Uncle Martin picked them up every Friday night on the way from his office and took them home for the weekend, which made me very envious. He would have done the same for me, but with petrol rationing it wasn't practical for me to be taken the rest of the way home.

I was happier in this school than in the Cardigan school, but Uncle Martin's predictions were only too true; the standard was not high, which made my reports look good, much to my parents' delight. One memorable term I reached top of the class in spite of my dismal mathematics. The school was very strong in music and drama, the senior girls put on marvellous plays and eisteddfods. Most of the girls could sing in tune, read music and tonic solfa. Mr Curtis took us for Art and Music, he was most impressed with my drawing but not with my singing. One day he told me I was 'tone deaf'. Probably a fit of pique on his part for my inattention.

He was proved wrong when Kathleen, M's musical cousin, tested me a short time later. At her instigation I learned the piano for a little while. I was very fond of my piano teacher because she gave me glowing reports and it took little persuasion to make her play for me. My lessons would be over in no time and I had learned very little except music appreciation. In one of my letters I said: 'I'm sad because our piano teacher is off sick with gold stones'. While she was off having her 'gold stones' removed her daughter came to teach in her stead, she was much stricter and remarked that I had made little progress.

Nov 16th: Sorry I did not write before, but I have been very busy. We have just been to beastly old church it was as dull as a doornail. Thanks for the sweets you sent, where the dickens did you get them, they are lovely. Have the apples you ordered arrived yet? If so please send me some if possible please ... On Friday the 28th you said I could come didn't you? Well I can bring a friend can't I? I bet bally Miss Hodges [headmistress] won't let her come unless you write her a letter ... Aunt Marjorie gave me a prisoner of war card so that I can write to Uncle John.

Every morning we trooped down to the school chapel for at least half an hour of prayers combined with assembly. In the evening the boarders had to undergo another short session in chapel. Every Sunday we walked in crocodile to the other end of the town to attend St. Peter's Church for a full service, once in the morning and again in the evening. We sat in a gallery next to the bell loft above the congregation, where we could watch the bell ringers if we wangled a seat in the back row. St Peter's was 'High Church'. On feast days there was a bit of extra pomp and ceremony to watch; lace vestments, incense and a very strong choir. We enjoyed singing hymns. Our Mr Curtis was choirmaster and encouraged us to 'sing up' so that our girls' voices rang out from the gallery to complement his all male choir in the stalls at the other end of the church. We found the sermons interminable. Almost invariably in my letters, I described them as 'dull' – with one exception: 'This Sunday morning the bishop came to our chapel and gave us a lovely sermon. I have no more news, the sermon was about not swearing, so love from Ann.' So much churchgoing was enough to put us off for life. To pass the time we made up stories about members of the congregation, read the prayer book and the Bible, and sent notes to one another. The choir boys were equally bored: one day I found one of their ditties in a prayer book:

The Lord said unto Moses,
All ye shall have long noses,
Except for brother Aeron
And he shall have a square-un.

Naturally this sort of thing reduced us to uncontrollable fits of giggles, and reprimands from an equally bored member of staff.

If we had a visit from the Bishop of St. David's or some other church dignitary, full service was held in our school chapel; the Jubilate Deo and the Creed all required dirge-like accompaniments on the organ, played by whoever was rostered that week. The less experienced became very nervous on these occasions, so we did our best to cover up for them by singing loudly through their mistakes.

My parents, like many of their generation, had never bothered to give me any information on what was always coyly referred by my grandmother as 'the ways of the birds and the bees'. I suppose they assumed that watching animals was tuition enough. However, M made a serious omission: she had never told me about menstruation. How I'd reached the age of eleven and had never heard of it astounds me.

I was soon 'educated' by my school mates. Being wartime, the assistant mistress took on the duties of matron; she did her best but she was pretty old-fashioned. For instance, menstruation periods were always referred to as

'Mrs Jones'. Girls were not allowed to wash their hair, swim or have a bath during their periods. When I told M she was shocked and vowed to have a word in the right quarter! I doubt if the subject was broached, or else the staff chose to ignore her.

Each week we had 'bug scrape'. One of the day-girls who sat in the desk next to mine continually infected me with head lice. If any were found we were confined to the isolation room until we had gone through 'a three-day black soap procedure'.

There was an avenue of tall sweet chestnuts in the school grounds, perfect for climbing; but this was not allowed. The punishment was 100 lines. Time and again I was caught, a second time at any misdemeanour earned up to 500 lines. This did nothing to deter our foolish ways, neither did it aid the wartime paper shortage. We helped each other to write them, by filling in all the I's' and the 'nots'. We were given lines so often that we became expert at forging. When they were handed in, I doubt if they were checked, because nothing was ever said about the fact that when we felt particularly rebellious we inserted the odd comment: 'This is a waste of paper during wartime', or 'I hate Miss So and So'.

I joined the school's troop of Girl Guides, and was assigned to the 'Nightingale' patrol! When it came to the solemn occasion of enrolment one of the senior guides took us through the procedure beforehand. She gave us a very accurate 'take off' of the commissioner. On the appointed day, a very large lady dressed in a shiny-with-wear, tight-to-bursting-point blue Guide uniform appeared. With her hairy face up very close, she fixed us with a bleary eye, and said 'Do you know your honour?' We found it difficult to give the occasion appropriate formality!

I enjoyed my short stint as a Guide because it involved

excursions out of school and agreeable outdoor activities. Later on we joined the Women's Junior Air Corps (WJAC). We thought it was much more glamorous than the Girl Guides, because of our Air Force uniform of forage cap and grey skirt, though I doubt if it was as practical. We seemed to spend a lot of time doing marches and parades and not a great deal towards the war effort.

The main school was a converted manor house. The bathrooms, a recent addition, were situated down a zigzag passage at the far end of the building. The authorities thought if the school was bombed or caught fire, the two main staircases would provide fire exits from the dormitories, but some sort of fire escape was needed for the ablution wing. We had regular fire practices, but the escape mechanism, which had been installed from a window in the main bathroom, had never been tested:

Dear M and D ... we had fire practice the other morning, we had to get our gas masks and put them on for 2 mins. Take them off quickly and prepare to use the bathroom fire escape, it is a long rope with a loop and you put this round your body and were let down, it was lovely fun! One girl, Lizzie Davies was so afraid she would not let go of the window sill ... How are the ponies? I forgot to tell you that one of my stirrup leathers has gone wonky so I need a new one ...

Most of us enjoyed lowering each other one at a time to the garden below. It took about three minutes to put on the sling, scramble over the sill and lower each person. Fortunately no emergency ever occurred or all but the first person would have perished. To my knowledge this exercise was never repeated!

I am sure the food we boarders were given was as good as

the wartime rations allowed. We had house blackberrying competitions, which were a good excuse for us to get out into the country without being made to walk in crocodile. One day a weekly boarder who had a brother in the Navy brought a banana to school. She gave several 'tastes' to her friends and the rest of us ate the inside of the skin! After a roast we used to have bread and dripping at morning break, which was very popular. Even so, the Ministry of Health must have been worried about our diet because suddenly we were issued with a tablespoon of cod liver oil each evening before supper. There were so many complaints about the taste, the smell and the way it repeated, so we were allowed to ask our parents to provide cod liver oil with malt. By the end of term there were very few pupils still braving the pure stuff.

My letters home were so often a litany of requests; I am staggered at the number of parcels my mother sent to me. Nearly all had some little luxury item of sweets or fruit tucked in. We had a craze for end of term feasts, after 'lights out' of course:

> Dear M, ... please would you do me a favour, send me a parcel which will arrive the Wednesday before the end of term, which will be November 15th or 16th. In this parcel I implore you to send a sponge cake, or small cake (sponge preferably). You see I want it for the end of term feast, and it's only for our dorm. and a few friends so please send it wrapped in a jumper or frock so as the prefect in charge can only see the jersey not anything else because it's a secret, I know this is a lot to ask for but it will be the last favour I ask this term, please don't forget to put the jumper round the cake, love Ann XOX

The school rules decreed that we were not supposed to

receive parcels until they had been inspected. Somehow I don't think the 'jersey' ruse fooled anyone, even if they bothered to look!

November and early December. I must have been home for the weekend of D's birthday, a day passed in talk and games of Lexicon, celebrated at Rhyd-y-gath. Next time I came home I found the mass of earth and stones against the north-east corner of the house, which was originally the north wing, had all been carted off to repair the causeway over to the kitchen garden. This made our sitting room less damp. Baron was unrecognisable with new teeth, and was in much better health now he had got rid of the bad ones.

From Cwmgloyne's top field there is a splendid view of the coast beyond Newport, where a gently sloping peninsula called Dinas Head sticks out into the Irish Sea. Although it is joined to the mainland by a swampy valley with attractive sandy bays at either end, it is usually referred to as 'Dinas Island'. Both M and D missed living close to the sea. They had walked round the cliffs of this peninsula before, and thought it would be a grand place to live.

At the beginning of December 1941 D read in the paper that Dinas Island was to be let by tender:

> four hundred and thirty acres with about a third in rough grazing on the cliff sides with some woodland. Buildings largely derelict, finance would be provided to start a working farm. Rent £140 per annum, application must be made to the War Agricultural Executive Committee.

Straightaway D obtained a permit to view the farm and wrote his letter of application, but he didn't tell them what he wrote in his diary:

> I have been completely converted to collective farming

by reading 'USSR Speaks for Itself', and I am thinking of ways and means of getting a collective farm established between Cwmgloyne and Dinas Island, and even other farms.

The road to the farm was atrocious, the lack of easy access being one of the reasons why the War Agricultural Committee did not want to farm it themselves. D rushed off to his mentor, Stanley James, who was on the committee and would give him sound advice. On December 10th he was summoned before this committee and thoroughly grilled. They must have been impressed with both the improvements and production made at Cwmgloyne, because D's application was considered favourably. However, he resisted the temptation to reveal to the committee how he and M had been planning to run both farms. I came home from school on 17 December with only an inkling of the finer details, but I was well aware that we were about to be uprooted again, and we had only been at Cwmgloyne for eighteen months! So much had been achieved in that time. The farm had improved immeasurably, so much was under cultivation by then. D was relieved that we might have some more grazing on Dinas Island. Gone were M's dreams of restoring the old house. She had done as much as time and resources allowed. She'd visualised the incorporation of the stream, causeway and waterwheel into landscaped surroundings. But in her heart she knew we had neither time nor money to realise such whims in wartime.

Christmas was very quiet with just M, D, one man, Baron and me. As before we had a turkey dinner in front of a roaring fire in the hall, and toasting absent friends (notably Uncle John, still a POW in Germany, and Uncle Ken in Burma). D says:

Ann's presents were much concerned with ponies and books on them ... she wrote all her thank you letters before bedtime ... [This was easy because I had written them all before Christmas in anticipation!] John's book of poems 'Westward' just published, Baron, after reading it, began writing poetry vigorously!

12

The Island Farmers

In the middle of January, en route to make calls for his job as Flax Officer for north Pembrokeshire, D took me back to school, 'this time without tears', he reported.

I was away while all the drama preceding the application, and then our exodus from Cwmgloyne, took place. I had heard my parents and Baron endlessly discussing a scheme for co-operative farming. I gathered Baron never thought it would work, but he was prepared to go along with my parents' revolutionary and hare-brained scheme.

Very briefly: D proposed to form a company to run Island Farm and Cwmgloyne for the mutual benefit of all shareholders, who must all be actively engaged in the work of the company. Each new member was to hold £1 share only, giving them the right to vote. Wages were to to be calculated by merit on a system of points arranged in grades according to the ability of the individual worker. Debenture shares were to be issued, without interest or voting capacity, to subscribers of stock, plant etc. A committee of four were to run the work, but major policy was to be decided at General Meetings.

Reading the diaries, D's scheme seems to have been beset with frustrations. On 28 January he met the Minister of Agriculture, Mr Hudson, who prophesied failure, particularly in Britain, pointing out, among other things, that D would be obliged to pay everyone a minimum wage if he was given government assistance. However, Mr Hudson would sanction spending under the Government Requisites Scheme: cost of repairs to house and roadway, implements for cultivations this spring, all possible assistance as if to a private farmer tackling the job, including a five-year tenure. He would NOT sanction a grant for the social side of the experiment with a wage unit plan such as D envisaged.

D failed to get any further articles published in the *Farmer and Stockbreeder* magazine due to the rabid conservatism of the owner of the paper, Lord Camrose, who said they would not risk any 'revolutionary statements'. However, he got a contract a few days later to write for the opposition, *Farmers Weekly*! When D went for his interview with the War Agricultural Committee he was granted most of what he requested under the Requisites scheme.

The first time I came home after the move, it was quite a surprise to find that we were not going to live on the farm. D had found a fully-furnished house in Cwm-yr-eglwys, a small village on the northern access to the farm. They thought this place would make ideal headquarters for their 'scheme'. The house, inaptly named Tŷ-Twt (tiny house), stands on top of the sea wall facing an attractive little rock-encompassed sandy beach, with an extensive view across Newport Bay. Just over the fence is St Brynach's churchyard. The sea had long ago claimed about half the graveyard and all but the tiny bell tower of the church. A notice on the gate said: 'This is consecrated ground', but no one stopped us playing among the tombstones, which stood at drunken angles as if in conversation with one another among the weeds and long grass.

Both M and D marvelled at waking up in the morning to the sound of waves on the beach, and the luxury of modern plumbing and electricity, which compensated for some of their sorrows at leaving Cwmgloyne. M had already tidied the small area round the house and started a vegetable patch among the scrub across the road. It seemed ironic that she had so many amenities here: a charlady to clean and polish the stairs and bare wooden floors throughout Tŷ-Twt, fewer mouths to feed, and time to lavish on a small garden, whereas at Cwmgloyne she had battled almost single-handedly, with no conveniences.

All sorts of people applied to join the scheme, the 'Pamelines' being the only ones from our original staff. It seemed to me someone new was recruited every time I came home. Neither of my parents was a good judge of character. I remember thinking even at the age of twelve, 'Where on earth did all these odd bods come from?' My parents never agreed about who they liked best out of the strange assortment who had read about the scheme and wanted to join. They turned away the obvious cranks and those who had nothing to offer in the way of any farming experience. To my knowledge no one was taken 'on trial', and they generally had only the applicant's word as a CV.

In February D appointed a Mr. Mills as manager for Cwmgloyne's side of the scheme. He had two teenage children, who for a long time I thought were rather tomboyish twin girls. I could be forgiven for my mistake: they were both the same height with ruddy complexions and short-cropped hair; the girl, called Bob, was nineteen, and the boy, aged sixteen, was called Hilary! I remember them well because I was home for the weekend with a friend from school. The ponies were still at Cwmgloyne, so we spent the weekend over there in order to go riding. Permission to have this friend to stay caused me much anxiety:

Miss Hodges stopped one of the girls coming home for the weekend, so she might stop me and my friend, so if she says no will you just quarrel with her and tell her we are both coming, we could hitch hike to Cwmgloyn and ride them down. We could start early and take sandwiches, because the hole idea is that Barbara can ride my ponies.

Sorry the last bit of this letter is written in pencil, but beastly Miss Clarke confiscated my pen and my books, it was jolly mean of her don't you think, just because I left everything on top of my desk. I often leave things on my desk on Saturday nights, I shall have my pen back in about a fortnight I suppose – this dashed school is a blowed niusence. How can one get on if ones books are confiscated , its dashed mean. Now I have no envelope to send this in, I shall have to borrow one,
Love from Ann

On 1 March D complained:

None of the co-operatives understand machinery very well ... there are frequent mishaps due to loose bolts and inexperience ... March 15th: I am a good deal overworked between the flax job, supervising, articles and an almost untouched book.'

By the end of March D seemed more optimistic:

picked up Ann from school, her report is good – she is top of her form and form leader ... a ramble round the farm with Ann, seeing wheatears and partridges gave me a pleasant refresher, especially as I felt that in spite of the rains we have done well with the work, and are now ploughing outside the main fields which are all done and most of them disced ready for sowing.

D and I nearly always went for a farm walk as soon as I came home.

In April Ruth Pitter, a friend of Aunt Enid's late husband, came to stay: author, poet, painter, gardener supreme and, after the war, distinguished member of the BBC Brains

Trust. D tried to persuade her to join us and take charge of the market garden. In fact she only came for a working holiday to see D's co-operative experiment. She would have been an ideal member. Years later I used to visit her in her spacious Buckinghamshire home, where she kept cats, grew unusual vegetables and published her poetry.

Early in June D set a few pots to catch a few lobsters and crabs. When he and M went to lift them they found one of our heifers, Baby, standing forlornly on a rocky ledge – she had slipped over a 90 foot cliff, luckily into deep water, where she escaped serious injury. They tied a rope round her horns and towed her round to the beach.

June 1942 was obviously very hot; a letter home refers to the above episode:

7/6/42 Dear M and D, How are you? I am feeling dopey and twp (Welsh for stupid) and my writing is going silly ... I am sweating and boiling with work, I got top in my monthly marks ... not bad eh!!!!!!!!!! The weather is scorching and I would love to have a bathe please let me come home and have one.

Thanks awfully for your letter, did Baby really fall over the cliff without hurting herself much?

Please send me my short sleeved blouses before Monday ... Please excuse the bad writing.

Love Ann.

P.S. PLEASE WHEN CAN I COME HOME FOR A BATHE.

A week later an epidemic of mumps amongst the boarders put paid to my swim. We must have been isolated for almost three weeks altogether. No ink was allowed in bed so our letters were written in pencil. We all badgered our parents to send soft sweets, jelly and fruit to salve our swollen throats:

June 25th: I expect you have had a letter from Miss Hodges to say I have mumps. Oh it is boring, we have to stay in bed such a long time, but there is plenty of company, so we are fairly happy. Now we have a suspicion of two more mumpys, that will make thirteen mumpy people. Have you been to St. Brides ... they have plenty of strawberries don't they? This is an awful request ... do you think you could send some, we can't eat much we are all too sore. Do you think I could come home for the rest of the term when I am better, because all my brown will come off and I don't want to look pale when Meriel and Terence come ... Anyway I want to come home for a rest, as I shall be terribly run down if I go straight back to school. I am the youngest one who has mumps so I am slightly scorned, but not much to worry about.

D reports: 'July 4th: In the afternoon a General Meeting went very well, some 20 co-operators present'. How the numbers had increased! I was staggered at the number of strange people who had joined. The flax contracts had proved very remunerative and 'we are now officially registered as an Independent Provident Society in the Register of Friendly Societies under the title Island Farms Ltd'.

M's charlady, Mrs. Clack, lived just across the churchyard from Tŷ-Twt. The whole family had been evacuated from Battersea for the duration of the war. They had three children, Lenny, Alfie and Rosa. Mrs. Clack really pined for the 'bright lights', but her children were very happy. I taught Alfie to ride. Ironically, the boys were strong swimmers, having always had access to the baths in London, whereas few local children could swim, despite living close to the sea.

Granny Lockley came down for a holiday. She took me aside and told me I was not to play with those vulgar evacuee boys. M told me not to worry; she always thought Granny was a snob. Poor Granny, she was a woman of her time. Looking back, I feel a bit ashamed of my admittedly hoydenish behaviour at that stage, just when she wasn't in the best of health.

During that summer holiday, I decided the ponies would have to work for the war effort, as they had become too fat. Every evening and weekend I gave penny rides, and the proceeds went to the Red Cross. In no time news of 'penny pony rides' spread among the locals, evacuees and young holiday makers. Some evenings there was quite a queue. It was good for the ponies, and I too had put on weight with stodgy boarding school fare.

Aunt Enid, Meriel and Terence arrived for their summer holiday. I had made 'detailed plans' for our activities, with ponies, the beach and a rowing boat at our disposal. D had said we would not be given so many chores because of the co-op. There was one drawback: Pauline's mare was away getting in foal, so we only had two mounts between three of us. Meriel and I rode over to ask a horse dealer I knew if he could lend us a pony. He offered a little black mare with foal at foot, hinting that I could borrow her for nothing if I managed to find a buyer for them both. Meriel and I had a nine-mile ride home leading the mare, called Bess, and trying to keep the little colt from wandering into the middle of the road. There and then we christened him Dumbo.

And so that summer passed ... and I was back at school again.

Most of the time I was blissfully unaware of the troubles which beset the co-op scheme, as shown by my letters home, which were still a litany of requests and horse thoughts just when my parents were undergoing a lot of angst with slack workmanship and dissension among the co-operators:

27/9/42 Sorry I left the harness outside, we left in such a rush I had not time to put it away, and I did tell M about the broken shaft on the trap ... I have been studying the book you gave me, and I think Bess may have mange as she had a scabby mane, Pet and Lolli might catch it ... I wish I could train horses when I leave school, because it would be awfully paying (says me the old miser) because I could leave school at fourteen then, you could agree to this because see how well I have trained Dumbo. Oct 2nd is Friday please could I come home then?

4/10/ 42: Why the dickens did you not let me come home this weekend. We were allowed down town on Tuesday, so I went to Uncle Martins office and I met Mary who said she would ring up and persuade you, as she wants me to go to the races with her ... I have not come home for some time have I? Please let me, as I need shoe cleaning outfit, table tuck, a sponge cake if possible and something to put on bread, blue wool for darning blue socks ...
Love from, Ann
P.S. Please can I come home?

The co-operative was doomed for a good number of reasons, even though it had worked quite well in the very beginning. Probably the biggest problems were lack of capital, lack of experienced staff, clashes of personalities, and the inevitable inattention to detail because no one actually owned anything. D naively thought people would act more responsibly if they thought they owned part of it, but it didn't seem to work that way. As the elected chairman he did his best to steer things in the right direction, then he was frequently accused of running things to his advantage – although in his mind he didn't think so: knowing him as I do, this was no surprise!

After the chicken brooder caught fire, M tried her best to see that the most disliked jobs were carried out properly. She had already taken over the vegetable garden up at the farm because no one was interested in growing anything in it. Small, uninteresting chores and the poultry were always the most disliked things, and therefore neglected. None of the members was particularly good with machinery, but they all liked anything which involved driving the tractor.

In October a couple from Lancashire, Albert and Alice Clark (collectively known as Al and Al) arrived. He was experienced and conscientious. Alice was a marvellous cook, and was put in charge of the hostel for single staff who were accommodated in what had, before the war, been the village guest house. Al and Al were the only ones who did not come in for some sort of criticism. Their only weakness was their black mongrel dog, 'Nig'. He took the place of the family they both longed for, but although they spoiled him, he was very well behaved. I remember him waiting patiently with his head on his paws and his droopy eyes fastened on a sponge cake temptingly close on the tea trolley, because he knew that there would, when Alice said the word, be a large slice for him!

D became despondent again:

The weather is very disheartening, the yards are a sea of mud on which nothing can get a grip except the spade-lug tractor. [Always referred to as 'bugger-lugs'!] Thatching and clamping potatoes.

Nov. 26th: This has been a disappointing time and year.

The hardest work and the greatest responsibility and so many setbacks, bad weather and bad co-operators. Mother is ill. Ann on her half-term holidays cut her leg open on barbed wire and had thirteen stitches put in, which she bore bravely without anaesthetic.

Alfie Clack and I had been out for a ride. On the way home we took a short cut down an overgrown path beside the co-op market garden, which was under the care of a new co-operator, Arthur Vinall. Too late we discovered the path had been much narrowed by a recently-erected fence. I remember telling Alfie: 'We'll have to get off'. I suppose the pony took a step forward at the moment I lifted my leg to dismount, I caught my ankle on the barbs which tore four long strips out of my lower leg. I could hardly believe how deep they were because at the time it neither bled nor hurt. I called out to Arthur who carried me to the house and rang the doctor. M nearly passed out when she was summoned from the garden and saw the now gory mess. D says I was brave, but I know I squealed every time the doctor dug the needle in – were local anaesthetics unprocurable with a war on? I still bear ugly scars because insufficient stitches were put in. This time I well and truly succeeded in missing three whole weeks of school.

In a meeting of the Nature Reserves Investigations Committee late in November, the best sites to be reserved as National Parks and Nature Sanctuaries in Wales were discussed. D put forward claims for the Pembrokeshire islands and its cliffs. This had long been a dream of his, which, many meetings and some years later, came to fruition. A week after that meeting he had to go to his mother's funeral. Then more trouble: D got a call from my headmistress to say I had acute appendicitis and was in hospital for an operation at once.

For about a week I'd had a pain in my tummy. I often had them, so I tried ignoring it for a day or so. When the pain persisted I told our so-called matron, who said I was probably starting 'Mrs. Jones', and suggested I would feel better if I stayed in bed. A day or two later a shooting pain hit me like the worst kind of cramp. I crawled to the bathroom feeling very faint and was violently sick before flopping back into bed. Fortunately one of the girls came up to the dormitory a few minutes later. I told her I really needed a doctor and quickly; she must have conveyed sufficient alarm to galvanise matron into action. In no time she called up a doctor from the local infirmary. He poked my tummy for a brief moment, picked me up, and carried me down the front stairs (which we were not allowed to use!) and stuffed me into the back seat of his car.

I was operated on almost at once for a perforated appendix and some peritonitis. The hospital was extremely full, so I was put in a ward with a lot of very sick women. I was there seventeen days. M stayed in Carmarthen for much of the time, but visiting hours were limited and strictly adhered to. I lived for her visits. The other women were very kind, but they had their own troubles and I had nothing to say to them. I begged Dr James to let me go home early. On 23 December he relented, even though the last drain had only just been removed and left a gaping hole in the base of my belly. When M saw the scar and the drain hole, she was so alarmed she summoned our local doctor from Newport, who seemed, M said, 'very vague about it'. I didn't care. I was so elated to be home instead of in that dismal ward over Christmas.

D reported:

The farm chores got through in the appalling mud at the farm. We had a busy Christmas with ten members of the co-op sharing a turkey dinner with us. The only wine available was some port given us by a friend, a drop of rum and some medicinal brandy. After which there were games and dancing to suit the rather mixed company of a boy of two, a girl of twelve and older people of above thirty!

Best of all, my wildest dreams had come true. My parents had bought me my cousin Mary's pony for Christmas – a half-thoroughbred gelding with the unfortunate name of Hitler. I had ridden him on visits to Rhyd-y-gath and had secretly wished he was mine. Soon after Christmas Mary brought him over. I was not allowed to ride him until I had the doctor's clearance to do so. So I drooled over him, groomed him, led him about – anything but ride him! He must have thought he had a strange new mistress.

On 7 January 1943 there was great excitement in the village. A mine was found on the beach at Cwm-yr-eglwys. The bomb disposal squad advised that all the houses nearest the beach front should adjourn for the night to houses further back. We all stayed at the hostel and had a marvellous party and card games which lasted until the small hours. Early next morning M decided the mine must have been dealt with and walked down to Tŷ-Twt to get eggs for breakfast. On her return she laughingly reported that we shouldn't treat the matter seriously, she had watched a man from the bomb squad nonchalantly trying to keep his shoes dry while he examined the mine more closely. We waited for the bang, but the mine was a dud!

D, in an effort to find peace and quiet, cleared a space in the scrubby woodland on the northern edge of the farm to make himself a hideaway where he could write without interference. The view was sublime, over Newport Bay with the craggy peak of Carn Ingli as a backdrop. He procured

RML at Island Farm, around 1943

the makings of a little cabin and furnished it with a table, two chairs, book case, and the wherewithal to make a cup of tea. M enjoyed painting an effective camouflage with murals of bushes and trees on the front so that no one would know it was there.

19/3/43 Dear M and D, Please could you send me some pocket money, I have none left, so Miss Wilson [form mistress] has had to lend me some ... Please can you send me £1 , because I have sent my shoes to the cobblers ... very expensive as it cost something like seven shillings, and then not very well done, also we went to the pictures, then stamps and church collection, we use a lot each week and I have to pay Miss Wilson back. Please excuse writing, but I am in an awkward position sitting in the warm kindergarten room where the sun is going down now over the towers of the lunatic asylum! [a distant building we could just see from the west windows] And the sky is a beautiful colour ... I have lots of news because we had a holiday on Tuesday because it was St David's day, we all wore daffodils and Cannon Pugh ... a preacher at St Peters took a service in our chapel. We nearly burst out laughing in the middle of it because we always think his false teeth are going to drop out. He has awful arthuritis and he finds it difficult to turn over the pages of his prayer books ... we saw Shirley Temple in her first love film, everybody thought it was very sad, but I did'nt though I was very sorry for her granpa because he had to do all the cooking and brushing and scrubbing of potatoes but Annie (Shirley Temple) used to help him dust ... Please tell me when I can come home next, Aunt Kathleen said in her letter something about D broadcasting.

I heard part of this broadcast: 'He did not sound ordinary' was my comment in my next letter home!

Even though it was wartime the skeleton staff at school did their best to make life interesting, even if we were not prepared to admit it. We had a number of guest speakers:

Thanks for the £1 note and now I have 6/10½d. left after paying Miss Wilson ... A missionary from China came and gave us a talk on what she did when she was out there and she showed us lots of their idols and embroidery, the first thing she showed us was a sort of death tablet, and a very valuable gold statue of Buddah, and a chinese shoe it was about 3 inches long and a girl of seventeen could easily get into it she said, and they never walked properly but hauled themselves along with whatever they could catch hold of ... Please let me know how I am to come home for the holidays by air sea or land or what ?!!!! Miss Hodges wants to know because of buying tickets ... we went for a walk yesterday in the Trevaughne woods, and we had super fun screaming at the tops of our voices and throwing stones over the quarry cliffs ... [we usually had to walk 'in croc' whenever we were on a road, but as a great favour when we reached the woods we were allowed to disperse and take a track up to this quarry] ... exams start on Tuesday worst luck, I hope I will be able to make up for what I have missed, I will do as well as I possibly can...we had rubarb for dinner and the juice of it was simply lucious ... Aunt Enid sent me some lovely chocolate biscuits and I will write to thank her ...

I have tried to make this letter three things a) neat, b) long c) interesting. By the way I bought some tooth paste yesterday too.

Whoopee home sweet home, we break up on April 6th,

Well, love from Ann.

On another occasion we had someone in to tell us about the night sky, after which I wrote :

we have drawn the blackout curtains after lights out to see the night sky, we have found O'Ryan because of his starry belt, we found his heel and his eye. We were also intrigued about how quickly the stars moved, because within quarter of an hour one large twinkly star moved from one side of a large tree to the other ... dying to come home now and cannot wait til Saturday, I cannot believe really it is the end of term. We come back on May 2nd I think, and then oh dear the long hot summer term, Why was school invented? Why? Why? Why?

When I came home for the mid-year holidays in April we were in the throes of moving from Tŷ-Twt up to the farm. I was really pleased because we would be closer to all the

The house at Island Farm

animals. The house was in a poor state with no one caring for it permanently. There was no plumbing or electricity. The War Agricultural Committee had promised to fund the provision of bathroom, internal plumbing, drainage and solid fuel range, and improvements to the farm buildings. It was a comfortable house, long and low, tucked into the head of the valley for shelter. We made one of the eight bedrooms into a bathroom – being over the kitchen made for easy plumbing, and it was accessible from both back and front stairs, although the latter created a problem if people forgot to unlock both doors. From the loo seat there was a splendid view of all that was going on in the yard, which encouraged people on the throne to linger! We pulled down a useless little scullery to enlarge the dining room, which had an inglenook, over which we put the *Alice Williams* wheel and my horse brasses. With M's usual cream distemper and wagon red strip this room had a lot of character. It was large enough for social evenings and accommodated the long refectory table brought from Skokholm.

The garden contained a few fruit trees. A thicket of self-sown bullaces grew below the house, which gave us many a feast of their delicious little plums. The rough cart track down to Cwmyreglwys was a delightful walk through the wood. Very rough vehicle access came from the opposite direction, across the valley that nearly makes the farm an island, past a sandy bay called Pwllgwaelod. Here is the famous pub that used to be called The Sailors' Safety – now The Old Sailors – where sometimes we went for a drink. The publican was a big Irishman, who never appeared to move from his armchair by the bar, where he held forth in his gravelly voice while endlessly chain-smoking. I was always fascinated by a glass vase of water he kept at his side, where he dropped his cigarette butts. It resembled some ghastly lava lamp, a slowly swirling, mixture of greens and browns. He had a portly housekeeper-cum-barmaid called Loycie, whose ample figure closely resembled the globes on our paraffin lamps.

We had taken on a couple of Italian prisoners of war to work for us. They were cousins, from an impoverished part of Calabria. They proved tremendously willing and capable workers. M was thrilled when, unbidden, they weeded all the kitchen garden. The younger unmarried one, Valentino, stayed with us for years and became part of the family. He told us his mother had named him after the film star Rudolph Valentino! He was not quite as handsome, and a little short in stature, but immensely strong, good-humoured and a great one for the girls.

About this time Mary brought over a female sheepdog pup from Rhyd-y-gath for me. She had already been named Blinkers, because of her square-shaped ear and eye patches. She became my constant companion during the holidays, I could not help feeling pleased when I was told she pined quite badly when I left for school, and she greeted me with such excitement when I returned.

On 30 June 1943 Island Farms Ltd ceased to trade. There is a gap in the diaries from the end of June until 1 September. This is hardly surprising in view of all the troubles with the co-op. I was not aware of how serious things were. I only remember that D seemed uncharacteristically impatient and preoccupied. Obviously neither of my parents confided their troubles to me, and none of my letters refer to them. I was too full of explanations as to why we should keep Petronella and Lollipop until after the summer holidays, because D had said they had to go. My pleas were in vain.

Possibly I was given Blinkers as a sop. I was getting too big for the two mountain ponies, and I already had Hitler. I was told owning three ponies was an extravagance. The idea of parting was too painful to contemplate. In the end, the ponies themselves caused their own fall from grace. Some inexperienced member of the staff had put them in a small field with two newly purchased rams. We'd already experienced this kind of trouble on Skokholm. Without exercise and naturally mischievous, they mauled one ram very badly and killed the other.

Some weeks before, while staying with friends in Neath, I had met a woman who wanted to buy some quiet ponies for her daughters. She would have given mine a good home and paid more than any dealer. I'd told her they were not for sale, because I'd hoped to keep them for one more summer. My duplicity brought the inevitable consequences, because it was I who had to take them to Dinas to meet the dealer's truck. I rode one and led the other, crying all the way to the village, and all the way back! That served me right!

My first letter of the autumn term:

19 /9/43 ... we have three new teachers, one of them teaches Domestic Science, I am not allowed to learn Domestic Science because I take Latin its --- [crossed out] jolly mean, piggish, heaps of other girls have dropped Latin. Lucky beggars ... Have you cut the other barley field yet and how are the horses? ... there is a threepenny raffle on at school and the prize is two real lemons. So if, and that is a very big IF, I have the luck to have them I will send them to you if they have'nt gone bad. The money is going to the Red Cross.

D's diary, 1 September:

Today I got signed resolution from the surviving shareholders of Island Farms Ltd. by which the company is dissolved as from July 1st. The difficulties had been all too great, but it had taken until now to realise it enough to force a decision. It had been a daring and innovative experiment. A profit sharing business which in principle seemed morally right, but just did not work due to the vagaries of human nature? ... The turmoil of a summer of unco-operative co-operation has left its mark in the first grey hairs on my head. But through this suffering I feel I shall emerge all the stronger ... The summer had its bright hours. The Huxleys are renting Ty-Twt for 3 weeks with Max Nicholson and Stephen Spender staying for a while ... we have walked and cycled much, and Julian discovered a rare centaury plant on Newport Head, we transplanted some on Dinas Head ...

D was in his element sharing in these writers' erudite discussions and endless sessions of a complicated word game we all enjoyed called 'Word Making and Word Taking'. D and Julian modified the rules to make it more challenging. In later years both Julian and D and the family took to Scrabble – to my mind, not as much fun.

Because D had been doing surveys on and off around the Welsh and Irish coasts for the Navy, he had some clout when it came to arranging visits to the islands in wartime. On 12 September we had a marvellous outing with some thirty friends, staff, relatives and their hangers-on. We filled the deck of the farm lorry with hay to make our transport comfortable. All the staff and the young piled in bound for Pembroke Dock, where we met those who had come by car. I am not sure which member of the Admiralty gave D permission to make this particular trip. While our gang were assembled on the wharf, a naval officer with quite a lot of gold braid came along and asked what we were doing in an area banned to civilians! I daresay D told him he had permission from the Admiral! We embarked on a Naval Examination boat called the *Pasup*. The sea was somewhat rough so there were some pretty poor puns bandied about concerning the name of the ship. Poor Al and Al were very sick. We landed on Skokholm, which was looking forlorn with no whitewash, roofless outbuildings and chipped woodwork. The house was a mess from occupation by a searchlight crew. The rabbits were back in force, but the birdlife was plentiful. Then we went off to make a circumnavigation of Grassholm. It was too choppy to land but we had a marvellous view of the gannets.

The crew gave us tea, liberally laced with sugar – we stared in wonder at their brimming sugar basins in wartime! As we returned at dusk we were stopped at the entrance to Milford Haven to await an outgoing convoy. It poured with rain, with thunder and lightning, and at the same time the outgoing convoy was having tracer bullet practice on parachute flares; a spectacular scene, making a fit ending to a memorable day. We returned in the lorry over the mountains by moonlight, those of us on the back snug on the hay under a tarpaulin.

The whole trip from beginning to end was such a fun day with a whole crowd. I didn't have time to mope about going back to Skokholm and then having to leave again. The state of the buildings and what it would cost to repair them did not worry a thirteen-year-old. In fact, I felt much the same during all subsequent visits – sentimental about visiting, but not sad. For Skokholm has not changed: the buildings have been modernised and there is a slight change in the dominant flora, but the rocks remain.

When I came home from school next I found we had acquired an Irish curragh, a traditional boat of similar construction to a coracle, but larger and longer. It had been built by the Irish Sea Fisheries as a present to the South Wales Sea Fisheries. At D's instigation it was delivered into his custody! Once we had got the hang of handling her, she was the prelude to many happy outings:

> met Ann at Fishguard station, she is 9th in a class of 23, of which the average age is a year above hers. She now likes geometry [news to me!] Science and English. She grows up a lovely-limbed child with dark eyebrows and lashes in a round rosy face ... saw a kingfisher on the diving board at Cwm-yr-eglwys ... Xmas day 1943 Hermia, my new secretary, Do, Ann, Baron and Valentino made up the Christmas party, the rest of the staff having gone home ... the farm kitchen looked good with decorations, cards , the shining Alice Williams wheel, long table and log fire ... a quiet day feeding stock and ourselves and listening to music ... Jan 30th 1944: Ann should have gone back to school today ... but a cold has detained her, very conveniently, as she is far from

being in love with school. However, she had to stay in bed to get rid of it, or would gladly have caught another today so as to stay yet longer.

Having been fairly complimentary at the beginning of the holidays, at the end of them D wrote:

She is a strong willed girl now, at the rather awkward 'don't think it worth bothering about anything, except horses' stage. We aren't too pleased with her progress at Carmarthen school.

In February a new landgirl called Phyllida arrived. She was not popular with M, Valentino or Baron, and with typical jocularity and some aptness Baron named her 'that Phyllandria'. There was no doubt about her talents: she was extremely good at drawing and watercolour painting, a capable cook, gardener and seamstress. She did exquisite illustrations for some of D's books. She was not an experienced landgirl; one day she cultivated a whole field without putting any 'set' on the discs – she had clearly forgotten to screw up the discs so that they would be at a slight angle and would thus scarify the ground as they were pulled through it. Baron went out to see if she had finished and could hardly believe his eyes when he saw all the little lines cut in the ground and no cultivation!

In February I was relieved from some more school: D and Pauline picked me up to do a BBC 'Children's Hour' broadcast in Cardiff. It was a long involved story called 'The Land of Castles'. Pauline and a boy called John Vernon Morris took the chief parts as a young boy and girl exploring Pembrokeshire and meeting different people in places of interest. They met D and me (who played ourselves) and we took them out in the curragh to local seabird haunts and seal caves. D said I did not suffer at all from nerves, whereas he and Pauline were not comfortable. I found the whole experience tremendously exciting. Afterwards we went to the waxworks, then a film, *Wuthering Heights*; D's comment: 'tragic and well done, if overacted'. I only remember Heathcliffe and Catherine, drenched to the skin, embracing on a rock on the moors, in dreary black and white.

Although D had done quite a lot of public speaking, and was to do more as time went on, he always found broadcasting, television or lecturing a nerve-wracking experience. On these occasions he never sounded confident or convincing, even though there was nothing he enjoyed more than holding the floor amongst a small group.

Part of my next letter says:

The broadcast was a marvellous experience and rather fun when I look back on it. Did Valentino recognize my voice? The girls at school who happened to hear it said I seemed to have a squeaky voice.

Well, I have no more news, except how are Hitler and Blinkers.

Love from Ann. XOX

D reports:

the end of February proved to be beset with troubles ... tractors, cars and lorries refractory, flat batteries ... lost a cow calving, snowing hard and settling white on the hills ... Valentino is moody and homesick just now, but has turned down an offer to go back to camp for a stint among his own kind ... he is in a frustrated state as none of the girls will play seriously at sweethearts; he has even tried to kiss Ann; but gets over these moods with sympathy and tact on our part.

Valentino had told me all about his girl back in Calabria and had shown me her photograph with tears in his eyes. Even so, he says he wants to go to America instead of returning home to Italy after the war. Little did D know that Valentino had, in fact, kissed me – in fact we even went in for a little harmless petting now and then.

13

The End of the Beginning

In mid May D wrote and told me that M had gone to stay with her friend Dorothy at Rhandirmwyn for a much-needed holiday. I enjoyed writing letters so it was no hardship to send them one each.

Dear D,
M came to see me yesterday she was taking Aunt Dorothy home to Rhandirmwyn, I wish she could be home for my half term, she said lets go out into the garden where we can talk, she told me you had been looking at agricultural schools for me, I do hope it is one with horses ... but even if it isn't I promise not to neglect my lessons ... I should like to be a horse trainer when I grow up ... I am coming home after school on Friday, I think the train is half past 5 to 6, please meet me if you can as there are no bus's at so late a time.

I came home for half term to find D had two new friends, a married couple, in the house. They had arrived in answer to an advertisement D put in the paper for someone to 'take a working holiday in a nice countryside environment'. I never found out what their real names were, they were always known as Bear and Froschel. He was a trifle hefty and bear-like; she, a flamboyant and extrovert German, who reminded me of a Clydesdale colt, tall and awkwardly long-legged, always flinging herself about and invariably dressed in Bavarian clothes. Subsequently they came to stay quite frequently at the farm. I was very doubtful about eating what Froschel prepared. She and her children Inge and Rolf were always helping themselves before anything arrived at the table. Froschel would invite them to 'licker-the-spoon', and after a smacking of lips they'd put the spoon straight back into the serving dish ... ugh! I thought they were most peculiar. When I told D I wasn't keen on his new friends, he implied that I was no judge of character, and they were some of the kindest people he knew.

Phyllida was very nice to me and made me a new dress. Pauline had left after long and faithful service, but temporarily she'd left her horse behind, so I was overjoyed at having another horse to ride. Baron had received a windfall from his Canadian ranch and had spent it on two grey Shire horses to replace Jewel, who had been sold.

The saga of me and Carmarthen school was to come to an end on 26 July 1944. Doubtless Aunt Kathleen was again on the warpath over my education. Various options were discussed, ending in the decision that I should go back to Brighton. I knew it was a better school, but was disappointed not to be going to an agricultural one.

Aunt Vi and Uncle Martin had recently left Rhyd-y-gath in the care of their foreman Tom Evans and moved to Vaynor, a better farm further south. This eighteenth-century farmhouse was well-proportioned, but rather cold, with modern plumbing but no electricity. The staircase, still with the nursery gate on the second floor, was lit by an elegant window extending for three storeys. The remains of the garden showed remnants of past grandeur too, which made M's green fingers itch to restore it. I was itching for an opportunity to see it. In July Miss Hodges received exam papers from Brighton. She made my class try them out, too, to see how the standard compared with her school. I am sure this was not a popular move with my classmates, but I did not comment: I was too busy at the time trying to get M to write to Miss Hodges for permission to let me off for a weekend at Vaynor with M:

I should very much like to come to Vaynor on Friday, please telephone or write to Miss Hodges and ask her to let me off. Will you say to her, or something of the same meaning. 'Dear Miss Hodges, Do you think Ann could come away with me for the weekend, she can meet her Uncle in town etc etc. yours Doris Lockley.' Please don't write the same words as these please, or she will think you never went to school. But tell her the time to meet Uncle Martin. She will probably never let me go, still you can try, I do hope she does ...

Obviously I did go, because my next letter to D says:

I had a super time at Vaynor ... [then I go into great detail on what we did and had to eat, which included home-grown strawberries and cream] I am writing this in the handwork room and everyone is doing different things.
1. one is playing the piano.
2. one is singing
3. one is mending her tie.
4. one is writing a letter (me).
5. One is reading.
6. One is doing club drill.
7. one is dancing.
8. one is smelling some roses and inspecting a hole in her shoe
Hope you won't be too long in north Wales ...

On 27 July I was due to go home for the summer break. M rang the school with instructions for me to take the train and meet her in Haverfordwest, so we could visit D in hospital where he had been during the past fortnight getting over an operation. When arrived he was sitting out in the hospital garden. They kissed and exchanged a few pleasantries, then D asked M when she was going to get a job in London; I thought this was a very strange question, but I said nothing and decided to question M later.

On our return to Vaynor I asked M what was going on. She burst into tears and told me that D did not love her any more. I was stunned, shocked and absolutely nonplussed, then I burst into tears too. My tears were as much for me as for her. Suddenly the import of recent circumstances fell into place and I realised this was final. How difficult life was going to become. Now I was going to have to spread my time equally between my parents. My school friends had remarked on M's prolonged holiday, but any possibility of a total separation happening hadn't occurred to me.

It had taken both my parents three months to tell me; I now suspect that the day M had called in to school she may have intended to tell me and funked it when she said: 'We will go into the garden and talk'. D was always evasive about distasteful subjects, and when I confronted him later, he was full of justifications. M was devastated, and still clung to a hope of reconciliation. She might have agreed to come back on any terms. In fact she did offer, but without success, which was very sad. I learned much later that her trauma was such that she suffered from migraines and insomnia for several years afterwards. As time went on I understood what had happened to their relationship.

D justifies his actions in the diary:

Do was neglectful of her duties towards both Ann and to me … Do was not demonstrative enough to either of us … to leave the housework more to the people I have provided. But no, Do must do the drudgery herself, must sacrifice us to the pots and pans, must push aside the willing helpers and get everything in a complete muddle … Do is to blame for not taking her opportunities. Poor

Ann has suffered much from neglect ... her personal cleanliness is of no interest to her mother ... Do never had the time or forgot ... God forgive me but my heart towards her is devoid of all feeling except pity ... there is no evil in my heart, nor is there in Do's. I have not neglected her – always asked her to come, but she could seldom make the effort, always held back by some vague uneasiness about finishing jobs at home ... I have told her she must go away with Dorothy and think about what she wants to do.

When I read D's words I knew there was truth in what he said, but he forgot that it simply was not in M's nature to be dictatorial. She was hopelessly inefficient when it came to time and motion, she was untidy, but she hated to see things dirty or half-done. She was not entirely to blame for the state of my personal hygiene at that time. I was going through a wayward stage. Besides, we had no decent facilities for washing clothes, nor was there any money to buy new ones or anything but the most basic toiletries.

What D fails to mention is that 'Phyllandria' had showed up what he says were M's weaknesses. Certainly Phyllida was extremely capable. D forgets that she was hired as a landgirl and did a bit of housekeeping if she felt inclined. D never mentions my parents' age difference: M was nearly ten years his senior. Phyllida was careful not to make a play for D's attentions in front of me, but Valentino told me she did so at other times, and it was reciprocated. D always laid on the charm for the endless procession of young staff and visitors who passed through our doors, and they were always ready to join in on the frequent outings which D loved to organise. Foolishly M did not comment. The fact that she took him so much for granted severely dented his pride. Later on I asked M why she did not protest when D lapped

Valentino helps me to pack up Hitler to go to visit M at Vaynor

up the attentions of all these females; her answer was: 'Oh, I thought it was a passing whim'. When D was in hospital people thought Phyllida was his wife, she was so attentive. The aunts got on quite well with her.

In July D moved back to Tŷ-Twt to get more peace for his writing and to leave the foreman and his wife with the house to themselves for a change. I believe Phyllida went too as hostess. But she tactfully vanished over D's share of my school holidays!

My cousin Mary was managing Vaynor for her father, which made life much more interesting for me. I have to admit that I was anxious to get back to Island Farm on this occasion because my other cousins Terence and Meriel had already arrived there, and I could not bear the thought of them going on any expeditions without me! However, I was determined not to let either parent say I favoured one or the other. In future I divided my free time between them equally, almost to the hour.

Most holidays I would ride my beloved Hitler over the hills to and from Vaynor, with a sack of clothes fastened to the front of my saddle. It is still a magnificent ride, through the lanes and high banks of mid Pembrokeshire, the sheltered woods of the Gwaun valley, onto the open moorlands east of Carn Ingli. There I could leave the road and gallop along the unfenced mountain across to the craggy rock which is Mynydd Melyn, usually referred to as Dinas Mountain. From here there is a splendid view of the sea all the way from Strumble Head and north towards Cemmaes. I always stopped for a few minutes to look down on Island Farm spread like a map below, to see what fields had been ploughed or what had been going on in my absence. I was to make this ride countless times and never tired of it.

Even though we were back with D at Tŷ-Twt, Terence, Meriel and I did not get off lightly this time. It was up the lane to the farm to do three hours of farm work each day before we were allowed to do as we pleased. Most of the time we were set to 'stooking', a boring job, nowadays almost obsolete because of combine harvesters. In the days of reapers and binders all the sheaves had to be set on end in bunches of six or eight in little tent shaped structures called 'stooks', heads up and butts down until the grain was considered dry enough to cart. I think we were often pretty slack. We never stopped talking or arguing, until the sight of D's approach would suddenly galvanise us into more action.

We had two horses between three of us. The odd one rode our communal bicycle. We bathed at Cwm-yr-eglwys every day and tried to time our work sessions so that we were free at high water, then it was deep enough to use the diving board at the end of the little jetty, where the Clack boys, Lennie and Alfie, would join us.

Back in May D had bought a little dinghy which he thought would be handy when there were not enough people to man the curragh. When he realised he'd forgotten to buy me a birthday present he said it was mine! I christened her, inappropriately, *The Pipit*. He was never an enthusiastic present-giver, even though he became very hurt if his own birthday got forgotten! That summer we had good times in *The Pipit* with the Clack boys, exploring the local bays and fishing with D's trammel net. One hot day we went skinny-dipping, a peculiar sensation to swim amongst the kelp with nothing on. We had a telling off from Aunt Enid, who'd spied us in our birthday suits through D's binoculars!

Aunt Kathleen brought her maid Margaret down for a week. At her request we seated her in the stern of *The Pipit*, her first experience of being in a small boat on a rough sea. I can hear her now as she screamed with mirth every time a wave came and tossed her up in her seat in the stern, neither did she mind when she received a wetting as we pulled *The Pipit* ashore. Aunt Kathleen watched from the beach 'in case we drowned her precious maid who had never learned to swim'.

Uncle Ken had leave from Calcutta with his wife Marie. It was just as well we were renting Tŷ-Twt, because they were both very averse to 'roughing it'. They played bridge in the evenings and smoked an endless supply of duty-free cigarettes. I often wonder if they knew how many we children filched – we took one each at a time from different boxes and smoked them behind the rocks on the beach. Uncle Ken had many adventures to tell about his walk out of Burma into India when the Japanese invaded. Before leaving Burma he buried all his valuables and silver in the garden. On his return after the war most of it was spoiled: the white ants had eaten all the containers! He became friends with Colonel J. H. Williams, who wrote books about his experiences with elephants in Burma and who was better known as 'Elephant

Bill'. Marie had been lucky enough to catch one of the last planes to leave before the Japanese came.

We had many good days in the curragh. We caused quite a sensation wherever we went because D had painted shark's teeth on the bows. There was room for eight people so she was the ideal craft for a houseful of guests. A frequent destination was across Newport Bay to Trwyn-y-bwa just round the coast, where the beaches are splendidly isolated and scenic. A book entitled *Seal Bay*, by Derek Davies, describes the true story of an international gang of smugglers, their hidden cave, and their eventual apprehension. Suspicion was aroused when some Newport locals reported odd goings-on round the coast, and strangers in the local pub. As soon as I read the book I was amazed to realise all this took place years later in our favourite bay round there!

We'd picnic, bathe and explore. Inevitably sooner or later D would set up piles of stones into towers, and we would, from a fixed distance, make war on them with smaller stones. Then we would climb the slope to see if the rare large-flowered centaury plant peculiar to the area, *Erythrea portensis*, was still thriving.

In the north of Pembrokeshire, apart from a few bombers practising their skill on buoys out at sea, we could almost forget there was a war on. However, we as children were still enthralled by stories about German spies landing on isolated coasts such as ours, and we knew D slept with a revolver close by the bed. In our wanderings one day we came across a dinghy hauled out on a little-frequented beach close to Pwllgwaelod. We were convinced a spy had landed. We wrote anti-spy messages all over it with a piece of charcoal and rolled a boulder against the stern to prevent his escape. We told D of our discovery, and were mortified to learn the boat belonged to a local fisherman!

On 22 September D paid a deposit of £40 for a farm in the Preselis called Hafod Tydfil, aiming to use it as summer grazing for cattle. From a distance it appeared as a green island on the mountainside. This little oasis in the moor became our new venue for picnics. When we took over, the tiny cottage still had most of its roof, but the outbuildings were almost derelict. On a fine day the place was idyllic. The track to the house was barely visible over the gently sloping marsh, which in winter was totally impassable except by horse and cart. It was not until the following spring on a golden afternoon that I had a chance to see it properly. D and I went to replace the missing slates on the cottage roof. There were two rooms downstairs and a half-loft above; a bank surrounded what used to be a garden, where a row of laburnum trees still grew.

I went back to Brighton to school, this time as a boarder. I reluctantly agreed it was the best decision. However, Carmarthen School had not quite finished with me: sometime right at the end of term I had picked up some head lice. There was wholesale panic: I, the headmistress's niece, could not possibly be responsible for spreading bugs round a school such as that! I was badly infected, so it was endless sessions of the black soap for me, which killed the lice, but the eggs, though dead, still clung on and they showed! M and I went up to Brighton and stayed with Aunt Kathleen for a few days before school opened. Margaret, Aunt Kathleen's maid, worked away with fingers and fine-toothed comb to try and scrape off some of the eggs. I slept in the same little room I had back in 1937:

Dear D ... I shall be going to the boarding house this evening, I am looking forward to it in a way and some ways not. Brighton is pretty well as I remember it, though of course the sea front is covered in barbed wire entanglements. Yesterday I turned out all the old toys I had when I was last here at school. What a collaboration! Pelicans, penguins, people, cattle chickens, wool, moths, monkeys, alligators, caravans, sheep and dust. Also all the toy horses I had collected, 5 carthorses, 1 brood mare and foal, one of the carthorses has an expression just like Ginny. Rather knowing and blank. By the way how is she? She was still ever so wobbly and lame when I left. I expect you have the harvest in by now ...

(Ginny was one of our carthorses. She had escaped from her stall one night and ambled into the barn and ate a quantity of seed oats treated with a poisonous dressing. She recovered eventually.)

It seemed strange to be sleeping in the same little bedroom after so many years away. To my utter surprise nothing had changed, everything I had left behind was still there as if I had never left, like the miniature barn, farm and zoo containing all the animals I had gone to such pains to collect. I gathered them all up and gave them to Margaret's nieces and nephews.

So many of my possessions became scattered and lost after my parents split up. Strangers slept in my room. Housekeepers came and went, tidying up and throwing things out while I was not on hand to claim anything. M had no place of her own and D was preoccupied. I was most chagrined when I discovered someone had thrown 'Bow-wow' away, threadbare and worn as he was. Somehow he seemed to be my last link with Skokholm. In future I learned to leave precious possessions with my aunts.

To my joy, my friends the Ashcroft sisters, who had also been away for most of the war, were now back at the Brighton school as boarders. However, daytime lessons were no more enjoyable than in any other school. The standard in all subjects was much higher than at Carmarthen. I still excelled in my favourite subjects: Art, Geography, Biology; I even held my own in French, and I enjoyed Games and Gymnastics, but I was woefully behind in Latin and Mathematics, both of which I loathed. An attempt was made to give me private coaching, but I let my mind wander during these sessions.

One of my first letters says:

> Dear D. How art thou? ... nearly a week has passed since I last wrote ... it is too wet to play games so here goes to write to my poor old père, have I got the accent in the right place? School is'nt going so badly. But of course maths are awful, I seem to be behind in Latin and its awful, I am sure if I dropped that it would be much easier for me, and in the places I did'nt have Latin I could catch up on my maths ... I am reading 'Tchiffely's Ride' it is lovely you know about the man who rode from Buenos Aires to New York ... It is nearly time for me to go to Latin coaching, Oh how I wish I had left school and left the horrors of Algebra and Latin behind. Will write next Thursday, Love Ann.

Never mind the French, someone needed to instruct me on the correct place to put apostrophes!

I was finally allowed to drop Mathematics and Latin so that I could concentrate on Physics, Chemistry and Biology, subjects I was determined to pass in order to qualify for agricultural college after leaving school, with a view to taking over Island Farm ... such are dreams!

How different life was at Brighton. On the whole I didn't mind being a boarder, it was a lot more interesting than boarding with Aunt Kathleen, and very, very different from being a boarder at Carmarthen. There were 400 day girls, but only fifty boarders. We were under the tender care of Miss Curtis (nicknamed 'Squirt' – because it rhymed with Curt). She was a very large lady who hailed from Yorkshire with an accent to match. Her announcements were breathlessly emphasised with that expressive north country 'ee'. She had the most unfortunate teeth. (Shortly after I left it was reported that 'Squirt has a brand new set of National Health teeth and we can't take our eyes off her new smile!')

Be that as it may, we had the greatest respect and affection for her and were fortunate to have her as housemistress. She lent us books from her personal collection and encouraged us to read the daily papers provided. We were often taken to matinees at Brighton's Little Theatre, where a number of performances destined for the West End were trialled. Three or four season tickets were also available for the Dome Concert Hall. We were even allowed to visit the ice rink, providing we wore our school uniforms, so we could be easily distinguished from some of the hoi polloi who frequented it! We walked on the South Downs. Joy of joys, we had to attend church only once every Sunday and never had to walk 'in croc' anywhere. When it was fine we made a point of leaving early for church so we could gawp at some of Brighton's Jewish population sunning themselves in deckchairs on their day off: they always looked too well-dressed to be on the beach. With permission we could attend services in other denominations; this was always interesting and, one would hope, broadened our minds and increased our tolerance.

Rationing was still on, but our cook Dorothy did her very best to make our meals interesting. We had horse meat occasionally. We were never told what it was, but it had that certain fibrous look!

My letters home were full of our activities. As usual, I never missed asking after my pony, the farm, my dog, my newly acquired cactus collection ... 'Please don't forget my cacti, they don't really need much water, but as soon as they get a bit dry they need water, and water the bottom or sides not on the plant'.

While M was working in London as a decorator she was only an hour away by train so I spent some weekends with her. I was conscious that both my parents strove to make life pleasant for me. I am sure I took full advantage of this. I know M spoiled me by booking seats to lots of West End shows which she could ill afford. D accused me of being over-protective towards her. I probably was, because she had no home to go to, no alimony, and D's family remained friends with her but did not sympathise. Joyce always remained her greatest ally.

I learned from a letter from D that my beloved Blinkers had had pups, three different colours so goodness knows who fathered them. I was very annoyed. She was too young and it showed that no one was looking out for her. At the same time his diary says: 'I am writing this round the fire – these are pleasant happy days. Ann has settled down well at Brighton. Do has quite an interesting job in London and sees a lot of my friends and relatives.'

I think M tolerated her job, decorating the interior of a couple of flats and a London Youth Club, but she was far from happy. But she most certainly did not restrict her social life to *his* friends and relatives – she had a number of her own.

I did not suffer too much from my parents' separation in that they never maligned each other. Certainly none of the facts I have since gleaned from diaries and letters were voiced to me personally, although I have become well aware, as time has gone on, of the situation that brought on the separation. M's only criticism was D's lack of conscience with money. Many years later D was to say no one could have coped uncomplainingly with the conditions on Skokholm and at Cwmgloyne like M did. This was brought home to him on his next two marriages! In some ways I gained from the separation. I was more indulged by the whole family, but also I learned to be very independent.

I have lots of memories of the next three years at school. There were certain disadvantages in being the niece of the headmistress. Any serious misdemeanours as a boarder seemed to reach her ears, so I got a double telling off, one from Miss Curtis and one from Aunt Kathleen! The worst was when three of us sneaked out without permission to watch some film which we were desperate to see, I daresay with an 'X' rating! Unfortunately we were spotted by matron, who reported us to Miss Curtis, who rightly pointed out that we were taking advantage of our privileges. I was pretty disgusted when I went to lunch with Aunt Kathleen the following Sunday and got another wigging for 'taking advantage of being the headmistress's niece!' I thought this unfair, because I probably behaved better at Brighton than at Carmarthen because I was her niece.

On 24 October D wrote in his diary:

I am now writing a second farming book ... Phyllida and I have moved back to the farm house as we expect to have to give up renting Ty-Twt soon, but the war drags on ... November 8th. I am 41, still feeling young and ready for adventure, six months single and not ready to change. I've had presents and Froschel made a cake for birthday tea ... we have started thatching...

At the end of November D went to Dublin to give a couple of lectures. I wrote:

Dear D ... there may be 2 or 3 letters waiting for you by

the time you get back from Ireland, but I am still writing to you as it is just the same as if you were at home at Island farm don't you think?

The music club gramophone recital was more of Chaikovski's records (can't spell his name for nuts) ... on Saturday we went to Lewes and saw the castle, the museum and Anne of Cleves cottage, it was full of lovely furniture and better than the museum, it was a lovely cottage ... Then we had tea in a café, it was very dainty and tasty but not filling enough. When you come back tell me what the Irish horses were like and anything you found out about them, and if you saw any of the places where they breed horses for the Newmarket sales ... I have done some Christmas shopping, trying to buy all my presents out of the pocket money I have left. Its going to be hard job with my sweet ration as well...

On 14 December D received a very long letter from me recounting my latest activities, then my usual discontent:

... I shall see you on Wednesday – Whoopee for the end of term, can you let me know where I am to meet you, stand behind whichever barrier it is so that I have no chance of missing you whatsoever ... Pauline tells me in her letter that Baron is very excited at the prospect of coming to Harpenden ... I hope that Hitler is not getting too fat, because when I ride to Vaynor it is a long way for a fat and out of condition pony of nearly ten years, poor Hitler he is getting old. I wish he'd live till he was thirty, then I could keep him in my stables and tell children about all the adventures, races, narrow squeaks and lumps and cuts we'd had when we were in our youth.

I am writing this letter in a free period, we are in the library, someone is whispering about the Cezanne painting on the wall ... one of your books is staring at me from the shelf opposite, it is *I Know an Island* by R. M. Lockley, it is next to Peter Fleming's *News from Tartary* which I enjoyed reading, next to that is *Ancient England* by E. Vale, Mr. Vale!!!' [The exclamation marks because we had enjoyed a visit from the Vale family at Island Farm during the previous holiday.] ... next is *The Romance of Mountaineering* and a jumble of books I can't see ... outside in the hall the juniors are having Greek dancing 2-3-4 thump giggle over and over again, if only it was the sound of the sea, the wind in the trees, the bulls moo and his chain rattling, and one of the ducks quacking who had'nt been shut in. But very soon it will be. Gosh I'll be glad when school is over entirely how I hate it. Prep, lessons, noise, prep, lessons, noise, prep, lessons, noise, a row. Pure monotony that's all. Ditto ditto. Well I suppose it has to be done. This is my last letter to you for the term, see you on Wednesday,

ta-ta-for -now,
love from, Ann XXXXXOO

December 1944 was D's turn for Christmas, and we spent it at Aunt Enid's home. D met me at Victoria Station, and we had dinner and a film. (D was a compulsive filmgoer.) Then in thick fog caught the 4.30 which didn't leave St. Pancras until 9 p.m.! The train was full of servicemen and we took turns to sit in the one seat we managed to secure. At Harpenden station it was dark and there was no transport, we were loaded down with Christmas fare from the farm. Between us, with many stops to rearrange our loads of four bags and a sack containing the carcase of a goose, we managed to hump all the bags the two miles to Enid's house. We dumped the bags and sang carols until someone opened the door, then we received a royal welcome.

Altogether it was a fun Christmas, with most of the family present. Gradually other friends joined us, including Phyllida. To work off Aunt Enid's effortlessly produced gourmet meals, we walked, played table tennis and, with neighbours and friends, hilarious garden hockey. There weren't enough sticks to go around, so we purloined an old set of golf clubs belonging to Uncle Ken and put Baron in goal with a spade!

We returned to Wales after enjoying an excellent performance of Shaw's *Pygmalion* at The Lyric Theatre, Hammersmith. I rode Hitler over to Vaynor to spend the rest of the holidays with M. It was good to be there, helping Mary with farm chores and riding another pony with which Uncle Martin hoped to make a profitable deal.

At the beginning of my second term I returned to Brighton in January 1945 and M to her interior decorating in London. Still having idealistic views, she had joined the Communist Party, but soon became disillusioned with their ponderous meetings. She was still depressed, but did her best to be cheerful for my sake. The worst of the blitz was over. London was recovering, but the buzz bombs persisted, and no one knew where they would land. In the late evening the underground stations were full of people lying along the back of the platforms preparing to spend the night in comparative safety. It must have been difficult to sleep with so many jostling people and now and then that hollow roar which heralds each incoming train.

Dear D. How are you? I hope you are well, send my love to all at the farm. School is not going too badly really. I am reading Mary Webbs *Precious Bane*, I have read all of hers except one. Another friend and I are trying to join the dramatic club, we have to act before their leader and one mistress to see if we are good enough, they are all Shakespeare we have to choose from worst luck.

Thankyou for sending the photos ... I would like to keep them to show to M. After the war when I can get a really nice photograph album I am going to stick all my favourite photo's in it, and then I can look at them in my old age if I ever reach 60!!! Because I'll probably be trampled beneath my own horses pounding hooves! Are'nt I absolutely cheerful, but still I think it would be a better death than dying in an office or somewhere indoors.

I hope this handwriting is better. I am looking forward to going to Joyces for half term, her village is very pretty ... I will tell you all about it in my next letter...

(I should explain that D had been very critical of my handwriting because it sloped backwards; to please him I gradually changed it.)

M and I often went to stay with her very dear and eccentric friend Joyce. She now lived in a delightful cottage in the village of Church Hanborough near Oxford with her husband David Green, who as his National Service had joined the Fire Service in London. (Joyce said it was because he liked climbing ladders!) After the war David did part-time guiding at nearby Blenheim Palace, which inspired him to write a wonderful coffee table book about Grinling Gibbons, whose carving can be seen there. Although Joyce had a modern kitchen and bathroom, she had thrown out the flush loo. Instead we had to go out to a little rose-bedecked Cotwold stone outhouse, where we were given our instructions. Inside were two buckets covered with conventional toilet seats, one for number one and one for number two. Beside stood a big bucket of fresh earth and a trowel!

Life as a boarder was considerably enhanced when the

aunts clubbed together and gave me enough money to go riding on free Saturday mornings. I went with another boarder, a headstrong Anglo-Indian girl whose parents lived in Madras and owned a big stable. We spent a lot of time trying to sneak in a good gallop while the riding master wasn't looking!

Three of Brighton's churches combined to produce a Passion Play from the Gospel of St Mark, in aid of 'Bombed Churches and the RAF Benevolent Fund'. They asked some of the schools for volunteers:

Dear D ... they wanted volunteers but I was'nt very interested, but they wanted someone who could imitate a cockerel, so my friends said I should go down and crow for them. I'm ever so glad I went because it is lots of fun ... poking round backstage at a big place like this, helping with sets and costumes and sound effects for angry crowd scenes, we all stand backstage saying: 'rhubarb, rhubarb', over and over again but not together for the crowd scenes ... the boarders came to a matinee, Some cheeky junior said she could tell we were saying 'rhubarb' – I daresay she could. Well you wouldn't want to say parsnips would you?

January on the farm. D wrote: 'Towards the end of the month it snowed heavily and chains had to be used to get up the farm road ... birds dying through cold and wind'. In February he went to The Scilly Isles for a week with Aunt Marjorie. They stayed on Tresco with the Dorien Smiths, who used to lease all the islands from the Duchy of Cornwall. D wrote: 'John warned me to take respectable pyjamas and underwear because their valet always unpacks the guests' suitcases!'

When I arrived home for the Easter break I was surprised

to find we'd hired a new and experienced landgirl, called Mary Abraham. She had brought Phillip, her big raw-boned hunter with her. Mary knew lots about horses. She was disgusted to find that I was still using my old original felt saddle. She promptly ordered me a beautiful new leather one. I was so delighted I dared not ask who paid for it. She let me ride Phillip whenever I liked and admired Hitler because: 'he had very good gait because he changed legs automatically at a canter'. All this went down very well with me: although I'd ridden most of my life I knew little about equitation.

There seemed to be constant change whenever I came home. Froschel seemed to come and go for months at a time. Just then she was at the farm and doing the cooking. She had invited a schoolteacher friend, Jill Stocker, down for the holidays. D wrote:

> Froschel had been matchmaking and thinks Jill would make a good wife for me. Froschel made great ceremony for Easter – at times her appetite for everything gay and entertaining is almost overwhelming: she imposes her loud voice, over-hearty spirits on the community, though if I told her this she would probably burst into tears. She and Phyllida do not really hit it off in the house, the one quiet and unobtrusive and the other rowdy and pushing
> …

I will never forget the day Froschel declared we were to have a 'Bavarian Easter Breakfast'. She cooked and coloured dozens of hardboiled eggs, then hid them all over the house. We were supposed to find them, and have them for breakfast, but no one wanted cold hardboiled eggs at that hour, so the interest was minimal. For some weeks afterwards people kept finding coloured eggs in all sorts of strange places; like the proverbial squirrel, Froschel had forgotten where she had stashed them. Well-intentioned though she was, I was reluctant to please her too much or I would be given a wet and smacking kiss and a cry of my name suffixed with some German endearment. Fortunately the receipt of these outbursts was more often restricted to her husband: 'Oh Bearli mein hertsli, smack, smack!'

June 3rd: Dear Twerp (Dear Daddy dumpkins)
You called me a stuffed heifer so I call you a twerp ... the definition of a twerp is: 'a fool but I love you'. I really don't keep anything away from you, I love writing letters, so Jill and Mary and I keep up a regular correspondence full of the latest news of the farm and Hitler etc. And I don't mind a bit who you know I write to. Why did you suddenly jump to the conclusion I wrote to them secretly? You are wrong about Parents letters being dull. M wrote me a super letter all about Mary's 21st birthday party. I never tire of hearing about what is going on the farm ... I Like to be well up in the news just as if I was there.

D had a jealous streak. I gather some mail went astray for a few days because it was delivered to Tŷ-Twt and wasn't passed on. Jill and Mary received theirs, so he accused me of writing to them secretly. I suppose it was all due to his enormous curiosity. D could not bear the thought of something going on under his nose which he did not know about. I don't think he had much conscience about reading mail not addressed to him if he thought it would be to his benefit.

Dear D

Your letter arrived this morning , so you cannot honestly say that I did not reply directly. I shall have to finish this letter later as we have to get ready for church, I will resume it when I come back – what a fag the sermons are so dull and Mr. Tomlinson annoys me intensely the way he smiles a smug, religious smile as he leans over the pulpit.

... you are going to the Society of Author's meeting on the 22nd are'nt you? So is Uncle John, why can't you persuade him and Aunt Marjorie and yourself to come down to Brighton for the weekend. I have not seen Uncle John yet either you know. That would be a bit of O.K. then I can see M the last two days.

On the 23rd June D came to Brighton. We had a great family gathering in Aunt Kathleen's flat with Aunts Enid and Marjorie, and Uncle John home from being a POW. He looked older and thinner. After afternoon tea in the garden, he and D went for a stroll and I tagged along and listened, spellbound by his descriptions of life in prison camp. We made an expedition to Chanctonbury Ring on the Downs, where D made notes on the birds and I climbed a tree and we gathered wild strawberries.

I was friendly with two weekly boarders, Daphne and Brenda Schroeder. They had a small farm near Henfield on the other side of the Downs. Their widowed mother, Ruth Schroeder, was a remarkable woman. She often invited some boarders out for weekends, and everyone enjoyed her free and easy hospitality. For me it was an extra delight because of the farm. Daphne was in my class, a gifted pupil who seemed to be able to handle every subject with consummate ease. Nevertheless she had a great sense of humour and huge tolerance of us, the less erudite. Brenda was younger. She and I had a lot in common, because she was keen to train for a farming career. On two occasions, Ruth Schroeder took us to Arundel Castle for Young Farmers' Club rallies:

July 7th Dear D.

I don't think I have done very well in my exams, no results yet, I will have to wait and see!! Last weekend I went to stay at Schroeders and we went to the Arundel Young Farmers Club rally, there were a lot of competitions and things. I had a good mind to go in for a few, especially one for 'horse backing and harnessing competitions', which no one seemed to know how to do properly, and the horses were as patient as anything. But we did not belong to a local club. Brenda and I judged the bulls and cows right too, you know, we did it between ourselves and then seeing if we were right by the results. There was sheep shearing ... tossing the sheaf (one man did 18ft) a straw sheaf too pretty heavy.) There was a very interesting forestry exhibition with photos of all the uses for British timber ... stakes, hurdles, mallets ... it was awfully good. [I was obviously very impressed by a man with a log splitter, because my letter contains graphic illustrations of it plus comment:] that man would be pretty useful at Island farm ... and he was'nt old either which is surprising 'cos most good hedgers and etc. are old now.

During D's many absences from the farm it was being run well enough by Albert, Valentino, Mary Abraham, Phyllida (when she wasn't swanning off somewhere) and Emrys (a local boy). D's diary is full of expeditions to London, and up the coast or to the islands, courtesy of the Navy at Dale.

Uncle John and the Huxleys had been to Pembrokeshire, cause for more expeditions. I wrote:

Dear D. You put in your last letter 'Dear Anna Karenina' what does that mean?
[obviously I had not yet graduated to reading Tolstoy!] You sound as if you have a grand lot of great ornithologists etc. staying at Island Farm, seems to be getting quite learnèd down there ... I am relieved to hear Blinkers is over her illness after having puppies, do try not to let her have any more My Dear Daddy, especially the mongrels she has been having lately! Mary promised to get Hitler in and fit for the races, which I will be home for. Don't let her forget – I know she won't forget anyway. We went to the film Henry V – it was wiz – but I agree with you that the castles were much too much cardboard, everyone says 'Oh but they were meant to be', but I think it spoilt it – but the battle scene with the French advancing was wonderful, and Laurence Olivier's horse, Gosh I wish he was mine, he was a dear when he shook his head at the suggestion of surrender ... I am looking forward to the holidays – lots of love Ann

D's diary states: 'July12th 1945. I am seventeen years married!' [By my calculations make that sixteen!] At a meeting of the Pembrokeshire Bird Protection Society, it was decided to change the name to 'West Wales Field Society'. Jill had decided to stay at the farm permanently. Somehow she had been co-opted into being the cook. In July D said Phyllida had left. (When I told M she said: 'Good riddance!')

When M finished her job in London she took up house-sitting and housekeeping, on condition her employers would allow me to stay during school holidays. Old

Skokholm friends Anthony (the Hengist of Skokholm days) and Mary Harthan asked M if she'd like to help pick plums on their orchard in the Vale of Evesham. I was pleased to see her away from the city smog and dirt of East London. I spent the beginning of my summer holiday there. I wrote to D:

Dear D.

I hope you and the farm are well. How is the new cutllift going? I hope the silage is as good as they make at Rhyd-y-gath, we never seem to make it like their super stuff, anyway have we any hay left because horses don't like silage much.

The frost killed most of the fruit here – but there is about half left ... I have been picking plums quite a bit, but I eat so much – every really perfect plum I come to is an awful temptation, so I don't pick as fast as those people who don't eat.

M borrowed a white heavyweight hunter from the neighbours for me to ride – he is a dear horse called Don, fleabitten grey in colour, he is just like Laurence Oliviers horse in 'Henry Vth.' And he would be just the horse for you D. He would suit you down to the ground except that he is already ten years old, but he is up to a big weight, friendly and easy to catch, he is a dear – don't worry I am not making you buy him, I can't see the owners parting with him ...

D's reply to any demands concerning horses was: 'We have enough animals about the place not earning their keep, what with Hitler and Pauline's horse eating valuable feed, we now have Phillip too.'

On 8 August Aunt Enid, Meriel and Terence arrived. They brought a friend, Micky Jeremy. He was tall, dark and handsome, and I was completely infatuated with him, an infatuation which I am sure was not reciprocated! All the same we had a wonderful summer of fun. Micky and Terence got into serious trouble on two counts that holiday. They procured some thunderflashes from somewhere and let them off in the hen house late one night, resulting in lots of loose feathers, but no eggs for a long time. The boys were put to extra work all the following week. Their other bit of mischief was not discovered straight away. A neighbour had offered to keep an eye on the Jeremy house while they were away. When he checked the windows he saw the dining table littered with beer bottles and some chairs overturned as if burglars had been in. He reported this to the police, who got in touch with Micky's mother, who was on holiday elsewhere. She came home post haste to find that nothing was missing. She guessed the boys had set it up before they left for Pembrokeshire!

On 12 August we filled the lorry with straw, and fourteen of us, not forgetting Al's dog Nig, went for an expedition to Skomer. This day was appointed for a sub-committee meeting of the Welsh Wildlife Trust to go into the question of moving Skokholm Bird Observatory to Skomer.

We ambled all over the island and viewed the old two-storey house, which was just about liveable-in, but the veranda across the front hung at a precarious angle. Unlike the cottage at Skokholm, it was in comparison an incongruously grand building. Built in 1700, it had been added to and embellished by subsequent owners. Skomer, being larger and far more accessible than Skokholm, was farmed for longer. At one time it had a reputation amongst the district's yeomen for its excellent partridge and pheasant shooting. On one of our sneak visits years before, when the irascible owner Mr Sturt was absent, I remember looking through the windows of the house and seeing a grand piano, which I believe came to a sticky end. Local legend had it that

Mrs Sturt suffered from schizophrenia, even going as far as brandishing a knife to prevent her own daughter and son-in-law from landing, and one day she started chopping up all the furniture during a fit of depression.

August 15th 1945 was VJ day. There was great rejoicing in the house. Plans were made at the breakfast table for a day out in the curragh and a bonfire on the headland. When we went down to the beach to put to sea in the curragh we found some friends had anchored in the bay in their big launch. They offered to tow us north to the small uninhabited and virtually waterless Cardigan Island, where D wanted to check on the fate of five young Soay ewes and two rams he had put there a couple of years ago. We all piled onto the launch and had an idyllic cruise all the way. We pulled up the curragh and had a picnic.

The sheep had increased by four. One of the rams had the appearance of a slight cross with a domestic breed. D decided we must catch it. All we youngsters, plus Valentino and D, gave chase, but it eluded us a number of times because the whole island is covered in long fescue grass, which is so soft and bouncy, making it impossible for us to run properly. We spent a lot of time falling down, sliding and somersaulting just for the pure intoxicating hell of it. Finally Valentino managed to grab the little ram with a flying tackle as it was about to escape for the umpteenth time.

By then with the wind increasing, we decided not to go home in the launch but go ashore on the mainland at Gwbert, the nearest beach, summon the farm lorry and go home by land, much to the relief of Aunt Enid, who was a very bad sailor. As soon as we got ashore we were accosted by a local farmer who complained that we owed him £40, as collector of landing fees for the owner of Cardigan Island. No one had any money with them, and in any case D said he already had permission to land ... I daresay he had, but probably not on an indefinite basis!

For our celebratory bonfire D sacrificed two, admittedly shapeless, stacks of oat straw reserved for wintering cattle, and there, started with a little waste oil, they burned fiercely for three hours, showing a light to bring day to the rows of flax mows nearby. By this warm light we played games: twos and threes, and nuts and May, with family, friends, staff and some of the villagers until 1a.m. Then we collected Baron, who was snoozing in the warmth of the blazing rick, and went to bed.

The next day everyone got back to work, cutting oats which we children had to stook. We had also grown a crop of seed clover. I remember it was all hands with every available rake or fork to turn it gently by hand in case we lost some of the precious seed..

Lots of visitors and family came and went, including Julian Huxley again, bringing with him Clough Williams-Ellis, the creator of Portmeirion. They were part of a five-man tour as members of the National Parks Committee. I remember Clough, an elegant figure with a monocle, pale brown breeches, chequered coat, bright yellow stockings and Stetson hat (which Baron insisted on calling a Stilton!). The house was pretty full at the time. Julian and Clough had camp beds in D's bedroom. I helped Aunt Enid make a folding bed long enough for the very tall Clough by putting a small coffee table at the end to accommodate his feet! For D this was a 'historic occasion'. The council for WWFS met the National Parks Committee around the long Wheelroom table. The eventual outcome was a very satisfactory one: altogether a sixth of Pembrokeshire was to become a National Park!

Most of the younger set were told to make themselves scarce during the late afternoon because of the meeting taking place in the house. Mary Abraham, Pansy our lorry driver, Valentino and we four teenagers grabbed pencil and paper and adjourned to the shelter of a haystack in one of the fields to play 'Consequences'. Without a more elderly presence the subjects tended to be more risqué than usual. Valentino never learned to read and write very much in English, so he would whisper suggestions, we rocked with laughter the whole afternoon.

I believe 'Consequences' is a parlour game not played much nowadays, but it was a favourite evening pastime of D's. 'Girl' meets 'boy'; 'venue'; 'she said'; 'he said'; 'the consequence was ...' and 'the world thought ...'. Each person had a strip of paper to write the first item, they fold it over and pass it on for the next heading, and so on. We always used names of famous people, topical characters from the news, family, staff, pets, flora and fauna, or friends. With such an inventive and imaginative mind as D's , this game could reduce us to such helpless laughter we had trouble reading them out at the end of each round. When the subjects got out of hand D would suddenly suggest some other game. Laughter is such an infectious thing, and as the game progressed the less witty episodes became subjects for hilarity. I quote the sort of thing which in cold blood seems so flat, but at the time produced so much hysteria: .

FIRST PERSON: Meriel
MET: Winston Churchill
IN: the cowshed
SHE SAID: Your fly is undone
HE SAID: Great Scot, I can smell burning
THE CONSEQUENCE WAS: They went to pick primroses in the glen
THE WORLD THOUGHT: That it turned out to be a waste of time

September 2nd was an expedition to Skokholm with the family and some staff. We took with us two Soay sheep that Reuben Codd wants to put on Middleholm: one a hand-reared ewe, and the other the ram we had captured on Cardigan Island. I remember we built a driftwood fire and had lunch in the little sitting room, then D organised a sheep chase, which was not successful. Even though we succeeded in driving the whole flock down to the Neck, just as we unrolled the netting to enclose them they broke back, ignoring our roaring and waving of arms, and all but one escaped.

As a parting treat at the end of their summer visit the boys were taken for a trip to the flax factory with Pansy. She was tall and strong and extremely capable. She spent most of her time carting flax. If the loads were inexpertly built, they would fall off on the road somewhere. Pansy would have to fork it all back by herself unless some kindly soul stopped by. She was greatly admired by the staff at the factory for her cheerfulness and capability. She was an outrageous flirt; she'd had affairs with most of our single male staff, Valentino being no exception. When Pansy offered to take Terence and Mickey for a ride to the factory, they jumped at the chance because she was so much fun, and they looked forward to being regaled with all sorts of off-jokes and juicy gossip as they drove along. There was no room for Meriel and me, so we were eager to hear about their day. Pansy told us it was the boys who had entertained her, when they engaged another couple of teenagers at the factory in an 'invective competition'.

Terence could be quite amusing at times. His letters to me while I was at school invariably began with revolting expressions of endearment. Somehow D preserved one: 'Dear maggot eaten bit of dog-eared cabbage, thanks for your letter, I trust you will in future refrain from writing such indescribable garbage ...' etc. etc.

However, he usually wrote some sense as well, generally about his favourite subject, aeroplanes. Then he would throw in some rude verse. By some freakish chance a letter from Terence fell out of my school blazer pocket and some friends read it. I suppose they might be forgiven for doing so, it was written on paper torn from an exercise book. I was sent to Coventry for a few days. What prudes, I thought – they obviously didn't have brothers!

On 14 September we ate the ram caught on Skokholm for a very good harvest supper, followed by games and dancing in the Wheelroom. D's dairy says: 'I find myself at nearly 42 as fond of the old waltzes and dances as ever I was at aged fourteen or fifteen; but not happy with the modern quick steps and foxtrots'. This comment made me smile: we didn't even own a single gramophone record with music for a foxtrot or quickstep; D just loved to career round our rather limited space to the energetic strains of our ample supply of Strauss waltzes!

The harvest supper was also a farewell for me. D wrote:

Ann seems on this holiday to be on the defensive about her mother, who seems to have played rather on her feelings making the child feels she must devote her life to her mother, which is not quite fair, but several quiet talks with Ann may help her to see my point of view without being unfair to Do.

Not true. I felt sorry for M, she went out of her way to entertain me, but she never discussed the separation, and neither did I until years later when the hurt had gone. She never tried to make me feel sorry for her. M's friends thought she had been shoddily treated and told me so, which is what put me on the defensive.

I was sent off to the station in a taxi to catch a train for

Reading. Here M met me and we went to stay with our good friends Starkie and Spider. They lived in the middle of a wood, where they had two wooden bungalows, one for living and a smaller one in which they did their work as public typists and accountants. A gypsy caravan was parked nearby, which they had bought on an impulse. I wrote:

Sept 21st 1945. Dear D, ... they have bought a gypsy caravan – a simply lovely one – they use it for holidaying in etc. it's a proper gypsy one with Tudor roses carved over the door, and all the big drawers and stuffy bunks the gypsies had, we decided that they must have put their babies to sleep in the drawers because they had a lot of kids and there was nowhere else to put them. Starkie says she wants £100 for it – Oh boy what a craft to go around England in with Cariad [one of our Shires] and Hitler. That is what I'd like to do ...

In the next letter I had to reassure D that I was only musing about the caravan: 'I only meant that it would be a lovely way to travel like that and you would have time to look at birds.' (This was a line from the last of my letters that D preserved.)

D developed shingles so he came down to Brighton to recuperate for ten days. He says he felt a lot better with Kathleen and Margaret looking after him. Some evenings I visited. Aunt Marjorie joined us to see *Madame Butterfly* by the Carl Rosa company. D called it 'quite a worthwhile performance'. I thought it magical but too sad. Apparently Jill rang from the farm to say Blinkers and another dog had killed twelve sheep. Albert advocated shooting both dogs. D wrote: 'I agreed, but could not tell Ann and spoil her holiday'. I was not on holiday and would prefer to have been informed at once.

November 8th: D was forty-two. He said he had presents or promises thereof all round. The best present of all was the return of our old sheepdog Jack, who'd been missing for two and a half years! We assumed he'd lost his way during the move from Cwmgloyne. D spotted him in Newport, where a kind lady had taken him in, but she agreed to return him to us.

After term ended I was at Island Farm for a few days, then went off on Hitler to spend Christmas with M at Vaynor, where I had such a happy time with all M's family home. Everything seemed so settled there, and I was pleased to be gone from a rather constrained atmosphere at Dinas. I learned about Blinkers when I came home. It was a terrible shock when she wasn't there to greet me. There is no cure for sheep-worriers, but I was very upset and more so because it had taken D so long to tell me. I guess he was trying to avoid a scene. It was good to have Jack again, but he was not *my* dog.

Valentino had always said he would emigrate to America after the war, where he had an uncle who had offered to sponsor him. He was very happy at Island Farm: he had experienced a high standard of living, been accepted by everyone as an equal, and he and Mary Abraham had fallen in love, or so D says. At the beginning of December he was suddenly called to camp for repatriation. Everyone missed him terribly. Valentino confided to me that he was very fond of Mary, but found her far too moody and knew it would not last. He had been with us so long, witnessed my parents' separation and quietly watched all developments since, so he had become my rock and my confidant. If I'd been away Valentino had been the one who filled in all the details of what had been going on, whereas D brushed aside anything he thought I might find distasteful. Perhaps it was D's optimistic nature that made him tell me what he thought I would like to hear: he generally looked on the bright side and expected everyone else to do the same.

Valentino was always polite and quietly spoken, he helped me with the horses when no one else would, he told me his hopes and fears, about his family, the girl he had left in Italy and his latest romantic conquests. He had a good wide vocabulary, but never learned to speak English grammatically. It was very difficult to prevent ourselves talking to him in his brand of English. We found ourselves saying: 'you like one cup tea?' or when he had a very badly infected thumb, 'How you sore finger? Me put new poultice on.' Several of our visitors brought him books written in Italian, many of them classics, which he would never have read had he stayed in Calabria. He had a wonderful sense of humour and was quietly observant, sometimes making us laugh with some dry and apt comment he made about the strange assortment of people who visited us.

Early in 1946 D reported: 'These are pleasant quiet days of happy work, going round the sheep, ... grinding corn to feed the stock ... and completing the first stage of my life since Do left me'.

In the middle of March Uncle John and Aunt Marjorie came down to assist with the start of the Skomer Field Study Centre. For a while D spent a lot of time commuting between Skomer and the farm trying to organise both. There were many vicissitudes. They nearly sank the *Storm Petrel*. The outboard failed, and she leaked where they had taken the centre board out to make room to carry a tractor over in her, and there was no room to row!

On a brief visit to the farm D found the staff in disharmony. He had engaged a mechanic. Baron was insanely jealous; understandably he felt that his place had been usurped, but there was more work than he could cope with at the time. Jill wrote me an hilarious account of the mechanic's arrival. Apparently he came unexpectedly at midnight. After he was shown a hastily prepared bedroom, he asked if he could have a bath. For the next hour the whole household was regaled with the strains of 'The Rose of Tralee' at full volume! I doubt if Baron heard; he was rather deaf.

In March 1946 D got his divorce. M was convinced at last that it was final and said she would not stand in his way. I never found out until much later that she never stuck out for her alimony. D started to pay her and was quite prepared to go on, until he discovered she was giving all the money to her father. She said it was in return for a sum lent by Grandpa Shellard when D needed to repair the Skokholm house before they were married. D said that sum had been a gift. M said it was a loan. Result: impasse – no money was paid again. I was furious with them both when I heard. I told M that after living with him and working so hard, she should know how little conscience he had where money was concerned, and she should have known better than to have given him an excuse not to pay. I pointed out to D that what she did with the money was her business, not his. D told me my recriminations were hurtful; M said I 'was not to cry over spilt milk'. I felt angry with them, mainly because there was nothing I could do about the alimony. At times I felt like banging their heads together.

In April I went with D to Skomer for a week. Visitors had started to arrive but the facilities were far from complete. An old friend, Winnie Bowman, was doing the cooking; she brought her two teenage daughters Tessa and Shirley. 'There is nothing to do on this barren island', they wailed. I was thrilled to be there and took them out to explore. We began at The Wick, accessible down the sloping nor-west side. I'd promised them a treasure trove, so I was relieved to find it still chock-full of flotsam and jetsam. We explored the seal caves in South Haven as far as we could without a torch, but there are no seals there in April. On our ramblings we discovered an old pony who must have belonged to Mr Sturt. Poor lonely chap, he was very tame and seemed to enjoy our attentions, we combed the remains of his winter coat and rode him with a halter made of old rope. The days flew by. The mornings were taken up with chores. After breakfast we had to peel vegetables and do all the washing up, assisted by a party of schoolboys from Bristol, who added to the fun. After chores we had to make our escape quickly or D would give us painting and cleaning jobs.

Two cows were transferred to Skomer, and one to Skokholm, the latter because John Fursdon, who had taken on the wardenship of Skokholm, refused to drink goat's milk! This cow, christened Caroline, became extremely lonely, and when she was in season she went a little mad and started frightening people near the edge of the cliff, especially at night when they were out after shearwaters. One night a victim of Caroline's attentions observed shearwaters climbing up the cow's legs and using her as a launching pad for that bit of elevation they need for take-off.

In May C. F. Tunnicliffe, the wildlife artist, and his wife came to stay at both islands, to do illustrations for a book D was writing. Valentino returned to work at Island Farm for a year. This was his decision, and welcomed by all. D 'took him to a tailor to get civilian clothes. He now earns £4.10 a week, and overtime, 23/6 for board'.

On the last day of July I came home to Island Farm. D wrote: 'Ann looked pale after sitting School Certificate, then a tonsil operation'. I had been allowed to drop the hated Latin and Maths. I took Art, French, Physics, Chemistry, Biology, History, English Literature, English Language and

Geography. We all dreaded this milestone in our school life. So much depended on passing.

I had invited a rather sophisticated school friend, Barbara Heron, to stay. Her visit was fraught with embarrassments. She was to arrive on the afternoon train to Goodwick. There was a fair on at the time, and D suggested we meet Barbara and then have a few rides on his beloved dodgems. We were late meeting her train. When there was no sign of her, we cleared off to the fair. In fact she was away in a telephone box, fruitlessly ringing us to say she had arrived! Fortunately one of our guests guessed where she was and rescued her before we went home. The house was so full D said Barbara and I would have to sleep in a dilapidated old hut in the garden which contained a rickety table and saggy double bed; not what I had in mind for my friend, who had never 'roughed it'. It stayed fine until the middle of her last night when the rain poured in – on Barbara's side, of course! Hastily we came inside. Just as I despaired of where she could sleep, she asked: 'Aren't I allowed to sleep in that empty bedroom upstairs?' Some visitors had departed and the guest bedroom had been empty for several days!

However, Barbara and I had some good times. One was the first trip in the curragh for the season. As we unfolded the sail we found three shrews hiding in the folds. D kept them in a glass globe and fed them on corned beef. They ate voraciously, fought savagely, and although given grass and earth cover, died in the night. All in the cause of science? Surely salty corned beef was not the best thing for them.

On another gloriously sunny day we visited the gull rock in a bay on the north of the farm; it is a narrow tower of loose shale, its crevices guano-streaked black and white by nesting sea birds. With some difficulty Valentino, Barbara and I climbed to the top. The temptation to throw a rock down to see the splash at the bottom was too much for us;

Valentino loosened an enormous piece of shale, which slipped out of his hands before he had time to aim. It hit a projection and made its 'splashdown' close to the curragh where the rest of the party were peacefully whiling away the afternoon snoozing and reading. There were curses and shouts from the drenched folks below. Three rather cowed individuals made their way down.

Meriel and Terence arrived soon after. Sadly it was the last summer holiday we would all have together on the farm; they were halcyon days, even if we did grumble about having to work three hours a day, which in retrospect was a paltry return for so many excursions and good farmhouse produce on our plates every day. Butter was still rationed, but we still churned our own and Terence lavished it thickly on his breakfast toast. D was heard to remark:

'Have some toast with your butter, Terence.'

'Thank you, Uncle Ronald, I will.'

Whenever chicken was on the menu, we three had to slaughter and prepare the birds. Terence hated this job, considering it beneath him and feigning uselessness by pulling out one feather at a time. The drawing was always left to Meriel and me. Terence would have nothing to do with what he referred to as 'their stinking innards'.

From entries in his diary for this time, it seems that D thought I preferred being with him, rather than with M. The aunts always made M welcome, but as always they seldom criticised anything their beloved brother did. I had a love affair with Island Farm (and still do). But it is not true that I 'preferred' being with him, entertaining as he always was. Life at Island Farm was often in a state of flux, with a constant stream of visitors making life very trying for whoever was housekeeping – a situation entirely brought on by D with his gregariousness, inability to turn people down or read their character. Nearly everyone was embraced with enthusiasm and optimism, but often they turned out to have failings which he did not foresee. A case in point was that of Froschel and Bear. Apparently they turned up unexpectedly one day in August and he called them 'an exuberant, vulgar lot and most unwelcome in the house at any time, especially when we have a houseful'. My thoughts a long time ago!

Terence and Meriel went on to stay at Skomer for the last part of the holidays. There Meriel met and fell in love with (at the tender age of fourteen) the man she was later to marry. I went off to Vaynor on my beloved Hitler. Before I left D said he wanted me to look at a crop of oats due to be harvested. When we reached the far end of the field he told me he was going to marry Jill on September 19th, just a fortnight hence! I could only think that Froschel would be pleased her matchmaking had paid off. I was non-committal, thinking it was strange he was going to marry again when he appeared to be enjoying his freedom so much. I did not say so. I seem to remember making very little comment. I liked Jill, she was always kind and listened patiently to my endless prattle about school or horses which I am sure didn't interest her. It is a wonder that I hadn't heard the news from the family, as, according to D's diary he had already told them and 'was afraid they would blab!' It is typical of him that he delayed telling me.

I didn't go to the wedding. I wasn't invited – nor was anyone else. I think witnesses were called in off the street. M was quite reconciled to him remarrying by that time – as long as it wasn't Phyllida! Jill had met D long after the split.

It was interesting to note that as soon as he did marry Jill all the aunts declared they did not like her. The feeling was mutual. From then on there was a 'scene' whenever they were threatening to stay. Big family occasions became few and far between, and those which took place were fraught with tension.

On 18 September I went back to school for my final year. D took me up to Brighton in his newly purchased Utilicon, a cream-coloured van of which he was very proud, and an ideal vehicle, being roomy enough to carry almost anything from goods to guests, family and livestock. The following day D and Jill were married in London before the Superintendent Registrar, a brief solemnization of ten minutes. They stayed at Julian Huxley's Pond Street house which was empty while he was in Paris with his job at UNESCO.

My Sixth Form year I found more enjoyable, because having passed all my school certificate subjects I could now concentrate on the biology, physics and chemistry needed for agricultural college; plus compulsory English and a couple of optional subjects.

It was D's turn to have me for Christmas, and it was a small party, just Baron, Mary, Jill, Valentino and a German POW. On 31 December D wrote: 'Ann went off to Vaynor on her pony in the morning with a bag of belongings tied to the saddle, looking the picture of health, big and broad backed now at 16, very independent but at heart very sound, accepting the love I give her ...'

I was relieved to be at Vaynor. They had a new landgirl, Doreen, who was as mad on horses as I was. She, Mary and I went out to a New Year party and dance that evening. We left Uncle Martin, Aunt Vi and M preparing to see in 1947 with drinks and snacks round the fire. We came home just after midnight to find them still there! Uncle Martin was standing with his back to the fire, swaying slightly, a whisky in his hand and a broad grin on his face. He gestured towards the two ladies in armchairs on either side: 'I have actually got these two tiddly for the first time in their lives,' he said proudly. Then waving his glass in the direction of

Mary and Doreen added: 'And how was your party? I suppose you two Shire mares were escorted by those two mountain pony stallions from next door again?' Uncle Martin was having a dig at the girls, both rather Junoesque, and the short stature of their latest escorts!

All my cousins were growing up, and we were all, including me at sixteen, taking an interest in boys. Cousin Mary, several years my senior, had already grown up. We went to the local chapel at Bethesda just up the road. The pews are like little pens and segregate the sexes, making us feel like piglets. It was all rather entertaining as the minister was full of fire, brimstone and hell; at one time he burst into tears. He delivered his services in Welsh, but when he saw me he'd announce: 'We'll speak English today, because Miss Lockley is here'. Then he'd forget and lapse back into Welsh. Mary was friends with his daughter, who was far from virtuous. We said we went to chapel for the good of our souls, but also because we might go for a walk with the boys afterwards.

I had one day at Island Farm before returning to school. On 19 January D had been reviewing his financial position:

> I'm making more money from writing than farming ... the farm losses due to falling prices of machinery, pigs and horses and farm goods generally, and a very expensive harvest....on the other hand some royalties were due to farming articles ... but it seems the sooner I give up large scale farming the better. I would like to settle at Fliquet, Jill's old home in Jersey ... Posted a revised fantasy called 'The Red Wilderness' to my agent Peter Lewin ... in the brave cold world which does not expect me to write outside the countryside and natural history, for the world did not acclaim my novels!

Dear D, how he longed to write novels. He had in fact, published two, both written in his early days, *The Sea's a Thief* (1936) and *The Island Dwellers* (1932). A novel called *The Red Wilderness* was rejected several times and eventually after countless revisions became the *The Seals and the Curragh* (published by Dent in 1954), part fact, part fantasy, with the most atrociously faked photographs. I remember seeing them on his desk and telling him, 'You can't possibly submit those in their present form'. As usual when I was critical he became very hurt and defensive. In 1974 another seal fantasy was published by Rex Collings called *Seal Woman*.

Most of April D had spent starting a book in novel form entitled *The Golden Year* (published in 1948). In it he describes the farming year from spring 1946 until spring 1947. All the characters are imaginatively disguised. I enjoyed the true bits, the descriptions of stock, harvest and nature, the things about Island Farm I knew and loved so much. The fictitious bits worried me to the point of hating it, and leaving me completely bewildered. He said: 'It was impossible for me to write a verbatim account of the farming year as far as the characters were concerned because of libel ... the only true features are the descriptions of crops, livestock and nature'. But I found some of those embroidered too. The book would have been so much better if D had stuck to the farming notes he kept so meticulously. Of course, this is my opinion, from one who knows too much!

I found an amusing letter sent to D in 1952, from one of the characters in *The Golden Year*, who had recognized himself in spite of the disguise. 'I enjoyed reading this book tremendously, I discovered I am the Swedish painter "Merk"; how we laughed ... the poor chap commits suicide a few pages later, while his reincarnation lives on near Newport ... I had to tell you this ... '

I came home in May for the last 'school holiday' I would ever have. The constrained atmosphere was still evident. Baron was unsettled because if the farm was leased what would he do? He told me for the umpteenth time that he wished M was back. She was so fond of him and looked after his needs, even though she scolded him if he forgot to change his underclothes and pyjamas often enough. She said if she didn't remind him, the fug in his room became unbearable: he always slept with the window tightly sealed, saying the night air was bad for his lungs and his bouts of malaria.

Almost at once, Jill, Mary Abraham, D, John Fursdon and I went off to Skokholm to get it ready for the coming season. We were joined by D's old friend Morrey Salmon and other faithfuls. There was so much to do, foremost to repair the Heligoland trap which the winter wind had knocked around. It was a difficult job to knit and hold the wire netting in place in a westerly gale. We hung doors and painted window frames. I touched up the figurehead of the *Alice Williams*, who had recently been reinstated above South Haven as a leading mark. We planted some shrubs to entice the birds into the re-erected trap and visited the Stack and Spider caves. The week passed very quickly. It was like old times, but the bad weather never let up. It had already been a cold, wet winter and late spring, which had caused huge losses in the rabbit and Soay sheep populations. There was hardly a blade of grass to be seen, and very few flowers. We collected a few early herring gulls' eggs. D says he made a sponge cake, but I have no recollection of this – he only cooked under duress, but says 'he did so because Mary and Jill did nothing but swan around the island with a sketch book while everyone else slaved. Ann worked well'. In spite of the weather I was in my element! I revisited all my old haunts and slept in my little bedroom, which seemed to have shrunk. Little did I think then that this would be my last long stay on Skokholm.

Peter Scott, the naturalist (later Sir Peter), was supposed to have joined us. He came halfway then turned back because it was too rough to land. I was very thrilled to meet him later when I travelled up to Cardiff on the same train as him when I returned to school for the last time.

14

Freedom

If we had had a ceremony for those of us who were leaving school that summer, it made no impression on me. I had no regrets at all.

M was very happily housekeeping on Caldey Island for Mrs de Reyes-King, where we had stayed back in 1934. At the end of term I took the train for Tenby expecting to have to make my own way over to the island, but to my surprise M had rowed a small dinghy over and had walked to the station. Typically, she had told no one, thinking nothing could possibly happen to her on her long row alone over partly open sea. Fortunately it was a calm day and we had a pleasant row back.

The Norse called the island Caldey, 'cold island', which is a misnomer, for unlike Skomer and Skokholm, which also have Norse names, it is much more sheltered, with 'real trees' growing in the valleys. Since early Celtic times it has been the site of a monastery. In 1906 one Father Aelred built the present one; he converted from Anglican to Roman Catholic in 1913, and joined the Benedictine Order, but they were unable to make the island pay. There are many 'tut-tut' stories told about the monks of that time being unduly liberal. In 1928 the island was sold to the present Cistercian Order. They are Trappist monks, so they maintain a vow of silence until Compline (evening prayers), rise at three in the morning for Matins, and have no contact with outsiders, except for one monk who acts as a go-between. To make the monastery pay, they farm the land, provide some of the products for a tourist shop, and take visitors' landing fees. There are also a few private houses scattered around.

Lots of people were having holidays with their Caldey relatives. I made friends with three young women about my age. Looking around for something to do, we decided the sleepy little village hall needed a wake-up call, and dreamed up the idea of a variety concert. The monks' go-between, Brother Thomas, was very keen to take part, so we made him Master of Ceremonies. Anyone who could perform any kind of party trick was pressed into participating. At the time we were fortunate that a group of young Dominican monks were guests at the abbey, and being a teaching order they were free to mingle with everyone. Their experience with young people added greatly to our meagre talents. The hall was packed: it had been quite some time since any one had used it for anything so light-hearted.

When Father Aelred had been abbot he had dedicated the abbey to St Samson. This famous Welsh bishop and confessor was once a monk here and 28 July is his feast day. That day, the Dominicans conducted a celebratory service

Some of the concert-goers on Caldey,
with Brother Thomas third from left

in the village church, and all the residents were invited to attend. I found it a memorable and haunting experience, enhanced by being out of doors under a clear blue sky. This church had been burned down in 1940; orange and brown wallflowers had seeded themselves in the cracks of the mellowed walls which still stood. The only artificial decoration, a blue Madonna, looked down from a niche above the makeshift choir stalls. There, the young Dominicans, looking so handsome in their white robes, chanted in delightful harmony.

Caldey has many beautiful bays. One beach on the east is a no-go area, reserved for the recreation of the monks. My favourite was Sandtop Bay on the west side. An interesting walk through the monastery farm where we could see the monks toiling (when we encountered them I always felt, even amongst ourselves, that we should maintain a vow of silence too), and past the old priory church, which has a peculiar sausage-shaped spire with a distinct lean. A path leads on down the western slope to dunes where green sea beet and sea holly grow. The sand is pale gold and whistles as you walk on it. At the end of the beach there are big caves.

One day a launch was organised to take a party of us to the neighbouring island of St Margaret's. The Dominicans came too; they talked about their work and answered the kinds of questions one always wants to ask a monk and does not dare. They did not seem to mind a bevy of giggling girls asking personal questions. They were so frank and good-looking, we girls thought it seemed a waste of handsome manhood.

St Margaret's is now uninhabited; a bird sanctuary under the jurisdiction of the West Wales Naturalist Trust. Only the ruin of an ecclesiastical building and several roofless huts remain. The island was extensively quarried round 1841; cormorants now nest in among the stones. The island is accessible at low tide if one is prepared to clamber across in a swimsuit, although exploration can be somewhat deterred because the island grows extremely healthy nettles. Years later D came in for some severe criticism for putting a flock of Soay sheep there.

After enjoying my time on Caldey I went back to Island Farm. The harvest was now all in thanks to a lovely spell of warm weather and the efforts of a team of Charterhouse schoolboys. They were a great gang. They camped out in a field near the house and did all their own cooking. Before they departed Jill prepared a scrumptious harvest supper for them. There was just room for us all in the big wheelroom and we played games afterwards.

I found that D was serious about leasing the farm. He had found Norman Perkins, a reputable farmer from the south of the county. It was amazing how D was so excited about a new venture, when at the same time he had so many regrets about leaving this idyllically-situated farm. I had heard some of his plans for Jersey. I foresaw some strife because Jill seemed to be getting increasingly nervous about the move. I was pretty heartbroken. I had still cherished the idea of farming Dinas Island myself, eventually; perhaps, I thought, all was not lost, if the farm was only going to be leased.

Soon it would be time to knuckle down to my compulsory practical for Agricultural College, but first D proposed a trip to Jersey with him. I was delighted.

On 17 September we picked up two ornithological friends, Bill and Penny Condry, who had been involved at Skokholm, and were now looking for a winter job. They were a dear couple, and I became very fond of them. We dropped Bill in Southampton to catch the ferry, and to look after the heavy luggage, which included a box of tools for the repair of the house, and their dog Badger. Penny, D and I proceeded to the airport. This was my first experience of flying, and it was such a thrill that I wished we had further to go!

Then D took us to Fliquet House. It was in an appalling state, but dusk was falling so we did not have time to make a close inspection. Penny and I settled in on the few dilapidated sticks of furniture left by a squatter. With no electricity in the house it was fortunate we had purchased candles. The defunct plumbing occasionally obliged with a little flow of rusty water from the taps or the loo. The well had been filled with goldfish by a squatter. We put our sleeping bags on the floor and lit a large fire in the kitchen grate to cook supper. D went off to eat and sleep in luxury with his birdie friends. D wrote that Penny and I 'were very game, I left them to a fire and to make the best of it'.

Next morning D arrived with Bill and the luggage off the night ferry. In spite of the conditions it was not surprising D had fallen in love with Fliquet. It is situated in a little wooded glen at the north eastern end of Jersey in the parish of St Martins. Down the drive stands a splendid Martello tower and a glimpse of the sea beyond. From the entrance gate I could see a row of rocks, the Ecréhous islets: they are famous, I learned later, for a small abalone called an ormer. At night the lighthouse at Carteret was visible across seventeen miles to the nearest point of France. The land is made up of little tiny fields, called 'cotils', set out in higgledy-piggledy fashion here and there. They are usually planted with early potatoes, closely followed by tomatoes. It was isolated and countrified enough, with a small acreage of land, to keep D happy. About 1990 I sometimes watched the detective series *Bergerac*, on television, and in one episode I recognized that the murder had taken place in the lounge at Fliquet!

We three worked every day at the cleaning. Penny and Bill were both tremendous company, and I was quite sorry to leave them, for they were going to spend the winter there, and the conditions were primitive to say the least. To make up for all our hard work D took us for a tour right round the island in the old Wolseley he'd been lent.

D and I flew back to Southampton 'in an 8 seater bi-plane over the Channel, we passed over the Cap de la Hague Lighthouse at Cherbourg with Alderney to the west and the white gannet crowned mass of Ortac very clear beyond. Then we entered a spectacular thunderstorm before coming out into calmer weather at the approach to the Isle of Wight'. I could hardly wait to tell Terence that I had experienced flying before he had!

Before going on to Pembrokeshire we picked up naturalist and author James Fisher. James was always witty company and lived life to the full. He had three children, Adam, Crispin and Selina, always referred to by James as Dirty, Filthy and Obscener. He and D were collaborating on a book on seabirds of the North Atlantic. The writing did not progress very smoothly. D had always been a morning worker: in fact he nearly always rose before daylight and did all his best writing well before lunch; James, however, was a night owl!

On this occasion James was coming to attend a meeting of the West Wales Field Society Council. The following day they set off in a Sunderland Flying Boat to do a three-day seal count, in an attempt to estimate the population of Atlantic grey seals breeding in British waters. Jill and I would have loved to have gone too, but it was for male natural history boffins only. On their last day we were instructed to drive post-haste to Pembroke Dock to meet them as soon as we saw the Sunderland 'buzz' the farmhouse on its return.

James Fisher, sadly, was killed in a car crash in 1970. A great loss. He had made his name as an author, editor, broadcaster and ornithologist.

A short visit to Skokholm was made at the beginning of October by Mary, Jill, D and me to evacuate it for the winter. A butcher came with us to slaughter Caroline the cow. The Trinity House crane on the landing stage proved a useful means of hanging her up in order to skin and gut her. The meat went to the slaughter house and the entrails into the harbour.

When we returned to Island Farm Richard Llewellyn came to supper, Richard had bought a hill farm up on Carn Ingli. I was very interested to meet him because I had enjoyed his book *How Green was my Valley*. I felt he was pretty self assured and slick. D wrote:

> he talked for 3 hours, a very worldly hard-headed man who is out for himself first, and the betterment of the world next. He talked privately with me about Island Farm and securing it as a Nature reserve and Home for convalescing children – an idea resulting from my query as to how he could assist W.W.F.S. [West Wales Field Society] to get it as a Nature Reserve. He arrived in a jeep and is most convincing about his work on the mountain – all idealistic, and probably, one feels, the basis for a novel ...

On 16 October Valentino, D and I went up to London. Valentino had to go to the Italian Embassy to get his passport endorsed for USA. I was on my way to a Land Army Training Centre near Hatfield for six weeks. It was run by the War Agricultural Committee. We had decided that being a member of the Land Army would ensure that I would earn standard wages during my twelve months' practical required for Agricultural College.

When I returned I went to work on a big dairy farm in north Pembrokeshire called Pant-y-deri owned by an astute business man and steel tycoon. It was interesting for me to experience a farm where the cows were milked three times a day and stock and machinery were the best money could buy.

I had digs with a local builder whom I disliked. He thought females should not be allowed in pubs, and disapproved of a very charming boy I had briefly dated, who was the offspring of a gypsy mother and a local lad: 'I'm going to tell your father about your pubbing and going out with a gyppo'. I waited for the tirade when next he met D, but the wretched man was nothing less than obsequious.

On the late shift we finished milking at 11.30 p.m. When my day off followed this shift I would cycle straight from work to one or other of my homes. At Vaynor my bed was always waiting for me; at Island Farm I sometimes spent the odd half-night on the couch because I discovered someone sleeping in my room. Much to my joy, I was given Christmas Day off among the delightful company at Vaynor.

Aunt Kathleen was on sabbatical leave in Chicago. In June she suggested I come out and work on a Summer Camp in Maine owned by two former lacrosse friends. I jumped at this exciting prospect, and went ... but that is another story.

D wrote:

October 11th: A week busily arranging for the sale. This is a difficult time and full of important decisions. Ann has decided to go on to Agricultural College for two years ... and between this and other considerations I decided to let Island Farm at £425 p.a.

I am reserving for myself the woods and the valley from Pwllgwaelod to Cwmyreglwys. Thus having no sons of my own and no immediate prospects of any, I have relinquished the responsibilities of a large stock and arable farm, though with many regrets and some relief.

I returned from the States on 14 October, dressed to the nines in all my cheap American regalia, on the very eve of the Island Farm sale. I was put straight to work helping Valentino make halters for the horses and our Pedigree Welsh Black cows. Apparently it had been the culmination of a week's struggle, sleeplessness and poor weather. Everyone was so busy with preparations and there was no time to catch up on the turn of events since I had left for America.

Next day a great crowd arrived, about 300 cars and about 1,000 people. The cattle being the big attraction, the stock were sold in the yard and the auctioneers stood on a lorry. Pigs and horses were slow, and some of the horses only made pet food prices. Machinery was dear, much of the second hand stuff fetching 100 per cent more than we paid for it. A side-rake bought for £1 fetched £21. With the sale, a betterment claim and other balances, D was in the black at last, and able to pay what he owed from buying the farm two years ago.

D was still undecided between living in Jersey or buying somewhere in Pembrokeshire. In the meantime he and Jill had re-rented Tŷ-twt. Jill was very tearful: she wasn't keen on moving to her old family home where there were too many ghosts. Valentino was nervous about moving to America, and wanted to hear what I'd thought of the Yanks! Baron had gone off to stay with his brother: D had told him he had to give the Public Assistance home in Pembroke a trial run; he said it was not fair on Jill to have to look after him.

In spite of his indecisions and some regrets D probably came out of this saga better than anyone.

I had a sad feeling that I would never fulfil my dreams of running Island Farm. In his diary D partly blames me for his leaving; I thought that hardly fair because we hadn't discussed the matter for a long time. Now he'd had enough of farming on a large scale. Although he still owned the place, it was obvious he would never go back to farming there on my account, and I knew I would never be able to make a start without him. Thinking about it, we would have had some fearsome differences of opinion if we had tried to work together as adults, which back then I did not consider too seriously.

Very fortuitously, the housekeeper and the land girl at Rhyd-y-gath had recently left. Uncle Martin suggested that M and I should take their places, which saved me having to find another farm on which to finish my practical. Working there seemed like a homecoming for both M and me. I had my pony there, the work was far more interesting and varied than at Pant-y-deri. M had a garden with which to do as she pleased. The house was still without electricity, but modern plumbing had been installed. The old two-holer was still there for emergencies, and to my horror I discovered the bathroom waste still went into the stream: the dairy inspector did not appear to notice this on his routine visits!

Tom Evans, Uncle Martin's manager, had been there so long he was known as 'Twm Rhyd-y-gath'. He rose each morning at dawn, seven days a week, and seldom went home before dark. If the pub was closed he would dally in his chair after supper or suggest a game of cards. The locals reckoned he never saw his wife in daylight except when they went to a funeral!

Also working there was Alun, a young man about twenty, and Ces, who was a likeable rogue, with a reputation as a womaniser and a poacher. He kept us endlessly amused with stories of his conquests and his illegal fishing. One morning he found out it was M's birthday and slipped half a crown under her breakfast plate. He was a terrible tease and loved making people laugh, but was always polite to M and me.

A travelling salesman used to call now and again, his van was a veritable emporium. M bought seeds from him and Tom would buy long woollen underwear. Ces always waited until everyone else had finished making their purchases, 'Because you see,' he'd say sheepishly, 'he keeps a stock of French letters hidden in his glove box!'

The nearby village of Hermon sprawls along the road for about two miles, with a school, two chapels, a pub and a shop. Needless to say the proprietor of the latter was known as 'Wil Shop'. He ran his business from his small house and sold just about everything. Goods were piled high in higgledy-piggledy fashion in the hallway, with just enough room to turn left into the shop proper. Inevitably someone would be leaning on the cluttered counter gossiping; there was a chair, but it too was stacked with goods. Behind the counter a bank of labelled shelves and drawers spewed forth their contents, although one could never be sure they were true to label. M used to say lamp glasses and mantles were the only thing she could be sure of buying because they were in such demand, and he didn't have time to lose them! I remember I found an extremely smart shoe. When I asked to try on the other one, he suggested I come back another day when it might have turned up!

I had quite a busy social life. Alun persuaded me to join the local Young Farmers' Club. The men were very persuasive: too often I went with them to The Lamb in Hermon. In those days, it was run by a dear old couple, John and Catherine; she spoke Welsh, and no English. The public bar was tiny with a counter squashed in one corner and couple of skews strictly reserved for aged regulars in the inglenook. If the bar was full we overflowed into Catherine's kitchen. With three a side at her kitchen table we would play hilarious games of 'Tipit', a subtle version of 'Up Jenkins'. I was quite sad to leave Rhyd-y-gath at the beginning of September to go to college.

Eventually D sold Island Farm. Years later he told me it was one of his biggest regrets. In 1942 he wrote these wishful, but prophetic thoughts: 'As I walked its rough fields and thought one day it might be preserved as a sanctuary for wild creatures'. In 1988 it was acquired by the National Trust, and 300 acres of the centre was leased back to the vendors with the Trust retaining the coastal fringe, which should augur well for a future nature reserve. Farming practice as it is today – with bigger fields, no hedges and large amounts of fertiliser in parallel with National Trust management on the cliffs – makes this difficult to fulfil.

I know exactly where D was standing in the little wooded valley below the farm house when he described this October scene from *The Golden Year*. I would like to think it may be forever relevant:

I sought the shelter of the wood when I had left the cliffs. There, too, I heard the rustle of the wings of passing flocks, but it was mingled with the melody of the tree-tops gently moving in the seaward zephyrs.

The metallic clatter of a dried leaf falling through the ash tree twigs was answered by a singing robin. A blackbird called, I stood and stared over the red bracken and the scarlet berried thorn tree shrubs, and the yellowing ash trees, to where the sea made quiet moan ...

The outermost leaves of the sycamore are tawny, or buff, or greenish yellow ... they begin to fall, with heaviness in the still air, and make a crackling carpet for the blackbirds which will hunt through them, for the plentiful insect life is quietly and unobtrusively going to ground for winter ...

Through the open heart of the valley comes sailing on short and heavy wings a bevy of gaudy magpies ... in the hawthorn tree I see the first redwing plucking the abundant berries, nervously swallowing them with little jerks ... a hundred little tinkling notes make me look up ... a great flock of linnets and greenfinches is moving southwards. The heart is stirred and full of joy at the sight.

D always was a man who lived on his terms. If something I had to say interested him he was all ears, and that went for almost anyone else too. In retrospect, I think I was in love with Island Farm, for the same reasons D loved it: the woods and cliffs, and above all its position, like a stranded pilot whale on the coast of Newport Bay. I can visualise it all now: one day when trying to make hay we watched in trepidation a shower of rain drifting over the craggy peak of Carn Ingli and drifting nearer over the rocks on Mynydd Melyn, but we remained stuck out on our peninsula in brilliant sunshine. If circumstances had been different, and I really had been in a position to run it as a farm, it would have been difficult, or a disaster, or I may even have funked it.

Epilogue

D and Jill moved to Jersey for two years, but returned to live near Tenby in 1950. I was pretty sceptical when D described his purchase of an old rectory with cottage and one field as 'being the last resting place for my old bones'. He was only forty-seven, and I thought this would not keep him happy for long.

After qualifying with a Diploma in Dairying I worked in Suffolk until 1953, when I went to New Zealand under their immigration scheme. I was given a royal farewell by the aunts before going to stay with D. He'd been overseeing the Orielton duck decoy in Pembrokeshire. He took me there to help one day, and we looked over the lovely old house, extensive grounds and farm. It was obvious that D was scheming to buy the place, so it was no surprise to learn that they had moved in by the end of the year! My half-brothers were born in 1950 and 1953 respectively. Jill never reconciled herself entirely to bringing up two little boys in this big house which, to make it pay, had to be run as a sort of hotel for nature lovers. D and Jill had rather an acrimonious divorce in early 1964. After that she took on various posts as matron of schools and institutions, finally retiring to live in Bath, Somerset.

I spent four happy years in New Zealand and became engaged to a farmer, Jack Mark. The family persuaded me to come home 'to collect the loot' and ensure, to quote Uncle John: 'I was doing the right thing in marrying a colonial'! I did marry Jack. We worked on his father's dairy farm for three years, then bought ourselves a sheep and beef farm in the same district. I love New Zealand. There are things I miss: the Pembrokeshire coast, the suddenness with which the spring arrives. It is offset by a pleasant sub-tropical climate here and a bounteous garden in which I revel. We have two sons, both of whom love nature and the outdoors.

In 1962 M built a cottage on our farm. By then she had travelled extensively and valued her freedom and independence. D married again in 1964 and came to live in Auckland permanently in 1971. He loved our farm, and would wander happily for hours with his grandsons in its bush-clad gullies observing birds. He would take a sherry with M and they would reminisce. D brought many of his friends to stay with us. 'We lived in shabby comfort', according to an article the author Richard Adams wrote about his sojourn with us in New Zealand.

M died in 1989. She refused to talk about her coming death or anyone else's. Just once she confided: 'During my early married life on Skokholm I was ecstatic.' Acting on this, our elder son Peter took her ashes to Skokholm in 1991 and scattered them on a little thrift-covered outcrop just south of the house. He laid a posy of sweet peas and wept a little, for they were very close.

When D heard about this he said: 'What a good idea, I'll have mine scattered on the Knoll!' On 3 June 2001, D's children and all but one of his grandchildren gathered to fulfil his wishes over the Knoll and 'Caroline's burrow'. There D rests among the birds, flowers and salt winds he knew so well. For one so restless, it was appropriate that we reserved a handful for the sea-girt reserve he was instrumental in creating below his house in Auckland, which looks out on more beloved islands.

With my half-brothers I unveiled a plaque set in the wall of Skokholm cottage, the last sentence reads:

> ... to dwell alone with birds and flowers in some remote place where they were plentiful and undisturbed was an ambition early cherished ...

Whenever I return to Skokholm I have a strange feeling, as if I am sleepwalking. I am not sad, just too many memories. When I return to the mainland everything is a blur. It is fortunate that Jack remembers to take photographs, so that I can enjoy the island all over again at a later date.

It is nice to think that both my parents enjoyed the company of their grandsons, and made friends with one another again here in New Zealand. Now they are together again on Skokholm. The full circle of their island life is complete.

Also from Gwasg Carreg Gwalch:

The Practical Islander

Ronald Lockley was born near Cardiff at the beginning of the twentieth century. Early in his childhood he became fascinated with the wildlife of his area, and particularly with birds. His other fascination, though, and one that was to dominate his life, was that of islands. In his twenties he took the lease on the island of Skokholm, off Pembrokeshire. There he lived until 1940, when he and his family were ordered off by the War Office.

To supplement the family's income Ronald wrote over fifty books about island life and the birds and people he observed, and then about farming on the mainland, near Newport, Pembrokeshire. R. M. Lockley was highly respected as an ornithologist and naturalist by the time of his death in 1990, and his passionate and knowledgeable writing is relevant to today's debate about the environment.

In order to introduce R. M. Lockley's writing to a new audience, the editor Jen Llywelyn has taken sparkling extracts from six of R. M. Lockley's books to illustrate his life story, and his relationship with the beauty of his surroundings, up to the end of the Second World War. There are essays, too, about other islands he visited in the 1920s and 1930s: Grassholm and Bardsey, and then Heligoland in 1936, where the Nazis were very evident.

Ronald Lockley's daughter, Ann Mark, has contributed a Foreword.

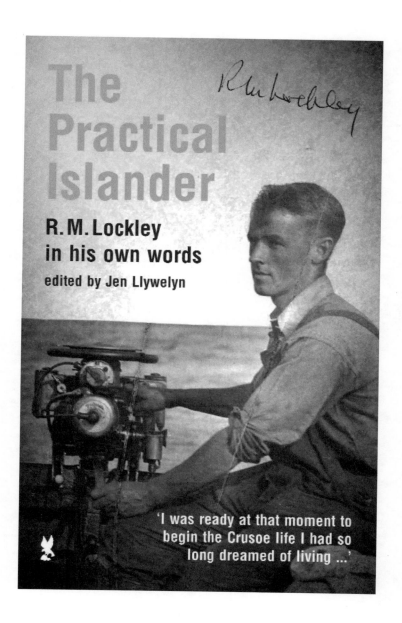

The Practical Islander

R. M. Lockley
in his own words

edited by Jen Llywelyn

'I was ready at that moment to
begin the Crusoe life I had so
long dreamed of living ...'